MATTHEW SMITH

MATTHEW SMITH

His Life and Reputation

MALCOLM YORKE

faber and faber
LONDON · BOSTON

First published in 1997
by Faber and Faber Limited
3 Queen Square London WC1N 3AU

Photoset by Parker Typesetting Service, Leicester
Printed in England by Clays Ltd, St Ives plc

A CIP record for this book
is available from the British Library

ISBN 0–571–17336–5

2 4 6 8 10 9 7 5 3 1

Contents

Acknowledgements

This book would not have been possible without the co-operation of Alice Keene, Matthew Smith's heir and copyright holder. She has been very generous in allowing me access to her collection of letters, Smith memorabilia, and the works still in her collection. Any serious student of Smith's painting will already know her informative book *The Two Mr Smiths* (1995), published to accompany the Barbican exhibition of those works her mother donated to the City of London.

Smith's nephews, Michael Royde-Smith and Peter and Paul Birkett-Smith, have also been extremely supportive and encouraging.

No book of this kind is written without calling upon the goodwill and time of many other people and I would like to thank in particular the following: Frank Auerbach, Adrian Berg, Warwick Brooks, Dr Lionel Carley, Stephen Chaplin, Christie's staff, Monica Clay, Peter Cochrane, Henri Corbeille, Corinne Cornish, Raymond Creuze, Felicity Dahl, Phyllis Dobbs, The Marchioness of Dufferin and Ava, Tony Estill, David Graham, Professor William Gerdts, Ann Goodchild, Mr and Mrs Christopher Halliday, Alfild Hansen, Josef Herman, Patrick Heron, Valerie Hobson, Ysanne Holt, Ken Howard, John Hoyland, Glyn Hughes, Iris Hughes, Jeremy Johnson, Andreas Kalman and the staff at the Crane Kalman Gallery, Vivien Knight, Leon Kossoff, Michel Le Harivel, Simon Matthews, Kenneth McConkey, Cecil Michaelis, Patricia Neal, Betty Newmarch, James O'Connor, Katerina Porter, Larry Powell, Lord Queensberry, Graham and Daphne Reynolds, Peter Rhymes, Elizabeth Royde-Smith, John Russell, the late Vera Russell, Mrs Sheridan Russell, Mrs Penelope Rosenberg, Sister Penelope

Salmond, Robert Sandelson, Peter Snowden, Marianne Steiner, the late Mrs Dorothy Stone, Sotheby's staff, Elizabeth and John Sutherland-Hawes, Alison Thomas, Dr Robert Travers and Julia Waddell.

I received a grant from the Society of Authors to help with this research and a donation from the Elephant Trust to assist with photographic costs. The University of Northumbria at Newcastle gave me two terms study leave.

My two editors, Giles de la Mare and John Bodley, pruned my excesses, and my wife, Mavis, supported me throughout the long struggle to bring this book into print.

Malcolm Yorke
Newcastle upon Tyne, 1996

Introduction

'It is hard to be born at the turn of the tide,' Matthew Smith told one of his mistresses.[1] He was referring to the flood of new ideas and the social upheavals which swept away the certainties of his childhood.

He was born in 1879 into a prosperous and cultured household and encountered in his childhood all the predictable Victorian attitudes towards patriotism, politics, religion, education, the family, sex, the social hierarchy, and what might be thought a respectable profession for the son of an industrialist on the rise. He was also exposed to the prevailing tastes of his class in literature, music and art. Some of these stayed with him all his life, others took decades to discard, whilst a few, particularly those to do with painting, he began to escape from at an early age.

During Smith's youth many forces were at work to undermine the great Victorian convictions, and nothing was more under siege than the kind of art with which he grew up. His father, Frederic Smith, had a taste for British academic pictures of the kind that illustrated literature or history and imparted moral lessons. Their style had to be realistic and full of details, all brought to a highly crafted 'finish' in which no brushstrokes were visible beneath the varnish. The year before Matthew's birth James Abbott McNeill Whistler had been accused by Ruskin of 'flinging a pot of paint in the face of the public' because he defied these rules. Whistler also offended connoisseurs like Frederic by saying, 'Art should be independent of clap-trap – should stand alone, and appeal to the artistic sense of eye or ear, without confounding this with emotions entirely foreign to it, as devotion, pity, love, patriotism and the like.'² A few English artists were converted to Whistler's radical, but unpopular and hence unprofitable, point of view.

In France discontent had stirred earlier than in England against traditional Salon subject matter and the conventional way in which it was painted. The malcontents asked, 'Why could there not be contemporary themes expressed in contemporary language?' A Realist group of artists emerged who believed in getting out of the studio and painting working people in the fields, clogs and all. In the year Matthew Smith was born another company of rebels, the Impressionists, were already on their fourth exhibition, showing in their bright dabby brushstrokes Parisians going about their business and pleasure in streets, theatres, suburbs, beaches, bedrooms and bathrooms with not a Greek god nor a Christian martyr in sight. These were the first ripples of the artistic tide beginning to turn into something later called Modernism, and by launching himself upon it Matthew had to throw overboard almost every artistic belief his father held dear.

He was a late and slow developer, first failing to learn anything of lasting value from two English art colleges and then plodding round the holy sites of French progressive painting such as Pont Aven, Paris, Aix, Arles and the Côte d'Azure, hoping something new would rub off on to his own work. Contact with Fry, Sickert, Matisse and O'Conor showed him further possibilities, but he was no intellectual and assimilated their ideas only gradually and piecemeal. In the end he found his own unique artistic voice, relying on instinct and passion rather than developing a system of principles. Through suffering he came to realize that his mission was to celebrate the good things of life: fruit, flowers, landscapes, but above all the voluptuous bodies of women. Each new picture meant a fresh struggle of a very physical kind that left him exhausted. Creation cost him too much effort to leave room for wit or irony or playfulness and he was constantly on his guard against what he called 'the Fake and Fudge road.' Consequently there were numerous false starts and slashed canvases and he was forty-six before he had assembled enough completed works for a one-man exhibition.

After that his reputation climbed steadily so that in old age the honours came thick and fast and almost every public gallery in England owned at least one Matthew Smith. By that time, however, there were fresh 'isms', new banners for painters and critics to rally behind, and art marched off in directions where Smith could no longer follow. His kind of subject matter and style were to be out of critical fashion for several decades. One of the concerns of this book is to pursue Smith's fluctuating reputation with reviewers and critics during his lifetime and to ask where it stands today, nearly forty years after his death.

Smith died in 1959 just short of his eightieth birthday. In those eighty years there had been radical developments in the subject matter and techniques of painting. The Impressionists' interest in spontaneity, in pure colours, in the visible gesture of the brushstroke, and in how paint behaved on a flat surface, had led by diverse and devious routes to Abstract Expressionism. Soon after that the tide turned again and the kind of modernism that Matthew Arnold Bracy Smith understood ebbed away, though he did not live to hear 'its melancholy, long, withdrawing roar.'

CHAPTER I

A Yorkshire Youth
1879–1898

Matthew Smith was a Yorkshireman, and he liked people to know it. He told 'wittily obscene Yorkshire stories'[1] in the Café Royal and enjoyed reminiscing about his childhood in Halifax with friends who had similar northern roots, such as the composer Delius and John Rothenstein, Director of the Tate Gallery. In later life when he met up with his two brothers in London they would shed their public school accents and banter in West Riding vowels about life up t' north. Smith gladly left Yorkshire at the age of nineteen and never lived there again, but when he revisited Halifax as a distinguished old man he assured local reporters he loved his home county, and though he had once thought Halifax 'the ugliest place on earth' he had now changed his mind. 'It was as enchanting as ever,' he told one friend,[2] and wrote to another: 'Halifax seems a wonderful place, wonderful scenery all round and the town itself solidly built of stone, not a brick to be seen, this seemed to give it a great character, and at night very Van Gogh like I saw the biggest half moon perched just above a rugged outline of houses and street that I have ever seen.'[3] Furthermore, he told the reporters: 'Manchester folk, in view of my family being well known in that city, have asked me why I don't call myself a Mancunian. The answer I give them is what any Tyke might say on being asked to call himself a Lancashire man.'[4] An emphatic no.

To be one of the West Yorkshire Smiths was certainly something to be proud of when Matthew was young. His relative George H. Smith explained just why in a pamphlet entitled 'The Smiths of Halifax'.[5] This Smithiad begins with the marriage of William Smith, Keeper of the

Monk Bar Gate in the City of York, in 1600. William's immediate descendants were turbulent Dissenting ministers who had established themselves at Mixenden near Halifax by the end of the century. A shoemaker, John Smith (1737–1828), emerged as the first Smith with more interest in profit than preaching; he also helped found the Loyal Georgean Society, a mutual insurance club for rich Halifax businessmen. The Smiths had begun to climb.

During John's lifetime Halifax was almost wholly dependent upon its wool manufacturing. The valleys were too narrow and the hillsides too poor in soil to support much beyond flocks of sheep. The wool was woven locally, on hand looms in the farmers' cottages, into pieces, shalloons and kerseys, then scoured, fulled, and dyed using the soft water from the local streams. With the coming of the Industrial Revolution the industry moved from water power to steam power as canal and rail links to the Yorkshire coalfields opened up. By 1850 there were twenty-four mills and the town was dominated by tall factory chimneys. Soon the whole valley was nicknamed 'The Devil's Cauldron' because of the constant pall of smoke over it.

One local writer looking back to the time when Matthew Smith the painter was a child recalls:

The atmosphere of Halifax – those days, whatever it may be now, was all of wool or worsted or cloth, or something similar, that scented the whole town. I have distinct recollections of the never ceasing whir and rattle of the machinery, of the clang of the wooden shoes at morn and night as the millhands went to work, of the great canopy of dun-coloured smoke which seemed to hang night and day above the grey old town from Beacon Hill to the edges of Skircoat Moor.[6]

The population increased rapidly from 6,000 in 1750 to 25,000 a hundred years later, and by the time Matthew Smith was a young man in 1900 to 100,000. After a nineteenth-century slump in wool the town diversified into carpets, furnishings, damasks and tapestries and, as we shall see in the case of the Smiths, into wire manufacture. Labour was pitifully cheap and the slums in the valley bottom increasingly squalid, but the emerging middle classes built mansions up the hillsides above the smoke and began to think rather well of themselves. An old Yorkshire rhyme seemed to confirm Halifax society's view of itself:

Bradford for cash
Halifax for dash
Wakefield for pride and poverty
Huddersfield for show
Sheffield what's low
Leeds for dirt and vulgarity.[7]

It was clear that in nineteenth-century Halifax there were fortunes to be made and steps up the social ladder on offer to any enterprising man with a bit of capital.

One such man was Matthew's great-grandfather Thomas Smith, one of the eight children of shoemaker John, who used the leather-working skills he had learned from his father to branch out into leather-based cards for carding the wool in the Halifax mills. His youngest son Frederick (1823–68) entered a rival firm of card manufacturers which also made wire, and acted as their commercial traveller. On his travels he met and married a lady from Aberdeen, but she soon died. Then in 1859 Frederick established his own wire works in Halifax, Frederick Smith and Company, to make steel wire to be turned into pins, needles, nails, screws or the stiffenings for bonnets and crinolines. In memory of his wife he called it the Caledonia Works and took a Scottish thistle as his trade mark. The factory is still there by the Calder and one remaining chimney still has SMITH written upon it, though the family lost ownership of it in the 1970s.

This Frederick was the man who established the fortunes of the Smiths of Halifax. To raise more capital Frederick borrowed from his brother Matthew (1819–80), who had also managed a wire mill in Birmingham and made a judicious marriage to Mary Sutcliffe Holroyd, a jeweller's daughter (there would be more intermarriages with the Holroyds later). Matthew then came into partnership, bringing his eldest son George Henry (1846–1931) into the business too. They soon expanded to make wire hawsers for the marine and mining industries, as well as fence wire, springs and high conductivity wire.

Frederick became a powerful man in local business circles and moved into politics as councillor for the North Ward, which he served until his death. Religious life was not neglected, as he was also a deacon of the

Sion Chapel where he married again in 1863 to Martha Sutcliffe, a local dyer's daughter. Then in 1868 he returned from a council meeting and died of 'apoplexy', leaving no will and his house at Skircoat unfinished.

Matthew completed the house, paid his brother's widow £10,000 for her inherited share of the company and assumed sole charge. Like his brother he was a pious man and the notes for his sermons in the Sion Chapel still survive, as do his lectures to the Engineers' Society and the careful records of expenditure during his tour of the Continent in 1877.[8] Matthew took his brother's place on the council as a Liberal and in 1879 was elected mayor in the very week in which his grandson the artist was born, and presumably named partly in his honour. However, he died suddenly before his mayoral term was completed. One of his sons was our artist's father, and the other four sons and four daughters who survived into adulthood had numerous offspring, so Matthew the artist was part of a vast extended family at the heart of Halifax society.

All the uncles and aunts married well and thrived. They were solid Yorkshire bourgeois: conservatives in politics, monarchists and patriots, nonconformists in religion, Freemasons, founders and joiners of civic societies, law-abiding, and devoted to money-making and good works. Along with the Crossleys, Appleyards, Ackroyds, Baldwins, Ramsdens and Whitleys, the Smith family ran Halifax, employing its people, controlling its institutions, financing its improvements and fostering its culture. Halifax was at its peak in the late Victorian age as men like these cleared the slums, erected fine civic buildings and endowed schools, hospitals, parks, model estates, libraries, workhouses, theatres and churches (though no art gallery). None of them were quite gentlemen as the Victorians would have defined that term, but they must have had hopes that their sons, given the right education and the right marriage partners, would aspire to that exalted status.

Matthew's third son was called Frederic (1849–1914), and he is crucial for our purposes since he was the painter's father and, if his son Matthew is to be believed, a malign influence on his whole career. Frederic had a good scientific mind and made several patented improvements in wire-drawing techniques in the 1890s. He also expanded the family business by opening his own Anaconda works in Salford, then later, in 1909, he merged this with The London Electric

Wire Works and also the Liverpool Electric Cable Company of Bootle, Liverpool. Family legend maintains he was sitting at breakfast when he read in *The Times* that Marconi had sent a message across the Atlantic by 'wireless'. 'This is the end,' he said, but in fact it turned out to be a new beginning since the wireless and telephone were dependent upon fine copper wire of a kind not yet widely available. From then on the original Halifax company concentrated on high grade steel wire and the Salford works on copper wire because it was near the Liverpool docks through which the copper ingots were imported and shipped along the Manchester Ship Canal. Eventually, long after Frederic's death, these Salford companies would be swallowed by even bigger ones, but at each take-over Frederic's shrewd descendants would retain their shares and reap their dividends.

Like his forefathers Frederic felt that his wealth and position brought with them public duties. He served on the Halifax School Board and other civic committees and joined the Freemasons in 1884. He also insisted on chapel attendance twice on Sunday for all the family and, his wife's diary informs us, he took the boys to a debate on 'Moral Degeneracy' at the local Literary Club in 1903. Photographs of Frederic show a lean dignified man in immaculate dark suits, every button done up even on summer days, his boots gleaming and his collars rigid with starch. He had a walrus moustache, blue eyes and a narrow bald head. In some pictures he wears a pince-nez. He does not look like a man to indulge in trivial pleasures, nor a man to cross in argument. Matthew later told people he was haunted by fear of his father's displeasure throughout his childhood. Yet at Frederic's funeral his close friend the minister claimed, 'None could be much in his presence without realizing that he was a personality of singular charm and winsomeness.'

Frederic Smith was no philistine in the way Arnold or Carlyle used that term: indeed he was a very enlightened patron of musicians, painters and writers. His passion was for violins, though he was himself an indifferent performer. He owned three Stradivarius violins (the Tuscan, Prince and Amhurst) and a priceless Guarneri which attracted to his Salford house such eminent violinists as Fritz Kreisler and Mischa Elman (whose playing reduced his wife to ecstatic tears). The German pianist Wilhelm Backhaus, who briefly taught at the Manchester School of Music around

1905, was also a visitor to Frederic's musical soirées and would have played on the two Bechstein grand pianos which Frederic owned. Henry Wood and Bernard Shaw also called in. Matthew would 'quietly disappear' on these occasions, perhaps as an act of defiance towards his father or because he had learned to hate violins.

So obsessed was Frederic by the master violin maker that he commissioned Seymour Lucas RA to paint *The Tuscan Strad*, which was shown at the Royal Academy, and Edgar Bundy to portray *Stradivarius in His Workshop*. Frederic himself also wrote a ten-page unrhymed poem 'A Soliloquy: Antonio Stradivari, Cremona AD 1734' which was published by Sherratt and Hughes in 1912. This was not his only literary production as his collected verse, *A Chest of Viols*, had been published in 1896.[9] These poems are typically Victorian in their preoccupation with God, death and the celebration of great men (Dickens, R. L. Stevenson, Mozart), but he also wrote a series of poems each inspired by the Stradivarius, Guarneri and Gasparo da Salò violins he owned. Occasionally real feeling breaks through the conventional language and set themes, as in this poem dedicated to his youngest son Maurice Stevenson who had survived only four years:

THE BIRTHDAY

On this first day that he beheld the light,
What greetings may we bring, or gifts bestow,
That he our tender, steadfast love may know?
Is there no speech, nor sign, by day or night,
No glance of love or pride or sweet delight,
That may rejoice him lying here so low?
Around us dead leaves fall and cold winds blow,
Earth heeds us not, and Heaven is out of sight.

O hidden under-world, so far, so near,
Veiled from our yearning hands, our searching eyes,
Within thy depths, in some abiding place,
Surely this little soul that knew no fear
Has found a Homeland, a child's Paradise,
Whose welcome is the vision of God's face!

Frederic's commitment to living authors is also evident from the way he called his third child after Matthew Arnold and his sixth after Robert Louis Stevenson. He even kept a cast of Stevenson's writing hand on his desk and he gave lectures on Stevenson's letters to various literary societies. At Frederic's death his 5,000 volume library was sold and amongst the predictable collected works of all the great English poets and novelists, from Chaucer onwards, and the bound volumes of just about every magazine published in Victorian times, there were some surprises. He had collected every English version of *The Rubáiyát* of Omar Khayyám, all the *Yellow Book* editions, Wilde, Swinburne, Darwin and Rabelais, and had also read widely in chemistry, botany, history, religion, art history, theology, golf, travel, motoring, philately, ornithology, photography, and gardening. His children could, if they so wished, acquire a liberal education without leaving the house.[10]

The walls were also hung with forty or more oils and there were thirty-two lots of mixed prints and watercolours to be auctioned on Frederic's death. Matthew later claimed he never saw a good picture until he was twenty-one; but this conflict in artistic taste between father and son is a topic which will be addressed in the next chapter.

When he was twenty-six Frederic had married his second cousin Frances (Fanny) Holroyd, four years his junior. She seemed very much under her spouse's thumb and Harold, one of her sons, later told how, when Frederic had once to go to London on business, the whole family – including Fanny – joined hands and sang ring-a-ring-a-roses all round the house. Then a telegram arrived announcing his return and all light-heartedness was abandoned.

Apart from the fact that she accompanied Frederic's violin playing on the piano and that she bore him six children, little seems to have been recorded about Fanny by other people. Matthew told one friend that she had a 'radiant and vivacious personality,' but another that he regretted 'the lack of a mother's influence.'[11] Her own diaries note the daily weather, her weekly 'at home', charity work, dress shopping, listening to sermons in chapel, dinner parties, the frequent family illnesses and her management of the six to nine women servants eventually employed in the house. A housemaid in 1903 cost her £6 per annum and a cook £25, but the turnover of servants was remarkably high. The chauffeur took her for drives and she arranged two family holidays each year in their house near Llandudno. It was a blameless life she recorded, entirely without gossip or malice but also without humour. Only cryptic entries such as 'Black Monday' hint at depths beneath the daily trivia. Photographs show Fanny to have been slight, pretty, dark haired and with a rather abstracted expression.

After the marriage in 1875 children came quickly: Hilda Mary (1876), Arthur Noel (1877), Matthew Arnold Bracy (1879), Harold Frederic (1882), Phyllis Marjorie (1887), and lastly Maurice Stevenson who was born in 1889 but soon died of croup. These siblings stayed remarkably close and supported each other, and the accident-prone Matthew in particular, all their lives.

Hilda, the oldest, married young but was soon widowed, leaving her with a mentally handicapped son to nurse. She then married a doctor and settled in Bowdon where her nephews remember her as 'flamboyant and dangling with earrings and beads and bracelets.' Noel, who one day in adolescence announced he was now to be addressed as Arthur, was the natural leader of the three boys, being good at sport and extrovert enough to be an amateur actor. Matthew came next, then Harold, who grew to be Matthew's closest male confidant and later, like Arthur, a snappy dresser and a joker with an eye for beautiful women. Phyllis was also close to Matthew, sharing some of the shyness their other siblings lacked and treasuring the brotherly letters and little drawings he sent her. When Matthew died her wreath at the funeral was labelled 'To dear Matt who coloured my childhood.'

All these children were nursed by Jemima (known as Annie) Mark who graduated to nanny and ended by staying on as housekeeper when they were grown up. When Frederic died Annie moved on to help Phyllis with her two children and stayed with them long after her working days were over. Matthew mentioned her frequently and with respect in his adult letters until she died in 1930.

Matthew was born at 5.45 a.m. on the chill rainy Wednesday morning of 22 October 1879 at 30 Elmfield Terrace, Skircoat, Halifax. This is a solid three-storey terrace house with a cellar and a back yard, but it was to be the most modest dwelling he was to occupy whilst growing up. A servant and the twenty-one-year-old Jemima lived on the top floor and helped Fanny cope with the three children. No doubt they were taken to run off their energies on the open field, now Savile Park, just at the end of the road.

Evidence about Matthew's early childhood is sparse, apart from photographs of him looking like a Botticelli angel with hair down to the lace collar of his Lord Fauntleroy dress, and stories about him kicking his brothers' shins under the dining-table. Most references are to his delicate health. His mother's diaries record the frequent visits of their physician, not just to Matthew but to the whole hypochondriac family. Matthew had frequent toothache and would wander from room to room and sofa to sofa holding a cushion to his face. His eyes were always weak and when he went to school he began to wear thick spectacles. Rothenstein describes him as 'constitutionally neurasthenic and given to insidious paralyses of melancholy – a condition that persisted many years after leaving home.'[12] Smith's letters as an adult are full of his illnesses and friends remarked on the weariness of his voice and bearing, but beneath it he was tough, just as his diffident manner concealed a steely determination to get his own way.

We know little of his imaginative life as a boy but it was a bookish household. *The Cloister and the Hearth* by Charles Reade is known to have been a particular favourite whilst other exciting and morally bracing books by Stevenson, Kipling, Conan Doyle, Henty, Marryat, Kingsley, Ballantyne, Wells and Mark Twain were standard fare for the Victorian boy and all stocked in his father's library. He is known to have played Indians in the garden, as well as the usual prank of ringing doorbells and running away, and brother Harold told his own sons about the boys shooting water-rats during a holiday in Kent.

Smith told friends of two luridly-lit episodes from his childhood which stayed with him all his life. At the age of seven he saw another boy have a fit in a Halifax street 'and for years the memory of the struggling figure at the foot of the lamppost, his contorted face picked out from the surrounding darkness by the yellow gaslight, was one he was unable to suppress.'[13] On another occasion he claimed he saw a shipwreck on the Scarborough coast 'when box after box was washed ashore and gold pieces . . . were to be had for the searching on the lamp-lit shore.'[14]

We should not conclude from the stories of his illnesses that Matthew had a dreary childhood – indeed it was a very privileged one and full of family theatricals, nicknames and jokes. His mother's diaries include notes of family excursions around the Lakes, the Yorkshire Moors and Dales, trips to Scarborough and Chester, weeks spent in their holiday home, Glenlyn, and expeditions by train to Manchester. The children would occasionally accompany their father on his London business trips and stay in the Metropole Hotel. Childhood journeys would have been in one of the family's horse-drawn carriages and later Frederic bought a thirty horse-power Silent Knight Daimler limousine which seated seven, including the chauffeur. There was also a succession of Rolls-Royces. Their homes afforded space and ample grounds to play the newly popular mixed games of croquet and tennis and by the 1890s they had the new-fangled bicycles. Materially Frederic saw his family lacked for nothing.

From Elmfield Terrace they moved further down the hill to 14 Elm View, where Harold was born. This was another large terrace house with three main floors, a small front garden, attics and a yard at the back. Then Phyllis and Maurice were born nearby in a very large house indeed, simply called Heathfield. In those days it had a long garden facing Beacon Hill and in this Matthew developed an early love of flowers. There were at least sixteen spacious rooms and in the 1891 census six live-in female servants are listed, though there must also have been gardeners and coachmen in attendance.

Frederic's education had been at King Edward's School, Birmingham, and he had gone on to become rich from his own endeavours. Now if his family firm was to continue and prosper he would need sons with leadership qualities and influential connections, and the way to provide those was by purchasing a good education for them. From the cosiness of home the boys were sent away to preparatory school, and Matthew's miseries began. First he went to a private school at Hilderthorpe, near Bridlington on the Yorkshire coast, though nothing is now known about how he fared there except that he was unhappy. At that time such 'boy farms' had dubious reputations because anyone could start one and recruit unqualified teachers to do as they liked, free from inspection.

In 1890 he returned as a day boy to the Halifax Heath Grammar School just up the road from Heathfield. This was founded in the late sixteenth century as a Free Grammar School and after many vicissitudes had been handsomely rebuilt the year before Matthew was born to accommodate 250 boys in twelve classrooms. Unfortunately, it did not recruit enough pupils and closed again until 1887, when it reopened with a new charter from Queen Victoria and the pledged support of local worthies such as the Smiths. Headmaster A. W. Reith and his five masters taught Mathematics, Science, French, German and History up to Cambridge external examination standards, while the caretaker supervised daily drill, and swimming in the local baths on Wednesdays. There is no mention of art in any school document and none of the Smith brothers appears on the Honours or Scholarship lists. Matthew hated these lessons but life outside school still had its pleasures: for example, when he was around fourteen Frederic allowed him to see *The Gondoliers*, which he found 'a paradise', and so he became a lifelong theatre enthusiast.[15]

By 1895 the family address was The Grange, Lightcliffe, the biggest property so far. This was in a pleasant village well away from the grime of the Hepple and Calder valleys, though linked to them by the railway which ran behind their walled garden and glasshouses. The house is now a home for the elderly but still imposing with its wide frontage, carriage drive and stable blocks.

It was from here that the three boys were dispatched on the final two-year polishing stage of their education. In September 1895 Matthew followed Arthur to Giggleswick School. This was an unexpected choice, since it was an Anglican foundation rather than nonconformist and in those days rather spartan, but eventually most of his male Smith cousins went there too. The school is set in a remote village in Ribblesdale and Smith was later to say 'the country around Giggleswick, where I spent my schoolboy days has some of the finest moorland scenery in the British Isles, though there was a time when I thought it the most depressing spot imaginable.'[16] His memories of it probably curbed any later temptation to plunge back into the Neo-Romantic, Palmer-derived tradition of seeing the English countryside as a place of Edenic innocence and bliss.

Giggleswick was even older than the Heath School, having been founded in 1507 and re-founded in 1553 by Edward VI. It served local needs until 1869 when it began to take boarders from the aspiring Yorkshire business and farming families. By the time the Smith brothers went the tuition fees were £8 and the board and washing £16 per term with various extras for the use of chemicals, the covered swimming-pool and the gymnasium, so Frederic was making a considerable investment in his sons' futures.

This was a boom period for public schools, since the expanding middle classes saw them as a means of giving their sons that extra something which would change them into gentlemen and leaders of men. From these schools they would go on to politics, the army, law, medicine, education, ruling the Empire, or perhaps running the family business. Other more creative ways of earning a living, such as art, music, the theatre or journalism were considered rather *déclassé* and were not mentioned in the Giggleswick prospectus. Character rather than intellectual development was what these schools stressed, and conformity to an agreed range of values rather than individualism was what they instilled. All used corporal punishment, and most copied the prefect system introduced by Thomas Arnold at Rugby as a means of teaching boys first to obey then to command others.

The curriculum at Giggleswick comprised Latin, Mathematics, Science, Scripture, French, History, and the option of Greek instead of German for university candidates. Lessons began at 7 a.m. and 'extras' such as joinery, gymnastics, singing, and swimming took place after 4 p.m. According to the prospectus of 1897 'drawing, artistic and technical, forms part of the regular work, except in the Fifth and Sixth Forms.' The lower forms had two one-hour periods with Mr Suddarts on drawing each week. What he taught them is not known, but copying casts and geometric models seems most likely.

Within this narrow curriculum Giggleswick achieved considerable success. The school history boasts that when the Head, Mr Styles, retired in 1904 'he left a Public School known throughout the land', rather than the 'small Grammar School' he had found on his arrival thirty-five years before. There were ten masters and around 150 boarders in Smith's day; between 1800 and 1900 they earned forty-two scholarships to Oxford, Cambridge, other universities, Woolwich and Sandhurst. None of the Smith boys contributed to this total.

It was only around the middle of the nineteenth century that team games began to have clear and widely accepted rules. Once these were in place, for example in rugby and cricket, such 'manly' sports became part of the public school regime. They fostered team spirit, fervent school patriotism and encouraged the subordination of individuality to the pursuit of a common goal. Arthur played rugby for the First XV, but Harold was no sportsman and by now Matthew had begun to have the eye trouble which would plague him for the rest of his life, and he was imprisoned behind fragile spectacles. His myopia meant he was useless at games so that his name appears only once in the eight editions of the *Giggleswick Chronicle* published while he was in the school, and that was for playing for his dormitory in an inter-dormitory cricket match. He scored o in the first innings, o in the second, took no catches and did not bowl.

For Matthew these were days of tribulation, especially as he was kept down in forms with boys younger than himself (one of them a cousin five years his junior) and only achieved form 4A in his last term, when he was well past the age of the boys in the Sixth Form. He was a timid boy, and as Dr Johnson sagely observed, 'Placing a timid boy in a public school is forcing an owl upon day.' A lifelong habit of self-deprecation began during these unhappy days.

The school did not neglect to instil Christian virtues into its charges and it was normal for many public school masters to be clergymen. At that time Giggleswickians had to attend services in the parish church, though before Matthew left he would have seen the site cleared for the building of the magnificent Byzantine chapel to mark Victoria's Diamond Jubilee. He seems to have emerged with no religious convictions and a rather flexible moral code.[17]

When the eighteen-year-old Matthew left Giggleswick in December 1897, it was with great relief, though he was a nervy young man with low self-esteem and no obvious talents. The bias of his education had been against the technology from which his family wealth derived and he emerged alienated from most of the things his father held to be self-evidently worthwhile. He had, however, acquired the accent, dress-sense and manners which in English society at that time signalled that one had had an expensive schooling and allowed one to pass as a gentleman.

He had no clear idea of what he could do with his life and even talks with his mother were no help. 'If you can't do anything, why don't you go into a shop?' she asked woundingly.[18] His exasperated father made the decision for him and as soon as Christmas was over sent him to work at Empsall and Firth, a Bradford woollen firm owned by friends, which made carpets and cloth. Most mornings he jumped on the early train with an empty stomach, so that when he drank gaseous ginger beer for lunch he was doubled up with indigestion. His duties were to wash skeins of wool but he seems to have made a mess of this. He was given no allowance by his father, presumably to teach him thrift and self-reliance now he was out in the real world and earning a wage. This rankled with Matthew, who told everyone who interviewed him in later years about his father's meanness at this time. He was soon sacked.

Within the year Frederic moved the family from Lightcliffe to another huge house with extensive grounds and its own tennis court called Dunham Lawn at Bowdon in Cheshire, just a few miles south-west of Manchester. There was a morning room, library, drawing-room, dining-room and music room on the ground floor, five family bedrooms on the second and extensive servants' quarters on the third. It was densely furnished in mahogany and walnut with aspidistras in most rooms and a fine collection of oriental carpets, screens and ceramics scattered throughout. It has now been replaced by a block of flats.

The middle class had by this date moved out from Manchester and Salford to places like Bowdon in order to escape the soot and squalor. Horse-drawn omnibuses, more paved roads for private cars and eventually electrified tramways all helped them reach their factories or the banks, clubs and the Exchange in the city centre. From this very desirable address Frederic, and soon his three reluctant sons, all dressed immaculately in suits and stiff collars, could commute the nine or ten miles to his new Anaconda Works in Salford. There the tubers, galvanizers, thick and thin drawers, thick reelers and annealers soon learned to address them as Mr Arthur Sir, Mr Harold Sir, and Mr Matthew Sir (soon shortened to MuzzArthurs, MuzzArolds, Muzz-

Matthews) and in later life when the brothers got together in London for a drink or two this is how they mockingly addressed each other.

Frederic took with him his family's company title so that he could claim his new company to have been founded in 1859. The letter heading now read: 'Frederick Smith & Co. Wire Manufacturers, incorporated in the London Electric Wire Company and Smiths Ltd'. This world of roaring furnaces, acid baths, water sprays, lime solutions and wire-drawing machines extruding smaller and ever smaller filaments of bronze, copper and aluminium now looked like being Matthew's future. He and his brothers were doomed to work under the stern eye of their father and learn the craft of making money.

CHAPTER 2

Manchester
1899–1904

In later life Matthew Smith was at pains to point out to anyone who asked him that he showed no artistic promise whatsoever in his youth. He said he spent this time in 'the darker ages of art' and that he never saw a good picture until he lived in London. He thought his father an implacable opponent of all things modern in art and it is true that Frederic's taste was very much of his time and class; nevertheless, he was hardly one of those parvenu manufacturers buying culture by the square yard.

Frederic had not grown up with Van Dycks, Titians or Claudes on his ancestral walls nor had he time to make the Grand Tour of European art centres, so he had no feelings of inferiority before foreign art and wanted to patronize the best Britain could produce – as he did with his Rolls-Royces. The Royal Academy dominated the English art market during Victorian times and it was natural that new patrons would consult the reviews in *The Times* for the names of those artists who had achieved critical success in its summer exhibitions and attained the status of Royal Academician.

Frederic liked the animal paintings of Briton Rivière,[1] the historical reconstructions and genre works of Dendy Sadler,[2] and was moved by G. F. Watts's allegory of blind *Hope* plucking her last lyre string in a darkening world.[3] Several RAs attended Frederic's soirées, and as we have seen earlier, he commissioned works from them. Julius Delbos, who was born in the same year as Smith, was a family friend and by 1906 had his genre works accepted by the Royal Academy – his success making Matthew's failure to get started all the more obvious. Perhaps as a way of rebelling against his father Matthew rejected his taste in pictures. Cathleen Mann, a friend of Matthew's old age, recorded in her diary:

His father took him one night when he was about 18 into his room like the Headmaster's, showed him some trees painted or engraved by Leader [Frederic owned the engraving *A Surrey Pine Wood* by B. W. Leader] and said 'That is the way you ought to paint.' I said 'Did you for a moment feel that perhaps you should paint like that?' 'No, no,' he said, 'not for one single instant.'[4]

If Matthew knew instinctively what he did not like he still had nothing to put in its place. He shared his ignorance of new Continental developments with Frederic and most of the British population, including the inward-looking art world in London. Nothing in the prestigious *Studio* magazine before 1908 indicated that anything other than academic Salon painting was being produced anywhere in Europe. However, Russell and Halliday's contemptuous comment that Frederic 'had no real feeling for the fine arts'[5] seems unfair when one considers that by the time Frederic died he had included in his collection not only originals or reproductions by Rossetti, Burne-Jones, Gainsborough and Turner, but contemporary works by the French painter Henri Moret[6] who had learned much from both Gauguin and Monet, and by the important Belgian Emil Claus.[7]

In spite of Matthew Smith's later disclaimers that his talent was 'only a tiny flame' Rothenstein tried to prove that there had been early stirrings of the artist's gifts:

At about the age of ten, Matthew Smith began to show a vague interest in painting. He collected invitation cards when they bore reproductions of drawings on them and stuck them into a book, and he copied elaborately a portrait of Lord Leighton out of 'the Pall Mall Gazette.' But he took no interest at all in the paintings by the popular academic artists that hung on the walls of his father's large gloomy house. His preoccupation grew in intensity, but it brought with it no definite aspirations, only a growing sense of isolation. He yearned to speak to someone about painting. One day a successful painter named Prescott Davis[8] called to see his father. As he was about to leave, the shy boy formed the desperate resolution of showing him his sketch-book, but the drawer in which it reposed stuck fast. After this humiliating, although unwitnessed defeat, his sense of isolation reached a pitch where he could hardly endure it.[9]

Smith told an interviewer that his father paid for private lessons when he was thirteen and that these consisted of painting flowers on tin plates. Frederic also financed Matthew's trip to London with a friend to see a Whistler retrospective in 1892. The same reporter wrote: 'When talking about himself his modesty is helped by a lively sense of humour. For instance when asked if any of his early drawings made in Halifax had been preserved he replied, "Good heavens! I hope not." '[10] This was not humour but plain truth. No work has survived from the first twenty-five years of Smith's life except one Christmas card of about 1895 which seems to be an inept copy of an advertisement. Amongst the surviving letters to Phyllis is one dated 5 May 1919 in which Matthew states: 'There is no kind of value to those early efforts of mine so please have them scrapped heartlessly as I do not want them and NEVER SHALL.' Phyllis, who normally treasured everything he gave her, must have this time complied with his request and, unfortunately, she seems to have understood that all the student work he did should be put to the flames too.

Rothenstein continues his tale: 'Believing that a business man ought to have intelligent interests to occupy his leisure, his father at first encouraged his predilection for painting, but so soon as it threatened to exclude all other interests, he began to regard it with hostile apprehension.'[11] This mounting tension between father and son must have been compounded by Matthew's ineptitude and lack of commitment as a businessman, which Frederic observed each day in the wire mills. Nor could he have been much impressed by Matthew's bumbling progress in his chosen hobby. Halliday and Russell pass on what Smith told them about the outcome:

Such was his [Matthew's] frustration, and despair, that at last he nerved himself to stand up to his father, choosing for this the solemn occasion of Sunday tea, at which the entire family was assembled at table. Might he, he asked, become a student of art? That excellent man, his father, put his own view cogently: the place of the arts was in those leisure hours when the serious business of the day was over. It was then, after all, that he collected his violins (and played on them) and wrote his verses. But Matthew remained adamant, declaring that he could not conform to his father's principles, and that if he was not allowed to devote himself to painting he would leave home. The family was silent, heads bowed, while Matthew and his father fought it out on their own. In the end Matthew won.[12]

For Frederic, art provided an escape from the industrial world where he spent his working hours. He collected paintings which aroused nostalgia for a rural or 'merrie' England he had never known, and which made no connection with the technology where his own creative talents lay. He would buy such works, but he did not expect his expensively educated sons to *produce* them. And what security could painting offer now that we had photography? Furthermore, artists associated with models who took their clothes off for money. There was surely something disreputable about artists: painters might visit socially, but it is clear from Fanny's diary that their wives did not accompany them. In his novel *The Newcomes*, W. M. Thackeray put into words the doubts of Frederic's generation:

The Muse of Painting is a lady, whose social position is not altogether recognised with us as yet. The polite world permits a gentleman to amuse himself with her, but to take her for better or worse! forsake all other chances and cleave to her! to assume her name! many a respectable person would be as much shocked at the notion, as if his son had married an opera dancer.[13]

Attempts were made to raise the status of Victorian artists by a crop of knighthoods (Raeburn, Lawrence, Wilkie, Calcott, Eastlake, Landseer, Millais, Poynter, Burne-Jones, Alma-Tadema, etc.), but people like Frederic were not fooled: for all their fame these people were still commercial artisans at the beck and call of their social superiors.

Frederic, like many of his kind, was more at ease with music for, as G. S. Messenger observed, 'Music touched a part of the Nonconformist's soul which the visual arts, with their suggestions of image worship, sensuality and "Popery" could never touch.'[14] This did not mean that the actual profession of musician was any the more respectable. A few miles away Matthew's future friend Delius had just fought a similar battle against his wool merchant father who would not let him be a musician. 'His sole objection to Fritz's decision . . . was that music as a profession was demeaning to a gentleman, a view by no means uncommon in middle class society in England.'[15]

Nevertheless, in spite of all his misgivings, Frederic Smith gave in. It seems unlikely that it was because Matthew's will was stronger, but probably Frederic and Fanny believed their nervy and delicate son would not survive for long if he did leave their comfortable home and plunged into the bohemian jungle of London. Frederic must have consoled himself with the thought that he still had two sons in the factory who showed no signs of rebellion. But before Matthew could begin to study art, in late 1901 he was sent on a summer cruise to St Petersburg, presumably to brace up his health since the doctor had diagnosed neurasthenia, or nervous tension. There is no further record of this trip beyond Smith's memory of seeing Rembrandt's *Danaë* in the Hermitage – one of the most intimate yet voluptuous depictions of a mature nude in art. Later he made drawings of it for his own pleasure.

Frederic insisted Matthew live at home and attend the local free college in Manchester: furthermore he must study applied design, not painting, because that way he would at least be doing something useful. He also telephoned the Principal and told him that on no account was his son to be allowed near any classroom where women were posing in a state of undress. Victoria had died that same year and the free-living Edward VII set a laxer moral tone for the nation, but Frederic was determined to maintain the chapel proprieties he had grown up with and he could impose the conditions because he was paying for Matthew's upkeep.

So Matthew went off each day by horse tram from his green suburb to the big city. Manchester had come through a turbulent century and emerged as perhaps the most important industrial conurbation in the world, not just a metropolis but a megalopolis. It had an astonishing boom in cotton goods early in the century but by 1900, when foreigners were catching up with their cotton production, Mancunians had diversified into engineering, chemicals, dyes, rubber, brewing, locomotives and armaments, all attracting new population, taking up land and polluting the air and rivers. In Matthew's time there it was so economically powerful that thirty-six foreign governments kept diplomatic or consular offices in the city.

A character in Disraeli's novel *Coningsby* (1844) says, 'Rightly understood, Manchester is as great a human exploit as Athens.' Certainly it had its cultural triumphs, but like Athens it also depended on a huge slave class. Friedrich Engels concluded that the local workers would inevitably rise up, as they had already tried to do in 1819, when they suffered the Peterloo massacre. The city had slums, drunkenness, racial tensions, crime and prostitution. Cobden, Bright, Mrs Gaskell, Dickens, Carlyle, Ruskin, Mrs Pankhurst and Morris amongst others had tried in their different ways to warn against the dehumanizing effects of such rampant capitalism. In 1901, when Matthew began his art classes, women and young people had just had their working week shortened to fifty-five-and-a-half hours.

In spite of its downtrodden workers Manchester was associated with liberalism. Many of the key figures in the Industrial Revolution, like Frederic Smith, were Baptists, Congregationalists, Presbyterians, Quakers or other kinds of nonconformist. They stressed industriousness (the 'Protestant work ethic') and self help. They trusted each other, intermarried, traded and carried out good works together. But sometimes their stress on reason, labour, thrift and self-discipline had a rather joyless side, as Matthew found with his father. He felt under constant pressure to produce something useful, uplifting and saleable which would justify Frederic's expenditure and excuse his own seeming idleness amidst the bustling world of Manchester's commerce.

He enrolled in autumn 1901 in the Art Department of Manchester Municipal School of Technology, which shared a building and some staff with the School of Art in All Saints Square. One of the teachers explained that 'the students in the Art Department of the Technical School are in the main of a humbler class and more in touch with industrial life, and there has been more opportunity at the Technical School of bringing the application of art right home to the student.'[16]

At this time provincial art schools and technical schools offering art courses were administered by the Science and Art Department of the Committee of the Council on Education (SAD for short), situated in South Kensington. Their inspectors also ran and examined an annual National Competition for Schools of Art which in its various sections reflected the curricula taught in these institutions. By 'industrial or applied design' it seemed mostly to mean drawing in a realistic manner for advertisements. Several of Smith's attempts to produce these have been found, though none of them is very good.[17] One of Matthew's sketchbooks preserved by Phyllis seems to contain poster roughs, and a letter to her dated 5 March 1905 indicated his contempt both for the tasks set and his own efforts to complete them:

Mr Waddell the sausage builder was over here a few weeks ago, saw some of my rubbish and gave me a commission to do him a poster though is only going to stump up two guineas for it – very meagre – considering the fuss he made about it and the bother I am having with it – got it on too small a piece of canvas to begin with and had to begin again.[18]

He also describes the poster he has done for a play: 'it ought to have been really good but it is really bad . . . it is shocking bad.' These seem to have been his first and last commissions; by the time he was a real artist painters were expected to find their own themes. Nor would there be any more 'applied' art from him – no book illustrations, no prints, no posters.

However, Matthew must have made some favourable impact on his teachers because in 1904 he gained two second-class certificates for free-hand drawing in outline and drawing on the blackboard (a requirement for trainee teachers). He must have also found ways to get round his father's prohibition against live models, as he joined the Art College evening classes in 1903 and took second-class certificates in drawing from antique sculpture and from life, and in 1904 a first-class award for the antique and second-class for life. In 1905 Smith won a commendation in the competition for the best nude from life, but sadly his submission has been lost. Later, on his application form to the Slade School of Art, he claimed Manchester Municipal School of Art as his previous place of education, so perhaps his surreptitious change-over from applied to fine art was eventually made official.

From examiners' reports on these annual competitions it would appear that to draw from the antique casts involved separate mechanical exercises on heads, hands and feet before the full figure was attempted. Again, with the living model the figure was approached piecemeal through studies of heads, hands, feet and drapery, and then timed sketches, rather as children were taught to read at that time by encountering letters, then syllables, words, and at last whole sentences that might mean something. The students were not allowed to include background, but had to set the figure in a white vacuum. Drawings were to be carefully shaded in charcoal and stump, or hard pencil, and might take weeks to complete. This tedious regimen was designed to instil the Grand Manner in future painters by showing them Graeco-Roman sculpture and Renaissance idealism in the work of Raphael and Michelangelo, all of which stressed the body's perfection rather than its flawed individuality. In the mindless reproduction of established poses and the limited vocabulary for depicting them there was a direct, if unconscious, reflection of the factory system outside.

Around this time another misfit appeared in the evening classes in the Art College, and his painstaking life studies do survive: this was L. S. Lowry, a local youth filling in his days as a clerk. Lowry mostly studied under Adolphe Valette (a French painter unusually inspired by Manchester's industrial scenery), who came to teach at Manchester School of Art in 1907, too late to have taught Matthew Smith. Matthew's middle-class upbringing had left him rootless and he was to remain a man without a base all his life. Lowry, on the other hand, never left England, never owned a car, and took all his visual nourishment from the few miles of urban sprawl round where he was born. He advised provincial art students to stay put: 'I can't think what you want to go to London for, you won't find any better lamp posts than you will in Wolverhampton! It's all a lot of nonsense! London doesn't *make* a painter any good just because he *goes* there. No sir, you can only paint where you belong – and that is where you are born.'[19] Matthew Smith never painted a townscape because he never related to any town in the way Lowry did to Salford or Manchester and, though he would live the rest of his life on the profits from manufacturing, his art would deny the existence of such places as the Caledonia and Anaconda wire works. Smith told a reporter in 1954 'that in his younger days despite his acquaintance with Yorkshire industrial areas, he had never had any desire to paint pictures with a social theme.'[20] His hope was that the college would soon show him something he might want to paint instead.

The Art School had already had an erratic history since its foundation in 1838. It had undergone several changes of title (and was to suffer more) and several changes of location before settling in the building

Matthew so disliked. From its early days it had tried to respond to the local textile industry's need for designers and draughtsmen whilst also teaching 'fine' art. Central to both was the discipline of drawing, though whether the subject matter was to be natural forms, the idealized nude, geometrical figures or the antique was a continuing argument. By the time Matthew arrived the curriculum was under the influence of Walter Crane, William Morris and the Arts and Crafts movement in a vain attempt to humanize the industrialization outside the college walls. Artisan skills in furniture, fabrics, glass, embroidery, tiles, enamel and china were taught, as well as wood and marble carving, but Smith never showed, then or later, any interest in doing such things. However, all students, whether full-time or part-time, trainee teachers, craftsmen or artists, had to attend drawing classes. The Board of Education Inspectors reported in 1904:

A healthy tone prevails in the School, and it may in part be attributed to the good feeling existing between the students and the staff, to the assiduous and enthusiastic efforts of the teachers, and the energetic supervision of the Headmaster [Richard Glazier]. The work generally is satisfactory, and much of it excellent. On the whole this School appears to be doing a great work in Manchester, and is worthy of the highest encouragement.[21]

Matthew later told people he resented the four years spent at the school as a waste of his time. 'Just think,' he would say, 'if I'd had those four years in London! Such a dreadful building too – made you feel as if a bear might jump out and eat you.' This is unfair to Manchester School of Art, which has a handsomely carved entrance and a stone-faced façade opening on to a square, which in Smith's time was dominated by All Saints' church. The problem was that he was not a natural student. The evidence suggests that the academic teaching and facilities he had were as good as any then available in England, but he could not fit in or take from them what he needed, because as yet he did not know what it was that he did need. The other students were from poorer homes and schools so that to them he must have appeared a privileged dabbler and a dilettante. His premature baldness also accentuated the age difference between them. They nicknamed him Mr Futile.[22]

Matthew hated above all the plodding style of drawing he was taught as he showed in this conversation twenty years later with Alden Brooks:

His story was that he had spoiled at least three canvases that day as he tried to get going on a still life . . . I gave him this advice: Why don't you for once just attach yourself to your subject, just try to *draw* it for once – just to get yourself going? A last gasp from Smith: 'One doesn't need to draw it. If one sees a thing truly one *does* draw it.' A few days later he showed me a painting he did in his pre-Slade School days – a bottle painted with photographic realism, painted for some medical advertisement, and said with heavy sarcasm: 'There's drawing for you.'[23]

Fanny Smith's diary for 9 July 1904 records 'Matthew went to join Mr Frank Caulderon's sketching class at Liphook, Hampshire – to be away two months.' The Art School encouraged these summer sketch clubs and again Frederic must have paid the fees rather than have his one unproductive son drooping round the house all summer. The sketchbook from this excursion shows pencil drawings of the muscles in horses' legs copied from a textbook, fragments of a figure in a chair and a simplified country lane heavily hatched right to left (Smith was right-handed). It was a summer of great heat and perhaps he was too enervated to get more involved. So, there was still no tangible evidence available to convince his father that Matthew was cut out to be an artist.

When he returned to Dunham Lawn he found Phyllis had been dispatched to a boarding school in Hendon. Matthew wrote a series of letters to her addressed to Sweet Little Phyl and signed Maffy. In his loopy uncoordinated writing he gave her the family gossip and little domestic glimpses like this: 'Mater and especially Pater are buzzing exasperatingly round the table Pater is dictating a letter to mater mater is fratchy with Pater Pater with Mater and I am a bit vexed with the two of them.' He asks Phyllis not to mention in her reply that he has sneaked off with Nancy Hutchinson, evidently his girlfriend of the moment, to see the pantomime in Liverpool, which he thought vastly superior to the Manchester ones he's seen.[24] In a letter of March 1904 he calls Harold 'generosity personified (hoh)' for giving him a watch and says the Pater has come across with a cheque for £10 which 'relieves my financial position a little though I am still crying out for cash.' He was by now twenty-five and still relying on his Father for pocket money, but when Phyllis 'came out' in 1905 Frederic provided a marquee dance for 150 guests, so he was not always the miser his son claimed.

Manchester offered several cultural opportunities at its Literary Club, Hallé Orchestra concerts, and serious theatres. Frederic took an active part in these as well as the Automobile Club. Matthew usually avoided highbrow cultural events, then and later, and preferred pantomimes, musicals, or Henry Irving acting in various melodramas. He and Harold clung to each other in terror on the walk back to Dunham Lawn after seeing Irving's performance in *The Bells*. In the last years of his life Smith painted two grotesque heads of Irving based on these early dramatic memories.[25] He also mingled with his social peers at tennis parties, dances and outings in the family cars.

The mature Matthew Smith declared, 'I think every provincial town should possess a few old masters. People cannot begin to know anything about art unless they see really worthwhile pictures. For instance a Botticelli in a provincial art gallery could teach people the true value of many of the other pictures exhibited. I think comparison, to some extent, helps to form people's taste in art.'[26]

Manchester in 1901–5 had no touchstone of this quality on display. It was rich only in those Victorian anecdotalists he already knew from his father's walls and bookshelves. Matthew felt some mild affection for the Madox Brown frescos showing the history (largely fictitious) of Manchester in the neo-Gothic Town Hall. He later recalled enjoying the outstanding collection of Pre-Raphaelites in the City Art Gallery, some in medievalist vein, and others sharply focused tableaux produced in response to Ruskin's injunction to the Brotherhood to 'go to nature with all singleness of heart, selecting nothing, rejecting nothing.' The academic painters in all their moods were also represented here, from Barrie and Leighton's frigid classicism, through Lady Butler's war pictures to the sentimental realism of Frith, Stanhope Forbes and Herkomer. William Etty, a sensual figure painter, whose copy of a Rubens nude Matthew later came to own, was represented then by a self-portrait and an apocalyptic scene of angels and devils. Their long poetic titles are crucial to the observer's understanding of most of these works, but Matthew Smith never wanted to become a story-teller or user of symbols, or concern himself with creating imaginary worlds, so that if we lost all his titles it would be of little consequence. His appeal would be direct to the eye and emotion, not to the intellect or to learning, but that breakthrough was still a long way off.

One of his letters to Phyllis reveals that he was becoming aware of artistic events beyond Manchester. In spring 1905 he wrote in frustration: 'I have been longing to go to the Whistler exhibition and to think that you have been, you must tell me all about it. Did you not think the portrait of Miss Alexander magnificent, his mother and of course Carlyle and no doubt crowds of others I know nothing about'.

The next letter shows he did get up to London and the New Gallery's Whistler memorial exhibition (Whistler having died in 1903). A very muddy portrait of Phyllis must date from this time and is perhaps his reaction to Whistler's crepuscular tones – he may even have copied Whistler's technique of painting on a black ground. It is his earliest surviving oil and now belongs to Phyllis's younger son Michael.

None of these haphazard explorations was very relevant to his studies as an industrial designer, and by now it was evident even to his father than Matthew was no more capable of being a designer of utilitarian objects than he was of being an entrepreneur.

By the time he was twenty-five Matthew Smith had lived in five houses, each more luxurious and heavily staffed than the last, attended four all-male schools and lived in Halifax, Bridlington, Giggleswick, Bowden and Manchester. His upbringing had left him rootless, and his long expensive education had not equipped him to do anything very useful in the world. It was time to eat humble pie again and to ask his father for yet another hand-out so he could study art in London.

CHAPTER 3

London
1905–1908

Frederic Smith, with great forbearance, and no doubt after several stern lectures, agreed that Matthew should be given a second chance to make a career as an artist. He would pay for his son to go to a London art college. There were about ten to choose from and apart from the first established, the Royal Academy School (1786), all the others were Victorian foundations. In the end Matthew, or more likely his father, chose the Slade School, a part of University College, London University. Frederic took his son to London, as Fanny's 1905 diary records:

October 3rd. Poor dear old Math left for London.
Fred went to London too.
October 5th. Fred came back from London. Math has joined the Slade Art School and is at the Gower Hotel until he gets rooms.

So long as somebody guaranteed to pay the annual fees of £21, entry requirements were not high nor procedures elaborate – just the presentation of a folio of work and an interview with Professor Brown or Assistant Professor Tonks. To the inevitable question 'Why do you want to come to the Slade?' the answer you were supposed to give was 'Because I want to learn to draw.'[1]

Before starting his course Matthew took a summer holiday with his brothers in Germany, but the only family memory of this is that he lost his passport, having put it in a safe place and then forgotten where it was. Around this time he also lost his evening dress on the way to a dance. Anecdotes like this come from all periods of his life illustrating his family's belief that 'poor dear old Math' was the family clown and not in charge of the little practicalities of life. He later told a friend that they always considered him to be an idiot,[2] yet it was he who gleefully told everyone about his various calamities,

Frederic took the risk of paying the Slade fees for the whole year rather than term by term, which put Matthew under pressure to stay and make a go of it. Since he was over twenty-one he was ineligible for the two scholarships or any smaller prizes the Slade offered, so once more he relied on his father's rather meagre hand-outs. Matthew may not have been affluent but there was no way Frederic would allow a Smith of Halifax to starve or go without a roof over his head. His term address was soon 10 Thurlow Road in fashionable Hampstead and he journeyed in by bus or tube to Warren Street and then walked to the Slade's Gower Street premises.

Felix Slade, a rich patron of the arts, had left £35,000 to endow two theoretical Professorships of Art at Oxford and Cambridge (Ruskin accepted the latter), and a 'Felix Slade Faculty of Fine Arts', to be run by and for practising artists within the University of London. From its inauguration in 1871 teaching at the Slade was meant to be different from those official Government Schools of Art and Design such as the one in Manchester, and also from the Royal Academy which at the turn of the century was going through one of its periods of stagnation. Even the conservative *Studio* magazine complained, 'The Academy is contented to plod on year by year in the same path, to hang what are to all appearances the same pictures, and to do things exactly as they were done in that remote period when its ideals were fresh and its principles were first formulated.'[3] Many Slade students, Smith included, remained hostile to the Academy all their lives, an attitude they absorbed from their professors (Steer had been turned down as a student and Tonks had failed to get the Professorship of Anatomy there).

In the year Matthew Smith joined it the Slade had 244 students, of whom 204 were female. This imbalance of the sexes was not then unusual in art colleges. Most of these were young middle-class women from the Home Counties (several had titles) filling their leisure hours acquiring genteel skills before marriage, but sprinkled amongst these amateurs were a few with outstanding talents, such as Gwen John. One feature which may have appealed to them (as it did to Smith) was that there were no formal written examinations, though it was claimed the courses were of degree standard. Instead, certificates for each of the various courses were awarded by the tutors on the basis of submitted work.

The prospectus insisted that 'No woman is admitted as a Student of the College except upon the recommendation of the Lady Super-intendent, Miss Morison, and upon producing a satisfactory reference or introduction.' The two sexes were not encouraged to mingle, the regulations stating quite clearly that 'the men and women Students work together in the Antique class only.' Professor Brown snarled at one male student he had seen talking to a female student: 'This is not a marriage bureau.'

Yet, in spite of their prissiness, the Slade staff had given priority to the study of the nude from the school's very inauguration:

The curriculum at the Slade School emphasized life study as the sine qua non of a serious art curriculum. 'Constant study from the life model,' said Sir Edward Poynter (a distinguished painter of the nude who would later become director of the National Gallery and President of the Royal Academy) in his opening address as the school's first director, 'is the only means of arriving at a comprehension of the beauty in nature and of avoiding its ugliness and deformity; which I take to be the whole aim and end of study.'[4]

He was referring of course to the idealization of the models' bodies into the heroic creatures of history painting, which for painters of his generation was, indeed, the whole aim and end of their endeavours. This process began in the Antique class.

Smith would already know from Manchester that the Antique Room contained white plaster casts of Greek and Roman statues. The male Apollos and athletes threw discuses, wrestled, shot arrows, aimed spears or throttled snakes, showing off their perfect musculatures and tiny hairless genitalia. The assorted Venuses stood or lay, calm and modest, their breasts unaffected by gravity and their smooth bodies proportioned as if by mathematical formulae. Apart from the technical skills to be acquired by studying bodies which never moved or needed a break there were subliminal lessons being learned here about the active male and the passive female.

It must have been a shock for someone with Smith's prim upbringing to pass from the sterile goddesses of the Antique Room to the real models in the life room. These were working-class women often past their youth and with bodies marked by bad diet, child-bearing, boots, corsets, sweat and body hair. It was a shock his father had tried, unsuccessfully, to spare him in Manchester. Ruskin, who had studied the classical world, Renaissance madonnas, and Victorian history paintings since childhood but had never attended a life class, saw the body of his bride for the first time and was allegedly made impotent by disgust. The difficult task set the art student was to see these real bodies in an idealized way, to see a Cockney miss as Venus, and then to put her into paintings which took their subject matter from classical literature, or medieval or Christian myths. Sir Lawrence Alma-Tadema, Albert Moore, Lord Leighton and Sir Edward Poynter himself were still widely venerated exemplars of this manner when Smith began his studies in the Antique Room.

Life classes were segregated, though in both classrooms the prospectus said 'Figure models pose every day and draped models three days a week.' Models could not be spoken to by anyone other than the tutors, and one student remembers that still in the 1920s in the Men's Life Room 'the model's throne was surrounded by a net, to catch any female model who might faint, so that no male hands should touch her.'[5] Even so the Slade was considered very advanced for the time in allowing the students to draw from living figures so relatively early in their courses.

All these prohibitions and regulations seemed designed to raise the sexual temperature and to make drawing the nude something special, towards which all the other courses led. For Smith the nude remained the most exciting subject for the rest of his career, but only the female nude, as there is no record that he ever drew from the male model after he left college. He also preferred to have a sexual or social relationship with his sitter rather than hire professional models.

Poynter set out to introduce the 'free and intelligent manner of drawing' (to use his own words) of those French ateliers where he had studied himself, for example under Gleyre, who in turn was a follower of Ingres. Poynter stayed only five years at the Slade before moving on to fame and honours and then ultimate oblivion as new ideas from Europe swept aside his brand of history picture. In Smith's day he was entitled Visitor. When Poynter retired he recommended a French painter, Alphonse Legros (1837–1911), as his successor in the professorship. Legros was a Realist much influenced by Courbet and Millet, and was also a friend of Degas and Whistler. He stressed the necessity for free but solidly modelled drawing – what William Rothenstein, one of his pupils, called 'a severe and logical method of constructive drawing – academic in the true sense of the word.'[6]

Drawing thus became the rock upon which all the Slade's teaching was founded. The next Slade Professor, Frederick Brown (1851–1941), ruled from 1892 to 1918. He was a minor artist perhaps, but also a teacher of high standards. In his time numbers rose so sharply that it became a policy to try to reduce them to prevent overcrowding in the limited space. He has been described thus:

This rather grim figure, with his greying hair, moustache and chin-tuft, his prognathous jaw and grave bespectacled eyes, was invariably dressed in a black frock coat. His masseter muscles were especially prominent, as if his teeth were permanently clenched, giving him the appearance of a man who would stand no nonsense – nor would he.[7]

He had studied in Paris in the early 1880s and his friend, the critic D. S. MacColl, described what kind of style he had picked up there: 'In Paris it is associated with the ateliers of Julian, and it may be traced back to a caricature of the mannerisms of Bastien-Lepage. In its extreme form this painting may be recognised by a swagging way of painting across forms, by a choppy rendering of planes and by attention to values at the expense of colour.'[8] MacColl was pleased that Brown later moved on from this grey-toned Realism and its concern with peasants to rediscover colour and the Edwardian pleasures of painting ladies lolling on sofas or leaning against pianos.

Along with other like-minded Paris-trained artists Brown founded the New English Art Club in 1886 to provide an alternative exhibition outlet to the stuffy closed shop of the Royal Academy, and to introduce French ideas of Realism and Impressionism to the insular British public. Brown and his friends were already out of date because in that very year the Impressionists held their last group exhibition and it was dominated by the Pointillists, first wave of the Post-Impressionists, who were determined to put some structure back into modern French painting.

Brown appointed one of his own ex-students from Westminster School of Art to teach drawing at the Slade. Henry Tonks (1862–1937) had been a qualified surgeon and Demonstrator in Anatomy at the London Medical School and Senior Resident Medical Officer at the Royal Free Hospital, and he brought this hands-on knowledge into his teaching of figure drawing. He was thirty before he could move from part-timer to full-time artist and lecturer. Once established at the Slade, Brown seemed to shrink and make less impact whilst Tonks came to represent the Slade ethos and style until Tonks *was* the Slade. He imposed a graphic manner on a series of brilliant students: 'What a brood I have raised' he would say, shaking his head. Those who were not so brilliant received the lash of his tongue.

Even his friends found Tonks a strange mixture of contradictions:

A dour puritanical strain, revealed by the thin-lipped, sour mouth, the chilly stare, and a fussiness in the ordering of his daily life (he smoked, for instance, at fixed times of day, usually with reference to his watch), seemed incongruous with his sometimes Rabelaisian humour, the faint strain of impropriety apt to reveal itself in his conversation, and the sheer prettiness of much of his art.[9]

What the awed students did not see were his funny caricatures of his friends and his shrewd political cartoons. He never had trouble with discipline and weeded out those who did not feel the seriousness of their calling. 'He stood for probity,' Adrian Daintrey said, and Smith might well have been reminded of his stern father.

Tonks believed anybody of normal intelligence, even duffers like Smith, could be taught to draw. Clear thought led to clear vision which led to clear expression. It was merely a practical problem of conveying round things on flat paper – but once achieved, 'The drawings of great men are like lines in Shakespeare, the beauty of which are beyond explanation.' Tonks revered the Italian masters as well as Velázquez, Ingres, Watteau, Millais and Rubens ('a prince of painters, richer and finer in his appreciation of what life can offer than almost anyone else, a pagan really with a passionate love of flesh').[10] He based his teaching methods equally upon his knowledge of anatomy and study of the masters' examples.

'Observe the construction of the forms and then explain it' was his basic message, only then was hatching or shading in pencil or charcoal used to add volume. Local colour was to be ignored. Tonks's methods were founded on the search for directions and egg-shapes. By 'directions' he meant the direction of the bones and by mastering these one had mastered the contour ('The word "outline" did not exist for him, and he would not allow it'[11]).

The egg-like shapes were more confined to the thorax and abdomen than the limbs; but sometimes Tonks would run his charcoal round the portion of a limb, especially a thigh. He then put in the shading in long light strokes slashing longitudinally, only occasionally running his charcoal across the form; this was getting the drawing 'set up' (securing a general light movement before working out a particular part) and should not, he said, take more than ten minutes. He believed in keeping the drawing open, not tight, and warned pupils against committing themselves to a contour until they were tolerably certain where that contour had to go, because 'error is man's natural tendency.' 'You must give God a chance,' he used to say, in connection with keeping the drawing light and open; and in the final stages he was very much interested in the subtle shadows and reflected lights that fall across forms. The master anatomist was seen in the way in which he drew his limbs. He would confess that he had no idea what the figure looked like to anyone who was unacquainted with anatomy.[12]

Smith was certainly unacquainted with it and his depiction of anatomy would remain shaky all his career. Unlike Tonks he had small interest in the analysis of structure and in his mature works there is little sense of the skeleton beneath the flesh or the skull behind the face. It is easy to find examples of hands like flippers, over-long arms or dislocated necks and he seems to have funked the depiction of feet altogether. His response to the body would eventually be of a fundamentally different kind from his tutor's.

Tonks also advocated the traditional checks of a plumb line for verticals and horizontals in the early stages and drawing sight size with measurements made by closing one eye and holding up the pencil to check them off against the model's body and the sight-size drawing. Nobody remembers Matthew Smith doing any of these drills in later life.

What Smith was being taught here was an objective way of seeing and drawing that was methodical, logical, painstaking, and realistic, but in the wrong hands utterly safe and dull. Tonks had moved Slade drawing on from Poynter's idealizing process only to replace it by a new set of formulae. Smith must have found this constricting and passionless, but as yet knew of no alternatives. He, like Wyndham Lewis, Spencer, Paul Nash, Nevinson and Gwen John, would somehow have to gain the confidence to defy Tonks's rules if he was to gain a graphic style of his own.

When the Post-Impressionists' brightly coloured but awkwardly drawn pictures began to be seen around London, especially after those people Tonks called 'the Roger Fry rabble' set up the 1910 and 1912 shows at the Grafton Gallery, Tonks fought a rearguard action against all things new in painting, whether Post-Impressionism, Cubism, Futurism, Vorticism, Abstraction or Surrealism, on the basis that none of them could draw. 'I don't believe I really like any modern development,' he declared with stubborn pride.

Tonks was not against Impressionism itself because, as a member of the New English Art Club, he obviously learned from it: he too was concerned with the fall of light on a young girl's skin, or fine cloth, or flowers, and his models were the same bourgeoisie at play. When Monet died in 1926 Tonks suggested to his students that they should lay a wreath before one of his works in the Tate Gallery. The Impressionists were analytic of light, even if by Tonks's standards they were not of form. They tried to record appearances objectively, basing their claim to a new kind of realism on the scientific colour theories of Chevreul, Rood and Charles Henry. Shadows were no longer built in layers or made by adding black to the local colour but, as Sickert put it, 'the colour in the shadow must be the sister of the colour in the light.' So the dark side of a red ball would contain green and the shade under a green tree in yellow sunlight might be violet. They were aware that colours in proximity modify each other; that local colour is changed by the colour of the light it is seen by; that an isolated colour, say red, is surrounded by an aureola of its complementary, green; and that if you put the primaries blue and yellow side by side on a white ground the eye sees them as a fresher green than if you had mixed them together on the palette. They made two other significant contributions to twentieth-century painting: they depicted modern urban subjects, and they applied their paint more spontaneously so their 'handwriting' showed in individual brush strokes.

What so enraged Tonks about the later Post-Impressionists such as Gauguin or Van Gogh or Matisse was that they rejected these Impressionist breakthroughs and made a virtue of being subjective. Forms were distorted and outlined whilst colours were chosen for their associations and emotional impact, not for their reference to the world out there. These later French pictures were all about messy feeling and these were not things you could teach methodically. Furthermore, he could never understand the importance given to the inept draughtsman Cézanne by those loud-mouthed 'Art Boys', Roger Fry and Clive Bell, whilst Bell's dictum that 'the representative element in a work of art may or may not be harmful; always it is irrelevant,' must have made him foam at the mouth. Tonks stated his own passionately held credo in this way:

Artists are perhaps as likely as any to come nearer to the meaning of life: why I hate Post-Impressionism or any form of subjectivity is because they, its followers, do not see that it is only possible to explain the spirit as long as we are in the world, by the things of the world, so that the painting of an old mackintosh (I don't pretend to explain how) very carefully and *realistically* wrought may be much more spiritual than an abstract landscape. There is no short cut to poetry, it has to be dug by the sweat of his brow out of the earth, and it comes to a man without his knowing it; in fact one must never look for it. Of course it sounds absurd seeing the dreadful things we do, but a painter who is not a poet ought to be put in the stocks.[13]

He was looking for a spiritual art expressed by earthly means and he was almost messianic in his fervour:

I want to have an Art Revival as they do in religion. I feel I could go and weep and rave in Hyde Park and beg people to repent and turn to art before it is too late and they are destroyed like Sodom and Gomorrah – we laugh, as we laugh at everything (curse us) but this is true, unless a man believe in art he cannot be saved, and *everyone* must as they did when Donatello lived and Brunelleschi.[14]

This, then, was the tyrannical zealot under whom the insecure and retiring Smith was to learn to draw. Superficially he and Tonks should have had much in common, having similar northern manufacturing backgrounds, sickly childhoods, miserable public school life, little natural facility and late starts in their artistic training. But Tonks was older, aloof, and not inclined to interest himself in students unless he thought they were as outstanding as Augustus John, or they were pretty girls – and Smith was obviously neither. Here was yet another domineering patriarch Smith would have to rebel against if he was to become master of his own fate. If he could cut free of his father by rejecting academic painting then one day, when he knew more about these things, he might be able to get back at Tonks by embracing Gauguin, Van Gogh, Cézanne and Matisse.

Tonks was famous for his cruel tongue (Rothenstein called him 'grim, sardonic, discouraging and bitter'). He addressed one woman student as follows: 'Your paper is crooked, your pencil is blunt, your donkey wobbles, you are sitting in your own light, your drawing is atrocious. And now you are crying and you haven't got a handkerchief.'[15] On at least two occasions he turned his pitiless eye on Smith, asking in front of the whole life class, 'What in the world made *you* think of taking up painting? I give you six months to see what you can do.'[16] Smith himself told of this humiliation with understandable bitterness later in life. Tonks's more considered evaluation of Smith was 'No sense of drawing, no ability to paint.' Tougher students could shrug this off and claim later that to be insulted by Tonks 'was an almost infallible proof of merit and a title to consideration,'[17] but to a spirit as sensitive and vulnerable as Smith's this must have been deeply wounding. We have no way of knowing if Tonks's scorn for Smith's student work was justified because none of it survives, presumably because he destroyed it himself in a fit of depression. Given Smith's self-deprecation and low morale at this time he probably agreed with Tonks's judgement of him.

Adrian Daintrey, another ex-student, saw this brutal denigration of student performance as deliberate:

The policy of the school was, as I see it now, to act as a means of purification by which all the triviality and vulgarity, which frequently accrues to the half-educated in the modern world, should be pruned from the student. For this purpose the sarcastic tongue of Tonks, sharpened by years of practice, was always at work. The trouble was that, thus stripped, the pupil had frequently in the process lost all self-confidence, so that he was now incapable of rebuilding on the flattened surface of his personality. The result was that, in my time, practically no-one was able to produce a finished picture of any kind, which was after all what one might hope to learn to do in an art school.[18]

Painting was a separate skill taught by Wilson Steer (1860–1942), who had worked at Julian's in Paris (though he does not seem to have seen much of the advanced work going on around him). He also painted at Etaples, a location favoured by Monet, whose work Steer came to admire. When Brown was appointed to the Professorship he asked the young Steer to join him as Assistant Teacher of Painting. Unlike Brown and Tonks, Steer was an important painter – even Roger Fry thought him 'one of the most gifted and purest artists that we have ever had in England.' Steer borrowed what he needed from Whistler, the Impressionists, the Pointillists, and his exact contemporary Sickert, but created wholly individual work, such as his beach scenes with girls paddling, running or shrimping. He was fond too of young maidens languishing on couches and was a painter of nudes, though some of these are rather frothy confections in the Fragonard tradition. He also did a number of small oil sketches outdoors in the early 1890s which rival Monet in their immediacy and rough handling of high-toned paint. His early Frenchified works stirred up the hostility of the critics but then, after about 1893, he turned back to the works of Turner and Constable for inspiration, and by his one-man exhibition of 1909 he was hailed as their natural successor and a defender of those native virtues of amateurism, escapism and lyricism against the brash incursions of French intellectualism and formalist experimentation.

In his long service to the college Steer became a legend as a valetudinarian, cat lover, a hoarder of beautiful china and Greek coins, and as a man of utter lethargy in mind and body. He fell asleep as soon as theory was discussed. For him 'muddling about with paints' was a 'job like any other, something one has to do between meals' and all the rest airy-fairy nonsense. 'Well, you can't do better than the old masters, we all know that!' was about as far as he would go. Other fatuous Steer pronouncements were that 'Watercolour is like a cow eating grass, oil painting like a cow chewing the cud,' and 'nasty colour never becomes nice colour. A picture has to be nice colour from beginning to end.'

Students had to learn from him by looking at his works, rather than listening for insights in his words. He thought Van Gogh 'shouted too loud' and was reduced to asking his students to explain the point of Matisse's painting.[19] He was obviously not going to be the teacher Smith needed to initiate him into modern painting.

Once Tonks thought a student had made enough progress in drawing he was allowed to begin oils with a dull palette of flake white, black, raw umber and yellow ochre.[20] All studies were to be made direct from the model, not from imagination, nor from squared-up working drawings in the way Sickert advocated. In spite of these prescriptions students complained that such simple techniques as laying out a palette, mixing, painting fat over lean, glazing or scumbling were not taught in any systematic way. Students at the Royal Academy were taught their craft better than this. Unlike the drawing classes, painting sessions seem to have been very *laissez-faire*. As Daintrey recalls: '. . . one was never told about the various mediums that can be used to make the handling of oil paint easier, and so for years one used to slosh about with turpentine in one compartment and oil in the other of the twin dipper on the palette.'[21]

Smith himself remained an inadequate technician long after he left the Slade, adding too much linseed and other oddities to his colours, which meant that some parts of them are still sticky fifty years after they were painted, whilst other parts were over-thinned and now suffer from craquelure. Flaking is a problem for his works of all periods since he often used inferior canvas which could not bear the load of paint, and some works he varnished and others he did not, seemingly without system. Compared to the rigorously trained Victorian painters he despised, Smith knew very little about paint craft.

Steer's advice to students was to begin with the extremes of light and dark, gradually linking them up, whereas Tonks began with the middle tones and worked back in both directions, towards light and dark. Unfinished works in Smith's studio show that he never did decide on just one methodical way of starting a canvas; each one remained a new struggle.[22] Tonks's main interest was in subtle effects of light, so if students tried unmodified colours in the new French manner, this was dismissed as 'tea-tray painting'. His early interest in the Pre-Raphaelites meant Tonks was also more interested in detail and 'finish' than his friend Steer, so the students received conflicting messages from their tutors. We can now see that the Slade style of painting, with its emphasis on tonality rather than colour, was another burden Smith would have to shake off, along with objective drawing.

To complement the practical work there were lectures in perspective and courses which drew upon expertise from other faculties in University College. Not all of these were compulsory, so it is no longer clear which Smith attended. In the second and third terms there were twenty lectures on the anatomy of bones, joints and muscles 'illustrated by demonstrations on the Living Model', followed by ten lectures on 'The Physics and Chemistry of Colours' and one might guess he gave these a miss. The influential critic (and later biographer of Steer and Keeper of the Tate Gallery), D. S. MacColl (1859–1948), was employed to educate the students in the History of Art, and in Smith's time these lectures covered Sculpture, Titian, Rembrandt, Rubens, and Velázquez, who was particularly in vogue following the 1899 study of him by R. A. M. Stevenson, showing how he stood in the tradition of Titian and Rubens and linked forward to Manet, Whistler and the Impressionists.[23] Then came French and English Painters of the eighteenth century; French and English Painters of the nineteenth century; Monumental Sculpture (Medieval to Modern) then Monumental Painting (Giotto to Modern). The course on the history of sculpture was strange, since sculpture was not practised in the school, and neither were printmaking techniques such as etching. Although MacColl had been to France and knew the Impressionists at first hand he shared the view of his friend, the writer George Moore, that 'the first step in the artistic education of this country is to persuade students it is not necessary to go to Paris' – hence perhaps the lack of any living artists on the syllabus. On paper Smith would seem to have been offered a demanding, if patchy, grounding in the theory and practice of art as it existed at that time in England, but virtually all of it he would have to discard.

We must presume that Smith visited the free public art collections of London such as the National Gallery, the National Portrait Gallery, The Tate, the Wallace Collection, Dulwich and others. The commercial galleries showing contemporary works were also available but he left no indication of what he saw, apart from the Whistler memorial show. Not that Smith was actively seeking out works much in advance of those on his father's walls at home. He was back at Dunham Lawn during January and February 1905 when the London Grafton Gallery showed the Paris dealer Durand-Ruel's collection of 315 Impressionist works, and nothing in his letters indicates he was even aware of what he had missed. The English avant-garde had by then largely assimilated Impressionism, though the general public had not and this show was not a commercial success.

In a letter of September 1907[24] to a fellow student, Smith reports his visit to Liverpool's Walker Art Gallery autumn exhibition and conveys his enthusiasm for it as 'an excellent one; all the best Academy pictures – the 2 best Sargents, 2 or 3 New English, and quite a lot of Salon pictures'. He particularly noted works by well-known but hardly progressive painters of the day such as Muirhead, Pryde and de Glehn. He attended the International Society exhibition of spring 1907 and picked out for praise the French Symbolist Puvis de Chavannes. At the same venue a year later he must have passed by works by Gauguin, Matisse, Cézanne, Bonnard, Denis, Van Gogh, Monet, Signac and Vuillard, but unfortunately without recorded comment. There were no signs yet that his long rejection of what Tonks and the Slade stood for had begun.

CHAPTER 4

Whitby
1906–1907

A school achieves its reputation through its successful students as much as from its teachers, and the Slade produced some of the best. Before Smith arrived in 1905 Ambrose McEvoy, Wyndham Lewis, Spencer Gore, Harold Gilman, Ethel Walker, Gwen Salmond, Gwen John, Walter Russell, and the child genius Edna Waugh (who entered at fourteen) had passed through in glittering succession. The drawings of Augustus John and William Orpen were still pinned to life-room walls to show what good students were capable of. These were of Smith's actual age group, born around 1878–9, but they were all more precocious than he was and sorted out their ambitions sooner. Eventually he would catch up with and learn from this cohort, but meanwhile he was doomed, as in Giggleswick and Manchester, to compete and fail against people younger than himself.

Smith's Slade period marked a lull before another peak just prior to the First World War, with Stanley Spencer, William Strang, Edward Wadsworth, Mark Gertler, David Bomberg, William Roberts, Alvaro Guevara, Jacob Kramer, Bernard Meninsky, Gilbert Spencer, Duncan Grant, William Wadsworth, Dora Carrington, Paul Nash, Ben Nicholson, and Christopher Nevinson to follow him. Smith's own college contemporaries were good but not outstanding or markedly adventurous, though they all seemed dispiritingly brilliant to him.

The most intimidating was probably James Dickson Innes (1887–1914), who would become a friend after they both had left the Slade and who would die tragically young. Then came Elliott Seabrooke (1886–1950), Malcolm Drummond (1880–1945), Thérèse Lessore

(1884–1945), Gerald Summers (1886–1969), Jessica Dismorr (1885–1939) and Derwent Lees (1885–1931) – the last an Australian who on graduation was asked to serve as a drawing master under Tonks and who was instructing by the time Smith left. There was also Randolph Schwabe (1885–1948), who in spite of his German name was the son of a Manchester cotton merchant. In 1905 he won the Summer Composition prize and eventually in 1930 he followed Tonks as Slade Professor.

Smith's fellow students conducted most of their social lives in studios and cafés around Tottenham Court Road, Euston Road, Charlotte Street and Fitzroy Street, where several artists, notably Sickert, had their studios (and where one day Smith would have his own). The female students were less likely to frequent pubs than in later generations and any mixed groups gathered in small cheap restaurants. Perhaps those with more money would have frequented the Café Royal in the hopes of glimpsing Augustus John holding court. We have no record of the part Smith played in this social side of student life, but it seems very unlikely he was one of the leading spirits. He seems to have made little impact on the school or his fellow students: he had already perfected that near-invisibility which allowed him to be the amused watcher from the touchlines of life.[1] He certainly had none of the artistic facility of most of his younger fellows and by the summer of his second year he had all too clear an idea of where he ranked in his year group:

I can see all these Summerses, Inneses, Leeses, Etchelses, coming into the Life Room with springy steps, bright . . . good colours and general refreshment . . . and here am I; I often spend a day entirely in my slippers, and all my works are going wrong inside as they do in London . . . my things are all miles behind the work done by most of the Slade people.[2]

It was becoming clearer to Smith that, two years into his course at one of the best art colleges in Britain, he was getting nowhere: he was still Mr Futile. This would be shamingly obvious for all to see when he submitted his vacation work for the next annual competition. Professor Brown set this task each summer and expected an ambitious imaginative work in oils to be completed by the beginning of the autumn term. Smith returned home and once more asked for his father's financial support so he could go to a summer school for extra tuition.

We know about the despair Smith felt concerning his own work at this time because letters he wrote to a fellow student from the summer school in Whitby have survived. Mary Gwendolen Salmond was one of the few people who saw anything in Smith's quiet virtues, and this was the more surprising because she was already one of the established stars of the Slade school – even Tonks admired her. She was two years older than Smith and had enrolled at the Slade in March 1893, giving her date of birth as 22 January 1877, her home address as 8 Green Street behind Park Lane, London, and her previous place of education as Düsseldorf. Her father was a Colonel in the Royal Engineers but marked for rapid promotion to Major-General and a knighthood over the next few years: her two brothers were also destined to make careers in the forces. Gwen won certificates and three Slade prizes, including £10 for Figure Composition in 1896. Augustus John later wrote of this work: 'Gwen Salmond's early compositions were distinguished by a force and temerity for which even her natural liveliness of temperament had not prepared us. I well remember a Deposition in our Sketch Club which would not have been out of place among the ébauches of, dare I say it, Tintoretto!'[3]

Gwen impressed John as 'a commanding figure among a remarkably brilliant group of women students' at the Slade, others being his sister Gwen and his future wife Ida Nettleship. These three independent and emancipated women had left the Slade in 1898 to go and share Parisian lodgings in the rue Froidevaux, Montparnasse, and to study under Whistler at the Académie Carmen, 6 passage Stanislas. They shared their dresses, painted each other and worshipped Whistler, who Gwen Salmond thought a brilliant teacher and 'well worth living for.' There he gave them the kind of practical teaching they had not received at the Slade: 'I do not teach Art; with that I cannot interfere; but I teach the scientific application of paints and brushes.' He insisted the palette was laid out in a precise order and all tones mixed on it before any paint was applied to the canvas with a generously laden flowing brush. This was tonal painting at its most exquisite.

On her return to London Gwen taught life drawing at the private Chelsea school of art run by Augustus John and William Orpen and also at Clapham Art School, in both being a popular and admired instructor. Her works were accepted at the New English Art Club and even the Royal Academy, but she still felt the Slade had left her ill-equipped to be a professional painter, so she enrolled for two years' further tuition under Leandro Ramon Garrido (1868–1909), who had a Spanish father and English mother but was essentially a French genre painter who aimed to inculcate the techniques of the Old Masters, particularly Velázquez and Hals. His works appeared in both the Paris Salon and the Royal Academy so he was by no means a revolutionary. His school was at Etaples on the Normandy coast and Gwen arrived there in autumn 1905 supported by her father with an allowance of £11 10s per month (Smith was allowed £6). However, Garrido soon found the Channel coast too damp for his delicate health and moved to Whitby, Yorkshire, in May 1906 – an eccentric choice, except he must have known that nearby Staithes had the most famous artists' colony in the north of England, full of 'Realists' painting fisherfolk. Gwen worked there on large figure compositions (all now lost) which were shown at the Paris Salon, the New English Art Club and the newly formed Allied Artists Association.

Smith went to holiday and paint at Whitby in the summer and autumn of 1906 and all summer in 1907. Obviously, when he met Garrido's star student, Gwen Salmond, she was a better artist, a more mature person, more widely travelled, from a higher level of society and more strongly opinionated than he was. She was also handsome, with wide eyes, a short slim figure and abundant blond hair. Smith did not have a lot to offer her in return, and he knew it. Perhaps Gwen saw he needed a push, or perhaps she saw potential where nobody else could. She may have fallen in love with his vulnerability and defencelessness, as many women were to do later, or her own insecurities found an echo in his – but, for whatever reason, from then on Smith had a sympathetic confidante for both his emotional problems and his artistic uncertainties. He was baffled that Gwen could 'understand me so well and still consider me WORTH understanding . . . It is only to you that I feel I can turn for real help and a sort of wonderful satisfaction of mind and a perfect relief.'[4] He must have been astonished and flattered by the attentions of this forceful woman who had all the skills he lacked, and wrote: 'It will be years . . . before I can nearly equal them (your own *achievements*). The goodness of your work and the high level of it, darling, keep coming home to me in spite of your quite wonderful modesty about it.' He pleaded: 'You must promise never to get so proud as not to love Maffles because he is going to do his best and if his best is never as beautiful as Gwenny's best – you will still try to love him and let him belong to the same Firm.'[5]

Just as the friendship was blossoming in summer 1907 Gwen had to leave Whitby to accompany Lady Salmond to Wiesbaden for an operation to remove one of her eyes. Matthew wrote almost daily in mounting fervour and though his letters were kept by Gwen her replies are lost. When her mother had recovered Gwen journeyed on to Holland to study Frans Hals, only returning to London and to the desperate Matthew in October.

Before then he was floundering badly. The students' paradoxical summer task was to use their realistic training in drawing to create an imaginative picture in oils. Gwen had won the prize with a *Deposition* and Augustus John with *Moses and the Brazen Serpent*, but now in 1907 the title was *Youth*. At twenty-eight Smith must have begun to wonder if his own youth had passed. He still felt ill-equipped to tackle a large figure composition, but he hired an old man and two children to pose for what sounds like either a Victorian tableau picture of the worst kind, or one of the fashionable 'Realist' peasant pictures. Smith wanted to set them outdoors but landscape inhibited him, as he wrote to Gwen: 'I saw something I wanted to paint this morning at Rushworth, but it was just a landscape. I think I am vaguely hoping that I shall suddenly see a subject for Youth that will be possible for me to do.'[6] His lack of paint craft is revealed in another despairing passage to Gwen:

I fear you are doomed to disappointment about the Youth – if it is ever painted I don't think either of US will like it. I'm getting on the wrong road – the Fake and Fudge Road while I am doing this Competition . . . I fear Youth is just going to be AWFUL . . . this morning I smudged colour and turps onto the canvas and painted a head more or less without a model, and in the afternoon I used Mona to paint it. I use what I think! are out of door colours inside! I don't know what the result will be – there will be none of the beauty of beautiful reality which I always try to go for . . .[7]

The child model Mona was clothed but the Antique Room and all Tonks's life classes had left him unable to cope with this. Gwen asked a friend to help: 'Miss George[8] came over and gave me very useful criticisms of my rather worried youth and made me see that I had not sufficiently driven the composition tho' I see lots of trouble ahead – the clothes still bother me for all Mona's are rags and no definite folds or creases; all a sort of patchwork of little aimless crinkles.'

As the vacation time ran away from him Smith realized how little he knew about transforming his sensations into paint on a canvas: 'One must be allowed a little time to make a few mistakes and recover again. I feel I am doing it pigheadedly but there seems no time to reconsider. I find going outside now simply confuses me. Shadows outside seem a yellow mauve! colour which somehow seems to me impracticable.'[9]

Had he not been so ignorant of the Impressionists' search for complementaries and coloured shadows he might have seen a way forward. He could also have tried what MacColl called their 'snatch technique' of trying to capture fugitive light effects 'with speed approaching the pace of a shorthand reporter keeping up with a fluent speaker,' by dabbing on primaries in swift little strokes,[10] but that would have meant a shedding of the paralysing self-consciousness that he felt in front of his sunlit canvas. He was also exasperated by the models' unreliability and his eye strain which was always worse under tension. Doggedly he continued trying to paint his outdoor figure indoors: 'I quite see that the right way to do the outdoor is to spend a month or two studying outdoor tones and noticing how they vary and why . . . but I haven't the experience . . . and I have somehow felt fussed and worried all the time.'[11]

A local artist known to Smith's father pointed him towards the obvious solution – why not study outdoor colours by actually working outdoors! 'I am just off to see Mr Jackson – my father will be annoyed if I don't go . . . [later] . . . Mr Jackson has some fine things in his studio . . . he made me feel quite sick of methods. He works entirely out of doors . . . he is going strong for light just now himself.'

Jackson was also rude about Tonks's paintings, which cheered Smith up. In spite of Jackson's advice to get out in the open *Youth* continued its downward spiral: 'A sort of resigned feeling has set in as regards the Youth . . . I have got such a horrid texture to the paint . . . shiny . . . as though it had been painted with a clothes brush – I think it is because I have not used oil and in places tried to paint slickly, being in a hurry, with thick paint and my white is old and stiff.'[12]

Another local painter, Frederick Walker RA, called in and offered the only realistic advice:

as regards my attempting to get my Youth anywhere near finished he practically advised me to 'chuck it' as he feels it is impossibly ambitious at present – I feel this very much myself it is really a sort of cheek to attempt doing it . . . depending so much on imagination as regards the landscape and light . . . when I know nothing about either.[13]

Garrido himself had a look at it though Smith had little time for him, calling his followers 'Garridiots' (Gwen excepted). Gwen's offer of encouragement by beginning her own version of *Youth* was rejected because he could not bear the inevitable comparison: 'Darling Gwendy is on top of her training and not underneath it,' he pointed out.

Smith's letters of this summer dwelled on other topics as well as his failing art, and in other terms: 'Dear Little Gwendy my sweet little 'squisite little all my own darly little singy sings Browny Gwendy.' Another begins:

Most beautiful Gwendiful, It is morning – Sunday. Don't know what to say dear but I have been thinking of the beautifulness of you and realised things a little dear and began to wish I had never once written a word to you except about the 'beautifulness of you' and the wonderfulness of loving you always remains though it isn't always that my unimaginative brain grasps it. I wish it would I should then always be so happy and different to what I am.[14]

Gwen replied more coherently but equally passionately:

Of course I want to charm you to the very end of your capacity because if there is a bit left I have not taken it, it is lying there quite possible for anyone else to take. That is why I ought to be with you all the time darling – if there is any 'capacity' left in you, uncharmed, through my nonentity and your dear faithfulness I am in some way shutting off your life. The only consolation is that I'm a woman and you are a man so you are the answerable one of us in the matter of being each other's Darling – and you must know your own business best.[15]

It seems unlikely he ever finished the *Youth* composition, but the struggle to do so further eroded his self-esteem and after his return to

London in the autumn his attendance at his classes became erratic, in spite of Gwen's continuing support.

Not only was his painting going wrong but so was his body, and he missed several long periods when he had to retreat north to be nursed. First for a painful operation on his jaw in early 1906, then the next Christmas he hurt his shoulder at a toboggan party and over New Year 1908 took to his bed for several weeks being unspecifically 'poorly'. Smith endured the artistic frustrations, illnesses, eye strain, and deepening depressions as long as he could, but the attendance books show he turned up less and less often at the Slade. He may well have learned Ben Nicholson's trick of signing in under the eye of the beadle, then sloping off to do other things – in Nicholson's case to play billiards. Smith was more likely to have ended in a music hall or moaning to Gwen in a cheap restaurant, though we have no direct evidence for this.

His records show that he did not complete the three years his father had paid for and his only academic award was a Certificate for Drawing for the 1906–7 session, though this may merely have signified he was competent enough to proceed from the Antique Room to drawing the live model. Twenty-six others in his year group were also awarded the same certificate so it was nothing special.

Smith returned to Dunham Lawn for Christmas 1907 and took his part in the family play the siblings put on for their parents, straggled back to London in late January and signed in the attendance book for the last time on 18 February 1908 – in an unusually flamboyant gesture he did this in red crayon underlined with blue. He had had his three years in London and they had been no more profitable than the four miserable ones in Manchester. He stayed on in London until his exasperated father came to collect him and his belongings on 10 April.

He had been seeing Gwen in London during the autumn and spring and she was invited to Bowdon in April. The Smiths must have been relieved that this vigorous young woman from a socially superior family was putting some life and ambition into 'poor old Math' at last, though her parents cannot have been impressed by Smith's dim prospects. She quickly became a close friend of Phyllis and would remain so all her life. At some time in that year Smith did a chalk drawing of Gwen which is surprisingly handsome in the Slade manner

17

8

and makes one wonder why he (and Tonks) doubted his abilities so much.

In spite of Gwen's support it seems that Smith's corrosive self-doubt led to another nervous and physical collapse during the summer of 1908 and he was sent to convalesce at Walberswick in Suffolk – coincidentally the scene of some of Steer's best paintings and a long established artists' colony, especially for those rural Realists who followed Bastien-Lepage. Smith did little if any painting there but again spent his time confiding his troubles to Gwen. Her letters do not survive but it is evident from his that she was trying to urge him on to take charge of his own destiny and make some decisions, possibly about marriage or sharing a house in Hampstead with her – an idea he found too shocking to contemplate.

Though her own teacher there, Whistler, was now dead, Gwen still believed that Paris was the only place where real art happened and she urged Smith to go, possibly with her. His response was at first typically timid and indecisive: 'I don't suppose I shall go to Paris sweet . . . unless I'm very fit, and perhaps I shan't be as fit as all that. You have very ambitious ideas . . . haven't you?'[16]

Eventually, after Gwen's urging, he gathered up the courage to confront his father yet again and to ask him for still further financial support, this time for a stay in France. The doctor also recommended that a period abroad might knit up Smith's ravelled nerves and once more his father agreed to fund him, though if the destination was to be France (the nearest and cheapest) then he had to go nowhere near Paris, which as everyone of Frederic's generation knew was a sink of vice.

On 26 October 1908, four days after his twenty-ninth birthday, Matthew left Dunham Lawn for Brittany, leaving behind his beloved 'Gwendiful'. Here, at last, he always claimed, 'My life began, my mind began to open out.'

CHAPTER 5

Brittany
1908–1909

Artists of the Paris Salon des Beaux Arts held very similar views and painted very similar pictures to those of their Royal Academy counterparts. However, from the mid-nineteenth century individual painters, groups, and sympathetic dealers had tried to break the Salon's monopoly of sales and its rigid views on art education. Stimulated to leave their studios by portable easels, tube paints, newly invented brighter colours and rail travel, the anti-Salon rebels began to paint outdoors in sunlight. They also began to depict the people they found there, at work or leisure, wearing modern garments. If these artists still wanted to show people without their clothes then why not depict them taking a bath, undressing for bed, working in a brothel, or frankly posing in a studio rather than pretending to be Diana surprised by Actaeon or Venus rising from the foam? In France the old gods and the old ways were in retreat before the battalions of Naturalism.

Well before Smith arrived at the Slade rumours of these French innovations were spreading. Senior artists the students admired, such as John, Sickert, Sargent and Whistler passed on the names of Manet, Courbet, Lepage, Degas, Monet, Cézanne, Van Gogh, Gauguin and Bonnard as men to watch out for. Besides, to paint with a modern French accent was guaranteed to annoy Tonks, and that was an added attraction.

It obviously made sense for Smith to study in France if he wanted to be in touch with modern painting, but why, with only Paris forbidden to him by his father, did he go directly to an obscure port on the Atlantic coast of Finistère, especially in October? And why did he stay for nine months? Presumably someone in London must have told him that he would find an artists' colony established there, and that his schoolboy French would be no handicap.

It was the nineteenth-century Romantic movement which first took artists to Brittany in search of a picturesque wildness not available in towns. Turner had travelled there in 1826 and Corot and Boudin followed. Balzac and Hugo set stories in this rural backwater cut off from the industrial and economic changes in France and the rest of Europe. There one could rebel against bourgeois mores, go into exile and seek simplicity, all in some comfort. The peasants wore picturesque costumes, were deeply religious, led harsh lives, and their cultural traditions and artefacts connected nicely with the current interest in all things Celtic. The locals also spoke Breton so that one had the feeling of being somewhere exotic without having to leave the shores of France. The coasts were rugged and the inland areas varied with moors, pasture and woods dotted with churches, calvaries, castles and megaliths. All this meant one could paint from life, yet not offend the Salon jury by looking too modern.

The first artists to arrive spent only summers there while the Paris ateliers were closed, but soon they began to winter in some of the bigger settlements. Pont Aven became popular with American and English artists in the 1860s and the Dutch, Scandinavians and Irish soon followed. By the 1870s there was an all year round colony of artists between forty and sixty strong alongside a native population of about 1,500. After 1862 visitors could travel direct from Paris to Quimperlé by train and then by coach the fifteen kilometres to Pont Aven.

There they found a pretty inland port which shipped wood and flour up the coast and exported granite and potatoes to England, a tidal river, a little wooded valley called the Bois d'Amour, a dozen water mills, the ruined castle of Rustephan at Nizon, rustic chapels and unsophisticated villagers. Concarneau was only fifteen kilometres north along the coast if more complex shopping had to be done. It too had a rival artists' colony, though this was spoiled by the stink of sardines.

The Bretons soon saw their chance and converted sheds and outhouses into studios, sold artists' materials and charged for their services as models – the men in baggy breeches and long hair and the women in elaborate white coiffes, aprons and embroidered costumes, and both in sabots. They even hired out their finery to visitors and there exists a photograph of Matthew Smith dressed in Breton costume 9 standing with three local women and two other artists. By now he had grown a moustache and appeared much older than his thirty years.

Not all the visiting artists were impressed with what they found. The English Realist painter Stanhope Forbes (1857–1947) described the average Breton as 'a very dirty, uninteresting, drunken sort of creature' and complained about 'the dearth of beautiful maidens in these parts.'[1] Even if you found one with a good figure you would never know because she would be bundled up in heavy black clothes, and there was no way she would take them off. No artist was going to specialize in the nude under such restrictions, unless he imported his own models from Paris.

Stanhope Forbes's disappointment with the place was shared by the Pointillist Signac who visited in the summer of 1891 and loathed the corruption the artists themselves had caused:

Yesterday I was at Pont Aven. It's a ridiculous countryside with little nooks and cascades, as if made for female English watercolourists. What a strange cradle for pictorial symbolism. Everywhere painters in velvet garments, drunk and bawdy. The tobacco merchant has a sign in the form of a palette: Artist's Materials [in English]. The maidservants in the inn wear arty ribbons in their headdresses and are probably syphilitic.[2]

When Smith arrived the place was long past its peak as a laboratory of artistic innovation. Today 'The School of Pont Aven' signifies primarily Gauguin and his followers, but in 1908 Gauguin had been dead five years and his acolytes had long dispersed (with the exception of Filiger and Jourdan), though their ideas would have still been a live topic round the café tables. It seems unlikely that Smith knew much about Gauguin's work in London at that date, though he might just have seen one of the Tahiti works in the International Society Exhibition in July 1908 or heard of him from the better informed Gwen. However, there were several of the more naturalistic Breton painters represented in this show, including Frederick Jackson, who had given Smith advice in Whitby the previous summer.

Gauguin had arrived in Pont Aven in summer 1886, broke and in low spirits 'to practise art in a hole,' as he wrote to a friend. He had had no formal training and, like Smith, he was a late starter. At first he did mostly landscapes and peasant scenes in a modified Impressionistic style learned from Pissarro, but he had an itch to produce works with big significant subjects and to tackle the fears and spiritual mysteries which the Impressionists ignored in their pursuit of sunlight falling through leaves. Soon Gauguin and a new friend, the young Parisian intellectual Emile Bernard, began to perfect the style of painting which came to be called Synthetism. They believed both Realism and Impressionism were now exhausted and there was a need for a new subjective art which went beyond the objective analysis of appearances. Gauguin spoke fiercely of 'The abominable error of Naturalism,' Maurice Denis of 'the Naturalist lie'[3] and Baudelaire, one of the heroes of the new group, had written: 'To us the natural painter, like the natural poet, is almost a monster. In our context, the exclusive pursuit of the True, so noble when restricted to its proper applications, oppresses and stifles the pursuit of the Beautiful.'[4]

Bernard painted the first picture in Synthetist mode, *Breton Women in a Green Meadow* (1888), and Gauguin responded with *The Vision after the Sermon*, both works being static tableaux compared to the Impressionists' lively treatment of crowds. Bernard believed in keeping colours few and pure because the more they were mixed the muddier they became and the less vigour they had. If they were applied in full-strength flat areas and surrounded by a sinuous blue-black outline they would have maximum impact. Gauguin was convinced: he used fewer colours, simplified details, flattened space, abandoned illusionistic perspective, reduced modelling, eliminated shadows, despised 'finish', and abandoned the direct painting from nature and divisionist brush-work he had learned from Pissarro and Monet.

Analogies were made by these Synthetists between the direct emotional impact of music and that of their new kind of painting; it too would have harmony and discords, counterpoint and rhythm; it too would synthesize vision and expression, feeling and form, and both appeal to and stem from 'the interior life of human beings.' In turn this linked them to Symbolism, a strong literary and artistic movement in

France at this time, also opposed to Realism and Impressionism. The stress was on the supremacy of the dream over observed reality and its heroes were Flaubert, Mallarmé, Baudelaire, Poe, Wagner, Moreau, Redon, Rouault, with connections to such British non-realists as Wilde, Beardsley and Burne-Jones. It is unlikely that Smith then knew much about any of these people, and the theories he heard round the café tables must have bewildered him.

A group of about twenty young admirers of varying nationalities, levels of ability and commitment, began to gather around Gauguin and Bernard, amongst them the Irishman Roderic O'Conor who was later to be Smith's close friend and explicator to him of Gauguin's theories. In Pont Aven these innovators were always a minority amongst the École des Beaux Arts 'hacks' (pompiers), as Gauguin called them, and could all be seated round one table at the Pension Gloanec or meet in the attic of the post office in the rue du Gac.

The key to this new approach was colour. In giving a lesson to the young Paul Serusier in the Bois d'Amour Gauguin told him: 'How do you see those trees? Yellow? So put yellow, paint it with the most beautiful yellow on your palette. This shadow? Blue? Paint it with ultramarine. And these leaves? Red? Use vermillion.'⁵ These challenging words struck sympathetic chords with Serusier's friends back in Paris – Bonnard, Vuillard, Maurice Denis and others who called themselves the Nabis (Prophets) and who were soon to be producing the most innovative art of the 1890s. Later the Fauves would also find inspiration in them for their own intensification of colour. Serusier did his best to disseminate Gauguin's advice and eventually in 1921 published his ABC de la Peinture, a curious treatise on the interrelationships of nature, painting, and mathematics which became one of Smith's favourite books.

Gauguin took extended trips away from Pont Aven but returned in 1889 to paint the masterpiece of Synthetism, The Yellow Christ, which demonstrated all the characteristics of the style he and Bernard had now evolved between them. A year later Maurice Denis famously summed these up in words which echoed Whistler: 'A picture – before being a warhorse, a nude woman, or some sort of anecdote – is essentially a surface covered with colours arranged in a certain order.'⁶

This did not mean he was advocating total abstraction, since Gauguin's group never abandoned literary, even portentous, subject matter, though it did imply that the pursuit of verisimilitude through perspective, local colour, chiaroscuro, and accurate drawing took second place to other, emotional and aesthetic considerations. The Pont Aven School set out to break with academicism, but not with the past: indeed Denis proposed they should call their movement Neo-Traditionnisme. Gauguin himself eclectically admired the Egyptians, Breton folk art, Japanese prints, Raphael, Ingres, Puvis de Chavannes and Delacroix, and all his group admired Cézanne.

This then was the artistic milieu that Smith had joined, one suspects without quite knowing what he was stumbling into. These startling ideas took a long time to absorb, but eventually they would change his own priorities and Gauguin would become a lifelong hero to him.

But his first problem as a shy foreigner was to settle in. The Pension Gloanec was for the rowdies, poseurs, and the poorest artists, such as Gauguin's cronies (today it is a newsagents). Foreigners went to either the Hôtel du Lion d'Or, or like Smith, to the Hôtel des Voyageurs. This was run by Julia Guillou, commemorated today by a plaque on the original site of the hotel as '*la mère des artistes*.' She kept a spotless house, advanced credit and had built on to it four studios for her guests, having realized that if she could keep artists occupied they would stay, and pay, for the whole winter. She was evidently very kind and motherly to Smith who remembered her as 'a superb woman.' She organized an '*académie*' with costume models in well-appointed studios, landscape painting in the open air, expeditions to collect mistletoe, sketching exercises, discussions, French conversation and musical evenings. It sounded like the summer school in Liphook again – except that there was no formal teaching and conversation was in a language Smith did not yet understand. But for the first time Smith was outside an academic framework and free to forage for his own ideas, though his diffidence probably kept him out of any heated discussions of 'theory'.

Friends claimed that Smith 'dwelt with delight, for the rest of his life, on the look of the landscape, the dress, bearing and speech of the inhabitants, and the humanity, tolerance and voluptuous simplicity of the painter's traditional life in France.'[7] Pont Aven had already lost much of its primitive innocence before he arrived, but Smith always remembered seeing the local women unselfconsciously crouch to urinate in the village streets.

Fortunately, he was befriended by an English-speaker who could initiate him into the colony and the most radical artistic ideas he had come across so far. On the back of the photograph of the six in Breton costume already referred to, one of the men is labelled 'Maynard'. This figure is short and stocky with a full beard, and like Smith he is trying not to look too ludicrous in his peasant hat and high-necked jacket. Alden Brooks, a later American acquaintance, thought Smith made only one real friend in Pont Aven and that was the Chicagoan Guy Ferris Maynard (1856–1936) who had come to Brittany via Paris and Grez-sur-Loing. He was based for a time in the port of Concarneau and claimed to have known Gauguin during his Brittany period. Roger Fry said he also knew Cézanne and 'was tremendously intelligent about art.'[8] Roderic O'Conor was another friend, so Maynard provided Smith with an invaluable introduction to the ideas and personalities of modern French art. Rothenstein and Halliday think Maynard had by 1908 taken to drink and indolence but still had a 'quiet, assured personality', indeed the 'most interesting personality it had yet been his [Smith's] fortune to meet.'[9] He encouraged Smith to read artists' journals, visit the museum at Nantes, and to paint still lifes of the modest objects he had to hand.

Maynard showed at the Salon, but nothing survives of his painting, or if it does I have been unable to trace it. Alden Brooks later described Maynard's work as follows: 'I know of no other painter than Maynard that Smith specially knew in his early Brittany days . . . Maynard sought to be a follower of Rembrandt . . . to imitate with colour the latter's effects of chiaroscuro.'[10] Though what this can mean beyond the Impressionists' practice of hunting for colours in the shadows is far from clear. Another American friend reacted to his choice of young boys as subject matter: 'The sort of definite queerness in his things bothered me a good deal.'[11] Smith valued Maynard's opinion of his work and they kept in touch throughout the years until Maynard returned to obscurity in the USA in 1922.

Once he had settled in, Smith must have travelled the few miles south to Le Pouldu where in 1889 Gauguin's group had moved to get away from the increasing number of hacks and tourists. He might also have sneaked away to Paris and met up with Gwen, but would not have mentioned this in his letters home. Phyllis wrote to him c/o Hôtel Julia, his father sent his allowance and Fanny no doubt slipped him a cheque or two and kept him informed of family events such as Arthur making a trip to New York on wire business and Frederic's worsening sciatica pains which drove him to take the waters at Bath.

In April 1909 Smith's parents went to Bayonne and Biarritz where Frederic had some kind of operation, serious enough to bring Harold and Phyllis to his bedside. It would seem strange if Matthew had not also made the trip since he was in the country. By 20 June Frederic was well enough to visit the Paris Salon and then to return home after an absence of twelve weeks. Arthur and Harold now ran the Salford firm between them and Frederic, increasingly an invalid, retired. Significantly Gwen's address was now recorded in Fanny's diary, implying she was seen as a potential member of the family.

It is difficult to see how Smith developed as an artist in Brittany, since only three tiny paintings survive. He still found the blank canvas inhibiting and Maynard spoke for them both when he said, 'Torture is the very birth of art.' In 1947 Matthew gave a *Still Life with Radishes* to the writer Roald Dahl with the words, 'That's one of my first efforts: I think it's the earliest there is.' This cannot be literally true since we know of the earlier portrait of Phyllis, and it seems unlikely that a thirty-year-old painter who had been through two art college courses had completed only a single picture! More probably he had destroyed previous efforts in despair. This still life was apparently painted in Madame Julia's kitchen on a piece of cardboard about a foot square mounted on panel. It is loosely handled, with the lilac shadow of the cloth and the primaries in the objects kept bright and pure, in contrast to the earth tones of the background. It also has a daringly tilted triangular composition.

There are two versions of this still life and originally there was *Portrait of a Young Boy* on the back of one of them. This is said to have been painted under Maynard's influence because the brown tonality and the modelling by light and shade seem to relate to the American's

10

determination to 'follow Rembrandt's example.' Small though it is, it has some confident, even bravura, brushwork in the sunlit part of the face and collar, nearer perhaps to Frans Hals than Rembrandt. Only the ochre background has gone muddy and is overworked. It is also uncannily like a head of a Breton boy painted in the same place about sixteen years earlier by O'Conor.[12]

Smith had heard what Gauguin had to offer (though he had seen few of his works) but evidently he had not yet assimilated this enough to apply it to his own practice. Later, in Cornwall, after he had seen the strange pinks and purples of Gauguin's South Sea works, he would draw more fully upon the master's example. Meanwhile, these little paintings show Smith was no longer a dithering beginner, and though we have no more examples to prove it, we must assume he had continued to advance since leaving Manchester.

Fanny updated her diary addresses when Smith left Pont Aven in June 1909 and moved via Nemours to stay with Mme Gervais-Sens, rue de Rivage, Etaples, near le Touquet on the Channel coast. Gwen probably suggested this since she had spent six months there in 1905–6 and she may have crossed the Channel to join him, though this is now impossible to prove. Smith had failed to produce a single landscape in Pont Aven so possibly, because he had heard that Sickert and Gilman had worked in nearby Dieppe, and Boudin, Monet, Dufy, Seurat and Steer had painted on this stretch of coast, he went there in the hope that their inspiration might work for him too. He seemed to have a belief common to pilgrims everywhere that if one went to a place where something significant had happened then it might just happen again for you.

In Etaples he made another friend in John Lyman (1886–1967), a Canadian painter who certainly knew more about events in Parisian progressive circles than Smith did. Whilst a student at McGill University Lyman had been converted to a career as a painter by seeing a 1906 exhibition of Impressionists in Montreal. He had come to Europe and in 1907 studied under Marcel Beronneau, friend and imitator of the Symbolist Gustave Moreau (Matisse's tutor). He had also visited England, the Côte d'Azure, and worked at his life drawing in the Académie Julian. Eventually he would become one of Matthew's

staunchest admirers, though when they met he was the more sophisti-
cated of the two.

1   It is likely that Smith painted his 1909 *Self Portrait*, his first
significant work, in Etaples. The moustache has now gone and he had
plumped out a bit from Madame Julia's cooking. As Rothenstein says,
here is 'a shy, friendly young face, with blinking eyes that peer out at
you with an expression of mild surprise.'[13] This is an impressive work
which gives a convincing, rather mocking, self-likeness whilst being
fully satisfying in the handling of paint. The black coat is a bold flat
shape relieved by the brass buttons and left hand; the right hand is
omitted to prevent total symmetry in the frontal pose. The cropped hat
brings a necessary dark note to the top of the picture and frames the
face. These darks are enlivened by primary touches of red, blue and
yellow in the waistcoat and buttons and by the green eyebrow. Edges
are blurred, colours blended and the brushstrokes are frank, juicy and
vigorous so that whatever he had understood of Gauguin's doctrine had
not been utilized in this canvas. Smith was beginning to have a personal
voice.

He must have made forays into Paris from Etaples, but now at last he
felt he was ready to settle in the capital of art. He sold his bicycle to raise
the fare and then, on 10 January 1910, he and Lyman moved to Paris
and a hotel on the rue Jean Bart. Paris was inundated when they
arrived: in the worst floods for 150 years the Seine had burst its banks
and 50,000 people were being fed from soup kitchens.

Lyman had attended the spring Salon des Indépendants in 1909 and
been impressed with a Matisse landscape, so it was presumably he who
suggested their next move: they would enrol in the school of Henri
Matisse. At last Matthew would be in the same room with a giant of
avant-garde painting and perhaps the magic would rub off.

CHAPTER 6

Paris
1909–1911

Matisse opened his Académie in January 1908 with ten students drawn from America, Germany, Hungary and Sweden. The international flavour of the school was to continue with intakes of Norwegians, Swedes, Icelanders, Swiss and English as about 120 students passed through it in the next three years. This was because Matisse's reputation as an innovative artist was growing rapidly abroad with exhibitions in New York, London, Moscow and Berlin, though to the conservative French he was still a figure of ridicule. The school began in the Couvent des Oiseaux but quickly moved to the eighteenth-century Hôtel Biron, another former convent, at 33 boulevard des Invalides, which had been taken over by the state and its rooms let cheaply. Isadora Duncan had lodgings there at one period and after October 1908 Rodin had a studio. Today it is a handsome museum dedicated to Rodin.

It was in this building that Smith and Lyman enrolled, probably in April 1910. Lyman described the routine:

Continental art teachers seldom criticize oftener than once a week; Matisse visited us only once a fortnight and then his criticism usually took the form of a long chat about fundamental principles and qualities. We were about fifteen in the school. The late Edward Bruce was *Massier*. Besides Matthew Smith there was Per Krog who became a leading painter in his native Norway, Hans Purrmann, a number of other Germans and Scandinavians, and some Austrian women whose most remarkable aesthetic gift was their own blond beauty.[1]

Smith recalled one lesson vividly:

The school had a very pleasant atmosphere. There were long windows looking onto a garden which we walked about in during the rests. Students who wished to have a criticism left their drawing or canvas on the easel, while the others carefully hid them. We all followed Matisse around to each student's work and listened to what he said. I do not remember very much, as at that time I had very little French. I remember him going up to a Signorelli drawing pinned on the wall (a drawing of four nude figures, two male and two female, a very beautiful drawing) and running his finger down the drawing in several places, saying 'Voilà l'architecture.' This impressed me very much, for up to that time in London I had only heard of construction, and I felt 'l'architecture' had a more aesthetic value. Matisse admonished one male student for not showing enough appreciation of the female form, and frowned a little at him and said: 'Et vous un jeune homme.'[2]

Smith was also a *jeune homme* and fully appreciated the female form, but as yet did not know how to convert this into paint. Predictably, crippled by fear of rejection, he did not offer his own work for criticism, though Matisse never treated his students in the brutal Tonks manner. As a teacher he had other faults, however, and even one of his oldest friends thought 'Matisse was the greatest living painter, the greatest living egoist and the greatest living bore . . . happier in his dealings with the muses than with his fellow human beings.'[3]

By the time the two friends joined the school Matisse was beginning to lose interest in it and attended less frequently. Smith met Matisse perhaps three times only, but the memory remained vivid and he continued to be an admirer of Matisse's work all his life, though to label him glibly as a pupil or even a follower of Matisse, as the English reviewers did, is not justifiable.

Smith and the other students had enrolled with Matisse because he was seen as a leading, even scandalous, exponent of 'modern' art. In 1908 a Matisse nude had been condemned in New York as 'malevolent . . . hideously at odds with nature . . . loathsome and abnormal . . . revealing the female model in all her shame and horror.'[4] Yet, paradoxically, his teaching consisted of traditional life-classes and constant reference to the great works of the past, including drawing from antique sculpture. Like Tonks he based everything on drawing, and thought this had to be mastered before painting could be attempted. Lyman wrote: 'He was quick to censure the superficial device, the merely decorative abbreviation, the lack of "density" as he

called it. That was the burden of his teaching. Students who came to
him to learn modern tricks got no encouragement. "Learn to walk on
the ground before you try the tightrope" was his constant reminder.'[5]

Unity was another of Matisse's obsessions:

Everything must be constructed – built up of parts that make a unit; a tree like a
human body, a human body like a cathedral. To one's work one must bring
knowledge, much contemplation of the model or other subject, and the
imagination to enrich what one sees. Close your eyes and hold the vision, and
then do the work with your own sensibility.[6]

This unity was not achieved by putting in everything one saw as the
Pre-Raphaelites did: 'It was in the decadent periods of art that the
artist's chief interest lay in developing the small forms and details. In all
the great periods the essentials of form, the big masses and their
relations, occupied him above all other considerations – as in the
antique.'[7]

The whole figure had to be included in each drawing, from top to toe,
because Matisse believed 'The value of this experience in the further
study of composition is quite evident.' This was a rule Smith later
learned to disregard, perhaps from conviction, or more simply because
he was so short-sighted he needed to be close to the model and
consequently she filled his whole field of view and her feet got lost.

Matisse invited his students back to his own prefabricated studio at
Issy-les-Moulineaux in south-west Paris where they could see his work
in progress, including the large *Dance II* and his sculptures *La
Serpentine* and *Nu De Dos I*. It is not known if Matthew's reticence
prevented him from going, but Lyman certainly went and saw amongst
others *La Desserte* and *Red Interior*, works showing the master's
current interest in vivid, unmodulated, non-descriptive colour. Lyman
must also have seen Matisse actually at work because he describes how
'Matisse rarely repainted, he began his picture again on a fresh canvas
five, ten, fifteen times, until the moment of final decanting was reached.
It was the same with his drawings: trial sheet after sheet fluttered to the
floor until, with final concentration, he condensed into the subtle
modulation of a line an incredible amount of content.'[8] This 'condensa-
tion' of his sensations was at the heart of Matisse's practice. Smith too

eventually learned to simplify and refine his drawings through working in series, but he rarely used them to sort things out before painting. Instead he solved (and created) his problems on the canvas itself.

Matisse published his *Notes d'un Peintre* on Christmas Day 1908. This set out the beliefs he was then passing on to students like Smith and these have been neatly summarized as follows:

Matisse stresses six broad points: his aim is a form of expression inseparable from his pictorial means; he seeks to condense his sensations received from nature, thereby to produce a more lasting and stable art than that of the Impressionists; he transposes colours until their juxtaposed areas create an intuitively found unity that does not copy nature but realises its essential character; clarity and order are necessary to a picture and will convey its significance to the viewer even before its illustrated subject is recognised; his art is intended to have a soothing, calming influence on the mind; by basing his art on nature, he avoids preconceptions and rules, but is nevertheless bound to the expression of his times.[9]

There is an obvious echo of Gauguin's belief in using colour in such a way as to evoke emotion rather than to make servile copies of nature like the Realists and Impressionists, but Matisse was utterly free of the Pont Aven school's craving for spiritual messages. His was an art without angst: there was no violence, no reference to contemporary events such as two world wars, no content at all beyond the conviction that life could be enjoyed for its 'luxe, calme et volupté.' Matisse said he sought 'an art of balance, of purity and serenity, devoid of troubling or depressing subject matter, an art which could be for every mental worker, be he businessman or man of letters, for example, a soothing calming influence on the mind, something like a good armchair in which to rest from physical fatigue.'[10] How uncannily like the belief of Matthew's father, Frederic, this seems – that art was something you relaxed with after a hard day's work! In the wrong hands this could be a manifesto for producing Victorian kitsch, but Matisse's works are tougher and more formally demanding than his words make them sound. Smith responded to this benign and sensual credo and would eventually arrive at an art very similar in its intent, though his nervous temperament gave it a disquieting agitation of surface that was never present in Matisse.

Smith would presumably have seen his teacher's large retrospective exhibition at the Bernheim-Jeune gallery in February and March 1910 though he might not have been aware of the French press's savage reaction to it. The same response followed the Salon d'Automne showing of Matisse's *Dance II* and *Music*. The simplified drawing, lack of modelling and use of three flat vivid colours were universally condemned and even the man who had commissioned them, Sergei Shchukin, had second thoughts. Immediately after this, on 8 November, Roger Fry opened his exhibition *Manet and the Post-Impressionists* at the Grafton Gallery in London. The English public reacted equally vehemently to the works by Matisse, Cézanne, Gauguin, Van Gogh, Vlaminck and Derain amongst others. The French painters' landscapes in particular were brashly at odds with the English public's taste for a verdant countryside full of streams, ruins, and dappled cows. 'The show stopped where the child would begin,' sneered *The Times* reviewer. Smith was in England by New Year's Eve and must surely have seen the exhibition before it closed on 15 January, but his reactions are not recorded. The same critical hot-air balloon went up again when the Armory Exhibition opened in New York in February 1913 and introduced these painters to yet another scandalized public. Art students in Chicago burned three Matisse nudes in effigy.

What was it that created such seismic reactions? In the Salon d'Automne exhibition of 1905 Matisse and his friends Derain, Manguin, Marquet, and Vlaminck had been christened 'Fauves' (wild beasts) by the critic Louis Vauxcelles. It is worth examining what these painters had to offer since one of the most frequent, and misguided, critical labels later pinned on Smith was 'the English Fauve.'

By 1905 Matisse was thirty-six but had been a professional artist for only ten years (he abandoned law against his father's wishes). He had already worked through an Impressionist period, then under the influence of Gauguin, Cézanne, the Nabis and Japanese prints he had experimented with expressive non-realistic colour, especially playing the complementaries red against green and orange against purple. Around the turn of the century dark colours had briefly returned to his canvases and only a trip to Saint-Tropez with the divisionists Signac and Cross in 1904 brought him back on course as modernism's greatest exponent of full-blooded colour. This was consolidated during a 1905 summer visit with Derain to Collioure, a sunny coastal village near Perpignan, when both painters squeezed and slashed and dabbed on astonishingly vivid hues, overriding local colour, ignoring traditional modelling and aerial perspective and leaving bare white canvas between the mosaic-like strokes. Vlaminck, Dufy, Van Dongen, Braque and Manguin also pitched their colours high, though there was no manifesto or even theory uniting these so-called Fauves. They had discovered in the southern sun a way forward from Impressionism, which had developed largely under the changeable skies of Normandy. However, as Braque admitted, 'You can't remain for ever in a state of paroxysm' and by 1906 Matisse was painting *Le Bonheur De Vivre*, all pastel colours, languid arabesques and Arcadian charm, the nymphs and shepherds drawn as much as painted, and signalling he was moving on to new challenges.

By the time Smith encountered Matisse in 1910, the French artist had worked his way through Fauvism ('the fugitive sensations of a moment') towards a more disciplined art and had lost his position as leader of the avant-garde to Picasso who, together with Braque, was now developing Cubism – though it is not clear if Smith was aware of this. However, Matisse still began from the encounter with a living model, and not from a theory. He wrote of his models: 'The emotional interest aroused in me by them does not appear particularly in the representation of their bodies, but often rather in the lines or the special values distributed over the whole canvas or paper, which form its complete orchestration, its architecture. But not everyone perceives this. It is perhaps sublimated sensual pleasure.'[11] Matisse so organized his initial sensations, refining shapes and harmonizing colours, that the erotic charge was dispersed and depersonalized. He confessed, 'There was a time when I never left my paintings hanging on the wall because they reminded me of moments of over-excitement and I did not like to see them again when I was calm. Nowadays I try to put serenity into my pictures and rework them as long as I have not succeeded.'[12]

Picasso, on the other hand, made no attempt to sublimate his arousal and was not content to caress only with his brush as Matisse did. Whole new styles came and went as he loved, fought, crushed, then discarded his women. Nor did he confine himself to a few themes as Matisse (and Smith) did, but looted art history, current events, literature, his family life, love affairs, even his dinner plate, for new things to say and new ways of saying them. Matisse was still in the French tradition of *belle peinture* but Picasso with his intellectual restlessness, savage draughts-manship and indifferent colour sense seemed determined to destroy it. Smith, who had little intellectual audacity and no aggression, found Picasso's work antipathetic from the Cubist period onwards.

Traditionally art students like Smith who were in search of the *dernier cri* took up residence in the Quartier Latin, now that Montmarte was spoiled by tourists, in order to enjoy the cheap rooms, studios, dance halls, artists' cafes and restaurants, and the proximity of the various teaching ateliers. They were there to commit what Max Beerbohm called their 'gaucheries on the Rive Gauche.' One writer calculated that just before Smith arrived £94 per annum was enough to cover paints, lodgings, attendance fees, living and incidentals.[13] Smith had yet to sell a picture and relied entirely on his father's meagre monthly allowance, so presumably he cut corners on lodgings and food. His mother's diary gives his first address for 1911 as the Hôtel de Nice, 155 boulevard Montparnasse, near Le Dôme and La Rotonde where Picasso, Rivera, Cocteau, Gris, Léger, Soutine, Chagall, Zadkine and Pascin could be seen and where Modigliani hawked his drawings for the price of a drink. Though he was eventually on chatting terms with Zadkine, Smith was far too self-conscious to strike up a real acquaintance with any of these French masters. Next he moved to 8 rue de la Grande Chaumière, and from Easter he took a cramped room with studio at 54 avenue du Maine where steel tramlines were hammered into shape on the floor below (it has now been replaced by a station). Lyman and his Slade friend Innes lived nearby in an area so full of English and Americans it was called the Quartier Anglais. No correspondence to or from Gwen survives from this period and it is possible she might have joined him, or taken a Paris studio for at least part of this time; though they covered their tracks, it seems certain that they were still in close communion.

It would be interesting to know how Smith's confidence and happiness grew during this period of freedom when he could follow up his own ideas and go wherever and do whatever he wished. Did he share the Parisian rage for all things Russian and talk of Diaghilev, Chaliapin, Nijinsky, Karsavina, Rubinstein and the barbaric designs of Bakst? Did he take an interest in the controversy over Epstein's tomb of Oscar Wilde in Père Lachaise cemetery? Or the theft of the Mona Lisa? Or the trial of naïve Henri Rousseau? Did he see Blériot's triumphal arrival after he flew the Channel? Attend the new-fangled cinema? Did he pop into the student hang-outs round the Boul' Mich or did his English reticence keep him isolated? Did he frequent the Café d'Harcourt, the Taverne Lorraine, or Bulliers and risk losing his sobriety, even his virginity, with a grisette? Did he get out of his cramped lodgings and stretch his legs in the Luxembourg Gardens, hire a boat at Courbevoie or picnic in the woods at Fontainebleau? We cannot say, but he would indeed have been a dull dog if he did not enjoy being a bachelor footloose in the most exciting city in Europe.

Neither can we say for certain what he knew of the new art seething into being in the streets and galleries around him. Impressionism was now *passé* with the avant-garde, though Symbolism, Post-Impression-ism, Nabism and Fauvism were still being worked over and exhibited. Cubism had now moved on to its Analytic phase: Surrealism was beginning to stir in the work of de Chirico; the Italian Futurists had an exhibition at the Bernheim-Jeune gallery and advocated war as a great purgative for Europe's troubles; Delaunay had followed Kandinsky in making totally abstract pictures so that shape or colour were now the whole point, not the 'subject', which no longer existed. Duchamp despised 'retinal' and 'olfactory' (i.e. oil) painting and began to make wit and intellect the point of art; Mondrian researched intersecting straight lines, and Braque used collage to enhance the picture surface. New possibilities were on offer all over the city if only you knew where to look: it was as if Smith had stumbled into an artistic supermarket.

After his brief sessions with Matisse he and Lyman had a holiday in Pont Aven and went back to Dunham Lawn together for the summer. On their return to Paris Smith did not seek out another master's private class but probably signed on at one of the Académies. A few life drawings survive from this period, one with the model's name (Odette Derval) scribbled on the back. These are competent linear works with the modelling kept to a minimum, representing perhaps a shift in loyalty from Tonks to Matisse. Normally these establishments ran three sessions per day, 8 a.m. to noon, 1 o'clock to 5 p.m. and 7 p.m. to 10 p.m. Students could enrol for as many as they liked and for any period from one month to a year. Unlike at the Slade the classes were mixed and fraternization with other students and even the models was not discouraged. Criticisms were held twice a week on Tuesdays and Fridays and each establishment held frequent exhibitions of students' work. Such places as Julian's and Calarossi's did little to further modernism, merely providing life models, and from the following description of these we can deduce that producing nineteenth-century Salon pictures was still the norm, in spite of the ground-breaking developments listed above, in a city where artists were numbered in their thousands and art was produced on an industrial scale for a largely conservative museum or middle-class clientele:

The Model Market on the Place Pigalle on a Monday morning is thronged by all types of men, women, and children anxious to get an engagement for the week. Here a woman with a Madonna-like head, and there a man with a patriarchal beard as their chief points, another, a girl, lithe and elegant, from whom an artist would be able to evolve a Psyche or Wood Nymph; yet another of truly classical proportions, who sits for Juno and Greek goddesses; there a woman and a baby, the woman with a sad expression – cultivated, of course, as she earns her living by posing as the Virgin Mary, whilst her child has appeared in many pictures as the Infant Jesus.[14]

This was the kind of art the French state continued to patronize until after the Second World War – all those movements which we now collectively call Modernism were still struggling for an audience at this time.

If Smith was tongue-tied in the presence of living masters at least he could encounter the dead ones in the Louvre. At the Slade Tonks had pinned up drawings by Ingres on the life-studio walls and Matisse revered him too, so Smith naturally sought out the Ingres works in the Louvre. Perhaps Matthew knew that Ingres himself had told Degas: 'Make copies, many copies. You can only become a good artist by copying the masters.' He chose to copy the 1805 portrait of plump, proud *Madame Rivière*, painted by Ingres when he was twenty-five.

13

Smith probably worked from a reproduction rather than by setting up a canvas in the gallery, where strangers could look over his shoulder. He later told friends how he had once set up an easel in the street in Paris but had been so embarrassed by the laughter and comments of passers-by that he had abandoned both canvas and easel and fled.

This copy was not a slavish attempt to emulate the waxy dust-free surfaces and the Pre-Raphaelite detail of the original. Three sketchbook studies show him working out the bones of this oval composition before starting his ambitiously large canvas ($45\frac{3}{4}$ × 35 in.).[15] The stress on rhythmic lines and the application of paint in broad separate hogshair strokes rather than by the sable-brush point show him making the picture his own and not a mere facsimile, since Ingres had decreed, hitting at his rival Delacroix: 'The brushstroke, however skilful, must not be apparent; otherwise it destroys illusion, brings everything to a halt. It shows not the object represented but the artist's tactics; not his idea but his hand.'[16] Frederic Smith would have agreed with Ingres, and it was possibly for Matthew's father that the copy was originally made, though he would have been surprised by how the creamy flesh of the original had been simplified into patches of yellow and orange, and how the cool tones had been heated up by a red background and surround. Perhaps Frederic refused it as 'unfinished' because Matthew kept this picture with him on his subsequent travels and occasionally reworked it. This was the only painting he chose to represent his work before 1913 when he had his first one-man exhibition in 1926, so it evidently meant a great deal to him.

Later he acquired a copy by one of Ingres's pupils, Raymond Balze, of the master's large *Charity*, a woman with nude breasts nursing three children.[17] Again he made his own much freer version of this and chose to be photographed with it in 1957. Many years later he told Rothenstein, 'that revolutionary painters such as Matisse ... had understood [Ingres] much better than his professed followers, and academic painters in general, especially his extraordinary *DELIBER-ATENESS* and his profound calculations regarding the division of space.'[18] At some time during this period Smith bought Henri Delaborde's book *Ingres: Sa vie, ses travaux, sa doctrine*, published in Paris in 1870, and in this Smith marked passages he thought important, so his French must have improved.

Smith came to be famous later for his Dionysian abandon and agitated paint so it seems strange he should be drawn to the Apollonian restraint and immaculate finish of Ingres. The older master, like Matisse, certainly felt the attraction of plump female flesh, but this excitement was sublimated for aesthetic ends. There was a cool idealization, an intellectualism and a calmness of surface about the best nudes of both masters that Smith must have admired, but could never temperamentally emulate in his own work.

When not in the studios or the Louvre Smith must have explored the modern art galleries such as Durand-Ruel, Vollard, Berthe Weille, or the Salle Caillebotte. There is evidence that he knew the works of the Nabis (or Intimists as they were also called) and painted at least one picture under their influence. This is his tiny ($8\frac{3}{4} \times 7\frac{1}{2}$ in.) *Self Portrait in a* 11 *Mirror* showing the back of his head and dark half-profile facing right. The murky brown tones are relieved only by a gleam of collar, red nose tip and touch of green in his waistcoat. It is claustrophobic in feeling but subtly painted and daring in its use of the mirror as a framing device. It is reminiscent of the early small dark interiors of Vuillard and Bonnard and perhaps of Matisse's *Self Portrait* of 1900 in which he too emerges from the gloom. Oddly, Smith never returned to this favourite mirror motif of the French masters.

Smith guided his old Slade colleague James Dickson Innes round the places where the newest art could be seen. Previously Smith had been in awe of Innes's precocious skills, but now he could demonstrate to Innes all the sophistication of a man about Paris. He took Innes along to see the collections of Lyman's friends Leo and Gertrude Stein, where it seems Innes was not impressed by the Cézannes and other Post-Impressionists on the walls, not even by Matisse's stunning *Woman with a Hat* of 1905. Presumably if Smith knew Leo Stein he would also have had entry to the collection of Matisse's friends Michael and Sara Stein, who were always hospitable to young artists. Smith's stance as the habitué of all the hot spots of Modernism must have been undermined a little when he took Innes along to Ambroise Vollard's gallery to see the Cézannes, and the dealer threw them out, perhaps because Innes's public behaviour was deteriorating as his tuberculosis worsened. Innes professed not to care for Post-Impressionism at all and to be a devotee of Turner, Constable and Steer, but the bright colours he began using in his few remaining years were in response to the sunlight of Collioure (just as Matisse and Derain had responded to it earlier), and what he absorbed through contact with such English Francophiles as Augustus John, Robert Bevan and Harold Gilman.

In all, with short breaks, Smith spent two happy years in Paris, enjoying his freedom, learning French, encountering the latest ideas in art and doing the occasional painting – he had evidently not acquired Matisse's relentless work rate. He was always slow to respond to new discoveries: they had to be tasted, ingested, and digested over long periods before emerging in his work. It was the same when he went to new places: he could never set up a canvas and paint the scenery until he had settled in and felt at ease in it. So now the works he produced in Matisse's orbit showed little of the master's revolutionary use of colour, line and space, and made no reference to the fact that he was working in Paris rather than London or Manchester. He was teaching himself more by looking, reading and thinking than by painting, since only six works emerged from his stay, just three of which were created in Paris itself.

All Académies and studios closed down during the summer so everyone scattered for holidays, or returned to their home countries, or went off to paint landscapes in Brittany or Fontainebleau or Grez-sur-Loing. Smith explored the Paris suburbs by train, sometimes with Lyman, and had days at the seaside near Dieppe where in summer 1911 he painted *Barns with Trees, Varengeville*, a vigorously brushed but confused attempt to confront a landscape in bright sunlight.[19] Better is the small *Coastal Landscape*, which is a straightforward exercise in Impressionism. Back in his Whitby summer school in 1907 he had been baffled and defeated by the way sunshine ate into local colour and caused shadows to look 'a yellow mauve colour' as he wrote to Gwen. Now he had seen Monet and Gauguin and Matisse he dared to paint cast shadows as purple and contrast them with the yellow of leaves and grass, or dapple a tree trunk in pink and yellow against a green-blue sky.

Family ties were still strong so he had returned home to Dunham Lawn in the summer and winter of 1910 where Gwen, now his fianceé, was a guest on both occasions. Fanny and Frederic went to the Riviera and Monte Carlo in March 1910 and might well have seen Matthew as

14

they passed through Paris, though Fanny's diary does not record this. They did visit him in Paris in 1911 and he met them at the Regina Hotel. Fanny wrote in her diary:

16th April. Another perfect day. Went to the Salon for a short time . . . Took a carriage to Matthew's studio. Gwen had tea for us. They came to dinner with us. I stayed in after the others went out.
18th April. Matthew went with us to Au Printemps and Rue de Lafayette. Disappointed with both . . . Thomas had a talk with us about Matthew.

This was Thomas Head Thomas, an American friend met through Maynard, but what he said is unknown. Gwen had obviously joined Smith in Paris by now, though she occupied a different address and studio. She had been to Madrid in the summer of 1910 and made a copy of Velázquez's *Las Meniñas*, but Smith did not accompany her or share her enthusiasm for Spanish painting. Halliday was told by Smith that his *Still Life with Forget-me-nots* was painted in Gwen's Paris studio so they were obviously in close contact even if not cohabitating.

Fanny's terse and unenthusiastic diary entries could cover disapproval of Matthew's lodgings, or his paintings, or his way of life, or indeed all three. Frederic was now an even richer man because he had amalgamated his Caledonian Works with the London Electric Wire Company on very favourable terms: nevertheless he must have demanded to see some return on his investment in his son because Smith stirred himself and submitted his Etaples *Self Portrait* and a work mysteriously called *Bolan Gosse* (now lost) to the jury-free Salon des Indépendants in 1911 and these, his first public exhibits, are what his parents had come to see. The exhibition might just prove to them that even if they did not appreciate his efforts other artists might.

However, Smith's modest little works passed entirely without comment beside those of Matisse, Léger, Signac, Vlaminck, Modigliani, Rouault and the foreigners Kandinsky, Feininger, Archipenko, Jack Yeats and the Scottish Colourist J. D. Fergusson. In 1912 he exhibited three still lifes and again it is now impossible to know which these were amongst the thousands of entries. Still lifes are easy to set up and work on over time, but they also carry none of that burden of association and emotion that history or religious pictures or nudes or portraits do. This neutrality is probably why the Cubists were conducting their radical research into this motif at this very period, though there is no sign that Smith learned anything from them.

One work which has survived from that year is *Still Life with Lemon*, which is in similarly muted earthy colours to his Intimist self portrait. Far more adventurous is his *Still Life with Forget-me-nots*,[20] where again the objects are seen at eye level, but this time they are broadly brushed on to a warmly coloured wood panel. A table-cloth is indicated in a flurry of white strokes, as is the inside of a china bowl. A solidly painted black teapot emerges from dark thin paint and the blue dots of the flowers are wittily balanced by a single red cherry. Perhaps it owes something to Bonnard's love of table-top arrangements and his patterns of brushstrokes, enjoyable for their own sakes rather than their mimetic function. This could only have been painted after a stay in Paris: neither the Slade nor the Royal Academy would have seen it as anything but a loose daub. But, in French terms, it was nothing remarkable and only showed that after two years in the capital of art Smith had not yet broken through to a style of his own.

CHAPTER 7

Grez-sur-Loing
1912–1914

Smith went home at Christmas 1911 for the usual family gathering and a very successful ball held at Dunham Lawn. His father's troubles of the summer, when the Smith workers had all been out on strike for a month, now seemed over. It was time for the newly confident Matthew to take a decisive step. He married Gwen on 10 January 1912 at St Mary's Church, Bruton, Somerset, near where her parents had retired to Whaddon Hall. Matthew's father had, perforce, to raise his son's allowance because there was still no sign of him earning a living from painting and there was no way he could support a wife or children by his own efforts. Major-General Sir William Salmond gave his daughter away and Matthew's brother Harold was best man. Matthew was the first of the brothers to marry and one suspects that it was Gwen's bustling personality which moved him towards such a major change in his life. It was a wedding and reception in considerable style and Gwen's dress was pictured in *The Queen: The Lady's Newspaper*.[1]

They had planned to honeymoon in Rome, but before they could get there Fanny caught a chill whilst visiting a poor family in the neighbourhood. 'Tell the doctors I'm too ill to see them,' she said as she lay dying. The newly-weds got only as far as Paris before Smith was called back, leaving Gwen behind. He wrote to her on 12 February:

Dearest and Beautifullest beloved,
Dearest Mother is making a brave plucky and desperate struggle but only a miracle can save her. They all say how much she loves you so I can't help wishing you could have come too. Dear G I hope I will be a better Matthew when I get back. Beloved Beautiful. Matthew.[2]

Fanny expired on the same day he wrote and the Rome trip was cancelled out of respect. She left only £945 gross in her will, presumably because most assets were in Frederic's name. A little of this must have come to Matthew, but Gwen also had her own money so they could afford to take a prolonged honeymoon elsewhere. They chose to return to where the art was, to France, moving restlessly around in a way it is now very difficult to trace. They probably began by visiting Brittany, which was new territory to Gwen, and then on to St-Jean-de-Luz, Argelès, and the Musée Ingres at Montauban. The rest of spring 1912 was spent in Paris where they most likely saw the Vuillard exhibition at Bernheim-Jeune in April, and Matthew had three still lifes on show at the Salon des Indépendants.

After some months the Smiths left Paris. One writer believes Smith was simultaneously inspired by the artistic wonders of the capital and paralysed by his lack of confidence:

In Paris after the initial discovery, he had been inhibited by the presence and the stature of his mentors; he was constantly confronted with the achievements of others and, as we have seen, he was constitutionally prone to torment himself with comparisons. Therefore, although it entailed the sacrifice of his personal stability, for the sake of his painting it was necessary to cut himself off from the source of inspiration and test his discovery in comparative seclusion.[3]

There were several changes of lodgings as the Smiths explored the Ile de France, but by August 1912 they had established themselves in a house rented from one of Maynard's friends at Grez-sur-Loing and made it their home until January 1914. However, November 1912 is unaccounted for and they might well have slipped across the Channel to see the second Post-Impressionists exhibition organized by Roger Fry in the Grafton Gallery. Cézanne, Picasso, the Fauves and Matisse made a big showing there, to Tonks's disgust because they stirred up his students. They also antagonized xenophobic critics who saw the new French attitude to landscape as a threat to our own traditions. Fry defended his exhibitors against the predictable charges of representational incompetence, on the grounds that 'They do not seek to imitate form, but to create form; not to imitate life, but to find an equivalent for life . . . in fact, they aim not at illusion, but at reality.'[4]

The Smiths were certainly back in Grez for Christmas 1912 because we had Matthew's affectionate letter home to his 'very dear Dad' thanking him for his 'very handsome gift' of a cheque for £25, and telling him that Gwen is now recovered from her illness (she had miscarried on 10 December), and that they were both looking forward to Frederic's visit in the Spring. This was Frederic's first Christmas as a widower and Matthew wrote:

It would be a sad Christmas for you dear Dad – it was difficult to think of Dunham Lawn without imagining dear sweet beautiful Mother flitting about among you all – such love as hers for us I think MUST still exist, as ours for her exists, a thousand times more sensitively than we could realize it before – you must let Mother's love for you comfort you sometimes.[5]

Frederic went to France in February, though they seem to have met up in Paris rather than Grez. The Durand-Ruel gallery receipt has been traced (dated 26 February 1913) for Frederic's purchase of two works by Henri Moret (1856–1913). This artist had worked alongside Gauguin and Bernard at Pont Aven in the 1880s and made a speciality of Breton subjects, though to judge by those now in the Pont Aven museum his later ones were indebted to Monet as much as to Gauguin. Since this represents quite a daring shift in taste for the conservative Frederic we might speculate that his son offered him advice. If so it is to Frederic's credit that he took it.

Smith returned to London, perhaps accompanying his father, some time in the first half of 1913 and took out a lease on a studio in Percy Street, but by August he was back in Grez with Gwen. He was restless and found it difficult to get down to work, but he did make some progress. Fourteen oils from this period have been traced, though several are unfinished, each representing a struggle to assimilate the lessons he had learned in France so far. Traces of Gauguin, Matisse, the Fauves and the Nabis are present in all of them. We do not know what Gwen's effect was on his work, but given that she was more self-assured it seems probable that she chivvied him out of his paralysing self-doubts and hesitations and forced him to stick to the task. Whether she drew and painted alongside him we do not know because none of her work from this period has been traced.

12   A portrait of Gwen survives from 1912 which shows Smith had been assimilating the example of the Nabis, Vuillard in particular. Smith made rhythmic patterns of the abruptly edged shadows of Gwen's hair and did not try for psychological insights in the way he did in the more realistic chalk drawing of 1908. The colours too are very restrained, being variations on browns and a deep blue for her high-collared dress. It is successful in the same way that his Pont Aven *Portrait of a Young Boy* was, but it was a style he was not to develop further.

Two landscapes in the Fauvist manner also survive – a rather slapdash one of St-Jean-de-Luz,[6] and another just known as *Small French Landscape*.[7] In both, but particularly the latter, he experiments with flattening devices, Fauve primary colours and the use of paint in visible single strokes applied loosely and drily over a white ground. Another very adventurous and large (39½ × 43½ in.) townscape, possibly of Argelès, is of interlocking flat shapes painted in thin washes of brilliant yellow, red and blue – another manner he was not to repeat.[8] At this time he also seems to have rediscovered his childhood love of flowers and there are bright rhythmic studies of sunflowers, tulips and lilies.

The choice of Grez-sur-Loing for their main French base arose from the same impulse which took Smith to Pont Aven. As we have seen already, one strand of the French artists' revolt against stuffy academicism was to move outside Paris in search of the open air, contact with the soil, and those uncorrupted souls who tilled it. This was a romantic rather than a political urge and though these artists were flying the flag of Realism they sometimes had to turn a blind eye when the peasants turned out to be dirty, bigoted, drunk, philistine, and very adept at getting money out of the visitors' pockets. One way round this was to form defensive self-sufficient colonies in which the artists dominated the community and the peasants provided the services – though of course this meant any solitude was lost and another café society, all talk and little work, soon grew up very like the one they had left behind in Paris.

The colonies at Barbizon and Fontainebleau represented the first timid moves in this direction. Both could be reached by rail from Paris within the hour so one could always retreat if the weather or the natives turned nasty. Corot, Rousseau and Millet worked in Barbizon until it was vulgarized by day-trippers and the prices went up. Fontainebleau suffered a similar fate after 1870 when R. L. Stevenson and his cousin, the wild R. A. M. Stevenson (the Velázquez specialist), enjoyed the bohemian life style there. In 1875 the Stevensons hired a carriage and prospected further afield, finding Grez, a sleepy village a few miles south of Marlotte on the banks of the Loing, between Nemours and Fontainebleau. There was only an old church, a stump of castle, a thirteenth-century bridge, a Mairie, and cheap property.

Grez soon lost its serenity and became an Anglo-American settlement reverberating with hearty river-sports, amateur dramatics and lovers' quarrels. A local historian lists 175 artists from all over the globe who had worked in the village,[9] though many were what R. L. Stevenson called 'snoozers' – there to enjoy the life rather than the work. The writer met his future wife there, the American Fanny Osbourne, who like many others had come to Grez to paint.

Carl Larssen, the popular Swedish artist, led a strong Scandinavian contingent and Strindberg the dramatist spent two summers there with his wife Siri von Essen. Edvard Munch dropped by in 1903 to see his friend Delius. Other, English-speaking artists arrived and stayed, such as Frank O'Meara (1853–88), William Stott (1857–1900), and the American Alexander Harrison (1853–1930), who was a friend and pupil of Bastien-Lepage and had already worked in Brittany. The most distinguished visitors, after Millet and Corot, were perhaps Smith's future friend Roderic O'Conor, who lived there in 1889–90, James Guthrie (1859–1930) of the Glasgow School, and Sir John Lavery (1856–1941), who painted the punning *Grey Day at Grez* – a view of the famous river with idlers and a dog on its bank.

The silvery grey tones of the bridge stones, roof-tiles, river and light suited those Realists who painted outdoors in subdued tonalities, as opposed to the Fauves who were largely sun seekers. Michael Jacobs gives a flavour of the early Grez style: 'The sun is rarely seen to shine in their paintings, the season seems to be perpetually autumn (*October* is a favourite title), the peasants depicted are invariably gloomy, and there is often much symbolism . . . suggesting the passage of time and the inevitability of death.'[10] So the Smiths were entering a now depleted artistic community where the strongest tradition was one of melancholy rural Realism. It might have suited Gwen but it could not have been further from Matthew's painterly impulses, which were now moving towards strident colour and lively paint surfaces.

There were two good hotels, Chevillons and the Beauséjour, both with gardens sloping down to the Loing. This river became a favourite motif of the resident artists and it inspired R. L. Stevenson himself to lyricism: 'The course of its pellucid river, whether up or down, is full of gentle attractions for the navigator: islanded reed-mazes where, in autumn, red berries cluster; the mirrored and inverted images of trees; lilies and mills, and the foam and thunder of weirs.'[11] Evidently it did not inspire Smith who never then, or later, rose to the challenge of depicting lights slanting across still depths or sparkling on waves. Water was not his element.

The Anglophone nature of the Grez community must have been one of the attractions for the Smiths. Gwen had possibly heard of it in Whitby from Garrido, who now lived nearby at Moret-sur-Loing, or Smith may have been told of its charms by Guy Maynard who had been there in 1886. However, just as with Pont Aven, he arrived long after the important artists had moved on and the whole creative drive of the place had been lost. Today that decline is complete and Grez has turned over and gone back to sleep again.

Two of the first friends the Smiths made there were Alden Brooks (1883–1964) and his painter wife Hilma, whom they met in August 1912. Alden was born in Cleveland, Ohio, but had passed most of his childhood in Europe and had his secondary education in Repton School in England, from where he returned to the USA to graduate and then teach at Harvard. He settled in Grez in 1908. He was a French correspondent for the *New York Times* and a writer with his own obsessive theories about who really wrote Shakespeare.[12] His artist father, Edward Brooks, had come to France to paint and became a friend of O'Conor and other exiled painters in Paris, and then moved to live in Grez around 1884. Alden had been raised among artists and had good contacts and a good eye: he collected mostly Post-Impressionist paintings and owned wood-carvings by Gauguin. The Brooks also owned a Paris apartment so the friendship could continue in town and the Smiths could be introduced to Brooks's wide acquaintance among the capital's intelligentsia. Alden became a lifelong friend and correspondent, constantly pulling Smith's leg about his hypochondria, his chronic indecisiveness and his love life, and provoking funny ripostes in return.

The snippets referring to the Smiths in Brooks's diaries for these two years show the friendship began slowly, and offer disquieting glimpses into a world not as stress-free and work-filled as it might have been. On their first meeting Brooks noted, 'Mrs S rather impossible, he perhaps possible.' Later, 'Smith was very shy and secretive.' 'Smith talked of himself and family. Rather brow beaten life poor chap. Subject for a novel.' 'Bicycle ride with Smith, rather dull affair. Joked Smith about his laziness, but it fell rather flat.' 'He talked about himself and his ailments.' 'Smith came. Talked idly. Conversation little thin and tired.' 'He in his usual "too much fog" state' (i.e. to paint landscapes). 'Just as I was working Smith came and busted up my morning. Talked of Waldo and Thomas . . . Smith came to ask about a servant . . . then to Mere Jules to look at studio. Thought it too dark. How fussy he is.' 'Suzanne is posing for Mrs Smith. Matthew has left her and gone off to Paris and of course she wants to show him she can get models here. Awkwardness is her chief demerit.' 'Mrs Smith blabbing all her secrets to Suzanne.'

Smith still did not speak good French so Brooks had to get help for Gwen's miscarriage, deal with the legal problems when Smith hired his house from a friend of Maynard's, and take part in the search for models and studios. The Brookses seem not to have taken the tactless and increasingly bossy Gwen to their hearts in the way they did Matthew, who was always popping round for tea, late night chats, or a mushroom hunt – any pretext rather than getting down to work.

Other near neighbours from this period were Joe Heseltine, brother of the composer Peter Warlock and friend of Lavery, who had been in Grez since 1874, and Lloyd Osbourne, R. L. Stevenson's stepson and literary executor, who was soon to be one of the first owners of Smith's pictures outside his family. If Osbourne paid for these, rather than receiving them as a gift, then they must have been the artist's first sales.

One of the most distinguished settlers was the English composer Frederick Delius who had set up house with his future wife, the gifted painter Jelka Rosen, in 1896. He was already suffering from the syphilis which was first to cripple, then blind, and eventually kill him in 1934. Delius lived aloof from the village in the former priest's house next to the church in rue Grande (now rue Wilson), with the Brooks next door to him, and it was Brooks who introduced Smith to Delius. In a letter written in 1960 Brooks recalled:

Smith first met Delius on the afternoon of 7 October 1913. I had wanted for some time to introduce him to Delius, but he had always shied away. However, he now met Lloyd Osbourne at the local inn, and the Osbournes were going to a tea-party at the Deliuses' and Lloyd urged him to come along, so Smith rushed over to me and got me to come as a second escort. Smith was of course an admirer of Delius, but he remained always . . . well, not frightened, but nervous and ill at ease in his presence. Though, as my wife says, who didn't remain so?[13]

Later, however, Smith gave Rothenstein the impression that he had 'formed a lasting friendship' with the composer.

Delius shared a similar background to Smith, but Delius's rebellion against his industrialist father took a more adventurous course and included running an orange plantation in Florida for a time. During his Paris days Delius had mixed with the avant-garde writers and painters and in 1898 had acquired for a mere £20 Gauguin's magnificent nude *Nevermore*, a work Smith must have admired on his walls since its pose was to be echoed later in several of his own nudes. Delius also knew O'Conor and Edvard Munch, whose works were also to be seen around the house – though Smith would not have appreciated the latter's guilt-heavy attitude to sex.

Smith and Delius both lit the Christmas tree at the Brookses in 1913 and then on Boxing Day Brooks complained, 'Smith broke in with a book on Gauguin. Has now thoughts of going South. Worked up. I'm always ready to travel in the spirit but rarely go. No place better than here. And I want to work. Stupid and dull and dreary very often, but we can't have everything.'

Smith obviously found it hard not to be a 'snoozer' in Grez. It was perhaps the distractions of French bucolic life, or the first taste of economic independence, or the strains of adjusting to being one of a pair after the freedom of his two bachelor years in Paris. He found it easiest to work on still lifes, particularly flowers, since they lent

1 *Self Portrait*, 1909

2 Frederic Smith, Matthew's father
3 Fanny Smith, Matthew's mother
4 Frederick Smith & Co, Caledonia Works, Halifax, *c.* 1895

5 Noel Arthur Smith aged 8, Matthew aged 6, Harold aged 3, Hilda
aged 9
6 Dunham Lawn, Bowdon, Cheshire, showing drawing room and
library windows

7 Matthew Smith as a young man
8 *Portrait of Gwendolen Smith*, *c.* 1908
9 Matthew Smith (second from left) in Breton costume at Pont Aven,
c. 1909

10 *Portrait of a Young Boy*, 1908
11 *Self Portrait in a Mirror*, 1908–9
12 *Portrait of the Artist's Wife, Gwen*, 1912

13 *Mme Rivière, after Ingres, 1910–13*
14 *Coastal Landscape, 1911*

15 *Flowers in a Green Vase*, 1913

16 *Lilies*, 1913

17 Matthew Smith and Gwen Salmond at Dunham Lawn
18 Gwen with Mark and Dermot
19 Gwen, Frederic, Geoffrey and Matthew Smith at Swinford Manor,
c. 1914

20 *The Arum Lily,* 1916

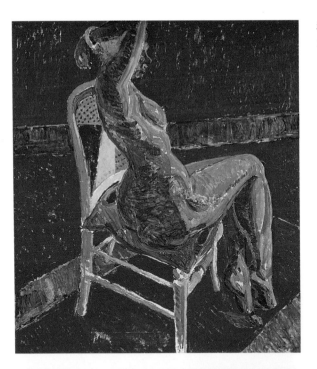

21 *Fitzroy Street Nude No. 1,*
1916

23 *Portrait of a German
P.O.W.,* 1918–19
22 *Fitzroy Street Nude No. 2,*
1916

24 *Steeple in Cornwall*, 1920

25 *Cornish Garden with Monkey-Puzzle Tree*, 1920

26 *The Wet Road*, 1920
27 *Cornish Landscape*, 1920

28 Vera Cuningham, date unknown
29 Matthew Smith and Vera Cuningham in the garden of the Villa
Brune, *c.* 1923
30 *Reclining Nude*, 1925

31 *Portrait of Vera Cuningham*, date unknown
32 *The Blue Necklace*, 1924

33 *Standing Nude with Fan,*

34 *Model à La Rose*, 1924

35 *Model Turning*, 1924

themselves to bold colour, simplification and experiment more than models or landscapes. The *Tulips* of 1913 (one of his very few dated works) has a vertical format and is only saved from perfect symmetry by a slanting skirting board behind the vase – a device he was to repeat later in his Fitzroy Street nudes. Again the canvas is filled in *Flowers in a Green Vase* (1913), this time by wild flowers and once more the white prime plays its part in keeping it fresh and light. This technique draws attention to the abstract relationships of the separate touches of pure colour and the implied space between them.   15

Smith was also still working on his copy of Ingres' *Madame Rivière* which he had brought to Grez, trying to make it yield up its secrets. He had turned his back on the Paris avant-garde to live in an artistic backwater and he retreated further into the past when he went on a second pilgrimage to the museum at Montauban which contained the 4,000 drawings and studio contents Ingres had bequeathed to his native town. This Salon painter still appears a strange hero for somebody trying to throw off academic strictures – with hindsight Ingres' rival Delacroix, with his message that 'One never paints violently enough', would seem a more likely candidate. Smith could surely have had no sympathy with the frigid historical works such as *The Martyrdom of St Symphorian* or *Antiochus and Stratonice* by which Ingres himself set such store, nor could he have seen much to admire in the simpering Virgins or the patriotic posturings of Napoleon or Joan of Arc. The *Turkish Bath*, too, was preposterous and dismissed by Smith's future friend Sickert as 'absurd and repellent, a suggestion of a dish of macaroni, something wriggling and distasteful'[14] – though these were the very qualities which made it a favourite of another future friend, Francis Bacon. Their glassy surfaces also reflect the way Ingres admired Raphael and the meticulous early Flemish masters, rather than those later more painterly masters such as Rubens or Rembrandt. 'Art never succeeds better,' said Ingres, 'than when it is concealed.' It was against this belief that the Impressionists were already beginning to rebel whilst Ingres was still alive.

As with Matisse, there is also something a little cold about Ingres' eroticism: somehow Ingres had mastered his concupiscence and contemplated the object of desire without desiring it. The spectator is kept at arm's length by an immaculate surface, decorous poses, the modestly averted gazes of his subjects and the pellucid, airless space in which they take up their sinuous but unlikely postures.

On a technical level the Ingres drawings in Montauban could show Smith that volume can be suggested by line alone, without resorting to heavy modelling in chiaroscuro – a lesson which would reinforce what he had already seen in Matisse, himself an Ingres admirer. Degas had been taken to visit Ingres when he was eighteen years old and had received the advice, 'Draw lines, young man, many lines.'

Smith could also learn from his growing library of books on Ingres that liberties could be taken if they heightened expression: what Ingres called 'correcting nature on her own terms' – and which showed in the elongated fingers, necks and spines of his nudes. 'Stress the dominant traits of the model,' Ingres instructed, 'state them vigorously, heighten them if needs be, to the point of caricature. I use the word "caricature" advisedly, to draw attention to a principle whose soundness is unquestionable.'[15]

It would still be difficult for anyone not knowing of Smith's devotion to Ingres to spot any trace on a canvas of the master's influence in Smith's work at this or any other period, beyond the obvious similarities in seated poses and the love of nudes. Certainly he never subscribed to Ingres's dictum that 'colour is merely the handmaiden of painting.' Halliday and Russell are surely right when they say: 'As with most of his admirations, it would be incorrect to speak of Ingres' "influence": "inspiration" was the word Smith preferred.'[16]

Back in Grez Smith had begun to accumulate the bric-à-brac that was to appear time and again in his table-top still lifes. One such prop is the torso of a female nude which appears in two versions of the 1913 *The Plaster Cast*[17]. These pictures were the outcome of many preparatory sketches and much deliberation, but the result is not a success for the reasons one critic gives:

The ingredients are dry studio stuff: the plaster cast, a metal statuette, an earthenware jug, a curtain, some drawings pinned upon the wall; but later less than these could be the vehicle of ardent expression. He has always had few needs in this respect. His subject matter is never complex, for he transforms it freely to make a design which is primarily imaginative. Here, however, the imagination has not yet taken hold. There is ample colour; but the sum of it is cold and grey. He is concerned too exclusively with the problem of realising experiences, and the result is scarcely more than photographic.[18]

Other flower paintings besides those already mentioned show Smith still struggling with Gauguin's and Matisse's powerful influences in terms of pure colour, simplification and composition. There is much use of the primaries, particularly scarlet and green, pinks and purples and yellows, and rather over-deliberate playing of organic curves against background angles in stretchers and table-tops.[19] One writer sums them up concisely:

In general the feature which distinguishes these flower paintings is their deliberate elimination of tonal effects, their flatness and their emphasis on design, bright colour and the lack of sensuous response to the texture whether of the paint or the flowers. The brushstrokes generally lack intrinsic interest, the loaded brush serving merely as the tool with which to fill in certain spaces on the canvas rather than as a potential means of expression or gesture.[20]

However, one painting, *Lilies* (1913–14), seems at last to have pulled 16 all these lessons together and to work in its own terms. Now there is no bare canvas showing through, with all the ambiguities that causes within the picture space; no pretence of modelling by shadows or highlights; no dry little dabs of brushstrokes without real purpose; no implied perspective deep into a room, only vestigial pinkish lines which might once have indicated table-top, floor and picture frame but which now serve compositional needs only. Instead we have a hymn to blue as each segment between these lines is filled in with intense streaky cobalt. The complex silhouette of the leaves and lilies dominates the top of the picture and the stubby grey vase the lower half, while the touches of red in both halves and in the proud signature chime back and forth across the blue. Surely it could not have been painted without a knowledge of Matisse's *Red Studio* of 1911.

Steer had advised any would-be colourist to 'lay it on like a breath' and to use small round brushes: Smith had now shaken off such Slade timidity and would never return to it. It was the first major picture Smith had painted and it was to bring him some welcome attention when he took it back to London with him. It was also enough of a breakthrough for him to feel he had something to build upon when he returned to figure compositions in his London studio.

Too soon the Grez-sur-Loing idyll was over. As Smith slowly emerged as a more confident man and painter he began to be irritated by Gwen: her suggestions and opinions which had once supported and charmed him now seemed like manipulation. War fever was also unsettling the village, tension ran high in the little community and suspicions gathered. Brooks had always had some reservations about Smith's early work as this 1912 diary entry shows: 'Afterwards saw Smith. He showed me his pictures. Very interesting in their way. No need to be discouraged, only little poorly drawn and ill balanced at times, needs to work that's all. Would have liked to have bought one.'[21] After the war, when Smith had served his prolonged apprenticeship, Brooks did indeed buy several. But one neighbour, Heseltine, thought the works so poor that Smith could not really be an artist at all:

Later, when war broke out, Joe took me aside and told me with the utmost seriousness that Smith's painting was only a blind – obviously so – that in truth Smith was an English spy sent out by the British General Staff, of which his brother-in-law was a member, in order to keep an eye on Delius, who though he pretended to be Danish, was actually of German extraction.[22]

The Smiths left Grez on New Year's Day 1914 and had one last jaunt round their favourite places in the south, joining up with the newly married Lyman in St-Jean-de-Luz, then hurrying back to Ashford in Kent where Frederic had retired to Swinford Old Manor. The news was that he was dying.

19

CHAPTER 8

Fitzroy Street
1914–1916

Frederic Smith died on 27 August 1914. Matthew informed Lyman that 'it was a very pathetic ending to a very full life.'[1] He was only sixty-five but had long handed over the day-to-day direction of his companies to Noel and Harold. Family legend has it that the day they returned to work after the funeral they changed out of the starched collars he had imposed on them and into soft ones. Nevertheless, they must have been grateful for his strictness with his finances. Each of his five children was left £500, every niece and nephew (twelve in all) was left £100, his nurse received £50, the gardener and chauffeur £10 each and all the indoor servants £5. Phyllis, still unmarried then, inherited the Llandudno house. Then his violins were to be sold, together with Dunham Lawn and all its rich contents, and the money divided. Most importantly his numerous shares were to have the profits distributed among his progeny for four years and then they were to be divided into thirty-five parts. Each son was to receive 10/35ths and the residue was to be shared between Phyllis and Hilda. From this arrangement Matthew received 1100 Electric Wire shares and 100 Frederick Smith company shares which ensured him a comfortable income for life, and which would be securely handed on to his widow or any children who attained the age of twenty-one. His father's industriousness and foresight meant Matthew never needed to worry about finance again, though he never seemed very grateful for this.

Very few artists indeed escape the trials (and rewards) of teaching, and even fewer are released from the pressure of sales. Smith always needed to exhibit and earn praise to sustain his self-respect, but he was reluctant to sell his work and left an enormous hoard of favourite paintings when he died. Now, released from all money worries, this archetypal slow developer could afford to work at whatever pace suited him.

He took a solitary holiday in Cornwall soon after his father died and later wrote to John Lyman, who had remained in France: 'The war makes one very unsettled in mind. At Plymouth I went to see a military doctor and he said I must put warfare out of my mind but still it is very difficult to settle down to painting when one's subconscious mind at least is *perpetually* thinking about the war.'²

He also told Lyman that 'Poor Innes died 3 or 4 months ago' – this was his precocious contemporary at the Slade whom he had shown round Paris and introduced to Lyman and the Steins. Innes had a studio in Fitzroy Street but by then his tuberculosis was so advanced that he could not rise without a stiff brandy, and his teeth had gone so rotten he could not chew. A last desperate trip to North Africa had failed to halt the disease and so Britain lost a brilliant colourist who was just beginning to exploit the lessons he had learned from his time in France.

Guy Maynard wrote to Smith to bring him up to date on events in Brittany – who had been killed at the Front, who had fled and who remained of their expatriate community. Concarneau was now a place for turning Breton peasants into soldiers and for nursing the wounded. The American Chadwicks had departed from Grez in the last auto-taxi, taking their Gauguin with them, and Hilma Brooks had wanted to flee with them but Alden had forbidden it. When she heard the guns in the distance she buried the silver in the garden. The Deliuses, after sneering at Chadwick for 'running away', had made a run for it themselves as far as Orléans, but had been turned back as too German-sounding and returned to Grez, where they decorated the house with flags of all nations to be on the safe side and declared they were now Danish. Maynard was reading Delacroix's *Journals* and recommended them to Smith. In another undated letter he assures Smith 'there have not been many killed from Pont Aven.' Alden Brooks had left his wife and baby daughters at Grez and gone off to enlist in the French army because the Americans would not have him.³

When the Smiths returned to England in January 1914 they had no home of their own and stayed with Gwen's parents in Somerset and at Dunham Lawn. Matthew needed solitude and a space of his own in which to paint and so hired an attic studio in London at 2 Fitzroy Street. It was a wise choice, since most of the progressive artistic and literary life of London was concentrated in the few streets and squares around him. He retained this cramped work space until the summer of 1920, though he constantly complained about it, as he did of most studios he occupied.

On 1 May 1915 the Smith's first son, Mark, was born. This was at 1 Greville Place, in the flat of Gwen's brother Jack who was away at the war and had offered it as their London base. Smith seems at this stage to have been a fond, but not very attentive, father who left the day by day nurturing of the child to Gwen. He did, however, do some very tender and simple drawings of her breast-feeding the baby[4] but, for the most part, he agonized in his studio or made new friends in the artistic community of Fitzroy Street.

Smith hired a model to work from and it was in the portrayal of the nude that he now made a major advance. There were first two experimental, drily painted, rather flimsy pictures in which the figures are hatched in with widely separated stokes so that ground shows through – a Fauve technique he had already used in his Grez flower-pieces.[5] Then in 1916 he painted two pictures which show him grappling with many of the lessons he had learned in France and forging a new style of his own. It was not, however, to be his final style, only a courageous foray up a side turning which proved to lead nowhere.

The subject was conventional enough, a nude female model seen from two different high viewpoints. She is seated on a kitchen chair but the pose with its raised elbow is as excruciatingly artificial as that of any Ingres or Matisse odalisque, though with none of their charm. His brother Harold's comment was that she looked like an insect changing its skin. The painter stood in close over the model and cropped the top of the figure in *Fitzroy Street Nude No. 1* and chopped the feet off in *No. 2*, possibly because of his short sight, or the cramped space of his attic, or on a hunch that the beholder would be more dramatically involved by being confronted directly.

21
22

The drawing is competently realistic (though the scarlet navel is far too low in *No.* 2), but done in emphatic green and blue outline. After that the whole interest of the painter is in strident colour contrasts, particularly those Derain had called 'deliberate disharmonies', viridian against red, and yellow against blue. There is nothing Whistlerian or Impressionistic about these brash, unmodulated primaries nor anything seductive about their application. The backgrounds exploit the discoveries he had made about solid colour in *Lilies* and use the perspective lines of skirting-board or carpet as flat strips to break up the picture into angular jigsaw pieces. Curious spatial shifts occur where the reds of the floor push up to the picture plane, and the blues of cushion and carpet seem to be continuous in *No.* 2. However, he cannot yet carry this bold simplification into the figures themselves, which he felt still needed to be modelled by light and shade and made to look round by brushstrokes which follow the form, for example around the cylinders of the thighs. Because of this, when they are reproduced in black and white they both look like perfectly conventional nude studies.

Having established the drawing he boldly filled in the *No. 1* figure with orange and *No. 2* with cadmium yellow, but then made the shadowed areas of both emerald green. In *No. 1* he has also made the half-lights blue, and in both made the hair blue as well – the old Fauve technique of heightening a local colour by transposing it from a darker to a brighter one, such as brown to red, ochre to yellow or, as here, black to blue. Both are startling works and nothing quite like them was being produced in England or France at the time. In Germany, however, the artists of Die Brücke were producing similarly harsh and expressive nudes, though Smith seems to have been unaware of this.

Ultimately, both are unsatisfactory paintings because they are confused: he has borrowed Gauguin's outlines and the Fauves' colours but not really understood them. The raucous hues seem arbitrarily chosen and both works lack unity because they employ two distinct modes of handling space. These paintings were rejected by the London Group later in the year, which is surprising because Roger Fry, its leading theorist, must have seen the French pedigree behind Smith's works.

The model for the pictures, possibly Nina Hamnett or Emily Powell, introduced Smith to another artist she posed for, Walter Sickert, the foremost English artist of the day, who lived in the same street as Smith. He had little time for Matisse, the Fauves, or Cézanne, but could see these two works were quite startling in English terms and paid Smith the compliment: 'You paint like a painter and you draw like a draughtsman.' He might have added *sotto voce* 'but not at the same time'. This was a generous compliment since Sickert himself eschewed such brilliant colours in favour of 'that mysterious fusion of coffee, sepia, chocolate, ochre and ambers with which he created his own particular brand of luminosity'.[6] Although Sickert was a friend of Tonks and Steer he disapproved of the Slade insistence on painting direct from the model instead of from drawings; and he advocated a slow methodical build-up of paint, often over a squared-up grid, until the surface was 'like the side of a matchbox', all totally unlike the 'one wet' method Smith was working towards.

Sickert urged painters to get out of the drawing-room and into the kitchen and the bedroom because 'the plastic arts are gross arts, dealing joyously with gross material facts.' This was a swipe at society portraitists such as Sargent and Orpen, as well as the aesthetes of Bloomsbury – though even Virginia Woolf conceded 'he makes us aware of beauty over the shoulders of the innkeeper.' In his female nudes sprawling in seedy rooms ('my own particular brand of frump') many thought this grossness overdone, and Professor Brown terminated his friendship with Sickert because of them. Apart from these unidealized nudes he and Smith shared few motifs, Sickert being a painter of proletarian life with little interest in unpeopled landscapes, flowers or still lifes.

In spite of their differing practices and very contrasted personalities Smith found his new friend wonderful company, constantly changing his appearance and enthusiasms, 'always thinking of wonderful things to do' and 'full of uncommon sense.' This friendship developed enough for Sickert and his wife to invite the Smiths to join them at Chagford, Devon, for the summer of 1916. The two men shared a love of eccentric company, the theatre, good food, wine, bric-à-brac and all things French, whilst their spouses, Christine and Gwen, endured similar problems in coping with their egocentric and impractical husbands.

Making Sickert's acquaintance opened up a new world for Smith. Sickert had two studios in Fitzroy Street, each named after former occupants. Number 8 was the Whistler, at one time Sickert's (and Gwen's) teacher and whose influence lingered on in Sickert's low tonalities. Here Sickert held his school, though Augustus John warned people off it because 'he'll teach you to paint chamber pots.' Number 15 was called the Frith after the Victorian painter of *Derby Day*, and it was in this huge studio that Sickert held his open house on Wednesday afternoons. One visitor recalls: 'He liked these afternoons to be as mixed as possible, to remind us of the world beyond Fitzroy Street. On a good day there might be Spaniards, Americans, actors, old pupils, dilettantes, the world of Mayfair, a sprinkling of French, besides the quartier and a never ending stream of khaki.'[7]

Sickert had spent many of his formative years as a painter in France, where he knew Monet, Signac, Bonnard, Vuillard, and Gauguin (who he had advised to stick to Sunday painting). But in 1885 he visited the studio of the man he admired most, Degas, 'the lighthouse of my existence.' From this master he had learned to be experimental in technique and composition, and to take city life as his subject matter. He had also noted how Degas had broken free of the classically derived poses of French academicism and found a new beauty in women crouching, scrubbing, yawning and scratching. Many in London were not ready for either Sickert or Degas: the National Gallery refused the gift of a Degas the year before Sickert came home in 1905 to jolly up English art, now that the impulses given it by Bastien-Lepage's Realism and Monet's style of Impressionism were running low or had been safely Anglicized. 'I am sent from heaven to finish all your educations,' Sickert said modestly.

Sickert stirred things up by helping start new groups ('these things are, and always have been, done in gangs' he declared): the Fitzroy Street Group which met on the first floor at Number 19 was formed in 1907, the jury-free co-operative Allied Artists Association in 1908, the Camden Town Group in 1911 and the London Group in 1913. None of these had a manifesto or a worked-out intellectual position – that not being the English way: indeed, the London Group had as its sole intention that 'all modern methods may find a home.' There were many overlaps in membership, but each group had the purpose of stimulating discussion and providing exhibition spaces in opposition to the Royal Academy and the conservative Bond Street galleries.

All these groups were exhibiting in the decade before the war and Smith could not have avoided being aware of them since their members all passed through Sickert's gatherings at one time or another. He must have met at this time such crucial figures on the London scene as Augustus John, Jacob Epstein, Henry Lamb, Robert Bevan, Harold Gilman, Charles Ginner and Spencer Gore – all indebted to Gauguin, Matisse, Van Gogh and the other Post-Impressionists for their brightened palettes and new visions. These men were Smith's age, spoke his language, and were eager to gain recruits for the war against Victorian academicism. Obviously Smith could learn a lot from the way they had adapted French discoveries to English visions and subject matter.

At Sickert's gatherings Smith could have eavesdropped on the Bloomsbury Group, intellectuals with private means, Cambridge degrees, unorthodox sex lives and a disproportionate influence in English art and literature. Clive Bell, the critic who had raised the whole issue of 'significant form' and its priority over subject matter in his book *Art* (1914), was one. He was rejecting Victorian 'story' pictures and trying to isolate what it was in Japanese, Pre-Columbian and African works which made them so aesthetically powerful, even though their 'content' was totally alien to the European viewer. His wife Vanessa Bell was another Matisse and Cézanne enthusiast who was simplifying forms and lightening colours under their inspiration. Like Duncan Grant, she was already painting totally abstract works by this time, following quickly after the showing of Kandinsky's abstractions in London in 1913, and their praise by Fry as 'pure visual music'. Grant was younger than Matthew but was already deeply involved in all the new groups and had shown at the Second Post-Impressionists exhibition in 1912, as well as with the Vorticists in 1915. Both Vanessa Bell and Grant became Smith's lifelong friends and were to share something of his later love of bright colour and rich decorative materials.

Just along the street from Smith's studio, at 33 Fitzroy Square, Bell, Grant and Fry ran the Omega Workshops as an artists' co-operative where painters could decorate handicrafts with startling abstractions which the public found acceptable on a tea-tray, though not yet in a picture frame. Like Ruskin and Morris they believed beautiful practical objects improved their users' spiritual lives. Etchells and Wyndham Lewis were founder members too and such artists as Gaudier-Brzeska, Paul Nash, Bomberg, Roberts and Gertler contributed in the pre-war years before it disintegrated into squabbling. There is no record that Smith took part in this, though the group's style would have appealed to him and he later painted two screens very much in their fashion.

The most influential single contact made at Sickert's soirées would be Roger Fry, in his role as entrepreneur and formalist advocate of modern French art, rather than as a painter – one who was 'a little dry, a little anxious, a little tame'.[8] Smith thought both the man and his work 'pleasant enough.'[9] Fry had moved on from Impressionism, which he thought too informal and lacking intellectual rigour, to proclaiming Cézanne as the apostle of structure. In his *Essay on Aesthetics* (1909) Fry had teased out 'the emotional elements inherent in natural form' and asked for a 'clear disinterested contemplation' by the modern artist to produce an art which did not serve morality in the way Victorian art had done, and did not cater for 'mere sensual pleasures' as the Impressionists did. The subject was irrelevant: it mattered not at all to Fry whether he was painting Christ on the cross or a saucepan, or so he claimed. The Bloomsbury intellectuals round Fry would have intimidated Smith, who flinched from theoretical discussion, especially such high-flown stuff as this. However, in Sickert's robust presence the Bloomsberries were usually cut down to size and kept in their places.

Fry was certainly then the dominant thinker in British art and would remain so until his death in 1934. He Anglicized French discoveries, sometimes taming them in the process to suit English eyes ('We are terribly tasteful,' Fry admitted). He firmly believed all art produced on our 'Bird's Custard Island' was necessarily inferior to that produced in France and so he blinded British artists, including Smith, to alternative traditions in Germany, Holland, Belgium, Austria or Scandinavia – though many in their Expressionist and Romantic manifestations were perhaps better suited to the English imagination than the 'plastic' merits of Cézanne. The jingle

The French have taste in all they do
Which we are quite without,
For Nature, which to them gave goût
To us gave only gout

more or less summed up the Bloomsbury credo.

However, Fry's favourite Post-Impressionists were soon challenged in Paris by the Cubists and in England by the Vorticists, a noisy group of individuals led by Wyndham Lewis and Epstein who combined the discoveries of French Cubism, German Expressionism and Italian Futurism. Alongside Sickert's circle, and the Bloomsbury coterie, the Vorticists represented the third growth point in English art that Smith came into contact with at this time. Their theorist, T. E. Hulme, urged artists 'to cleanse the world of these sloppy dregs of the Renaissance' and kick out the whole 'humanist' tradition. They showed in the Dore Galleries in June 1915 and Smith probably saw their work (he certainly owned a copy of their magazine *Blast*), though its angularity, aggression and lack of sensuality would have repelled him. He knew the insides of factories better than they did and so did not worship the machine, nor did he see the war as a great cleansing adventure as the Vorticists and Futurists claimed to do. Nor, having just begun to work from life models again, would he have allied himself with the Futurists' declaration: 'We fight . . . against the nude in painting, as nauseous and tedious as adultery in literature . . . we demand, for ten years, the total suppression of the nude in painting.'[10] They had no time for landscape painting either, which the English liked to think was their particular glory.

In spite of all these alluring possibilities opening around him Smith continued to work out his own destiny in his own studio. *Dulcie* is a further, more elegant exploration of the Fitzroy Street Nudes manner of combining flat unrealistic colour and modelling. This time the clothed figure is posed against a singing red brushed over a yellow ground. Again he has been so close to the model that he has lost the top of her head.[11]

Another work of this period, and possibly of the same model, is the bright yellow *Nude in a Cane Chair*, painfully posed and with her bare stomach curiously left as bare canvas.[12] One work which must have come after the 1916 nudes is *The Arum Lily*. Now he has the courage to abandon the safety net of outline and work in colour areas alone. These are still strong but not as wilfully brash as before, and he has made an astonishingly bold composition, worthy of Degas, by drawing a brilliant blue line one-fifth of the way in from the right margin to separate the foreground still life from the background kitchen. It represents as big a breakthrough as the 1913 *Lilies* and should have given Smith some prestige amongst his new friends in Fitzroy Street.

Sickert's only rivals as larger-than-life personalities were the younger men Augustus John and Jacob Epstein. All three had the animal vigour and confidence in their own abilities that Smith so conspicuously lacked, but all three came to respect this quiet nervous creature as their equal in talent and made him a companion in their revels. Epstein made contact by encouraging Matthew to exhibit his *Lilies* with the London Group in 1916. Smith had striven with this for a year so it had none of the spontaneity of his later flower works, but it became the first of his works to be shown in London. 'The only painter with guts' was Epstein's verdict on this work, and when it was bought by a discerning collector of modern painting, Walter Taylor, Epstein pursued him to his house and bought it back for himself. This was to be the first in his Smith collection, which eventually grew to thirty works.

Epstein was a year younger than Smith but he was physically and emotionally more resilient and made himself the frailer man's protector. He was a tough survivor who had fought his way against parental opposition up and out of the New York ghetto to become Britain's first modern sculptor. He had a precocious start and was attending life-classes by the age of thirteen and earning a living in Paris by twenty-one. He arrived in London in 1905 and soon had the press in uproar over his nude sculptures in the Strand, his Oscar Wilde memorial in Paris and his sinister Vorticist masterpiece *The Rock Drill* of 1913–15. Like Smith he distrusted theorizing (hence his hostility to the Bloomsbury chatterers and Fry in particular), but also like Smith he was a great enthuser. He shared with his friends Modigliani and Picasso an admiration for African art and collected tribal carvings with even more recklessness than he acquired Smith's paintings – though he failed to persuade Smith of the merits of primitive art. It was Epstein's rejection of the Graeco-Roman-Renaissance-Academic tradition of the idealized figure in favour of the 'primitive' which so outraged the art establishment. Smith now had a friend for life. Usually Epstein quarrelled with all his male friends sooner or later, but never with Smith, whose cause he continued to promote.

Epstein had a studio in Emerald Street and a house at 23 Guilford Street, each within easy walking distance of Fitzroy Street, and now Smith had open access to both. There he found the patiently enduring Margaret Epstein, who managed her husband's bills, taxes and sales, and generally kept the bailiffs from the door. She also housed and fed his models, whom he liked to have on hand, and raised the illegitimate children he had by them as if they were her own. This, and Smith's subsequent entry into Augustus John's bizarre domestic arrangements, gave him an insight into ways of life and styles of marriage he had not encountered before in his middle-class upbringing. It must have made him think about his own increasingly uneasy relationship with Gwen, who was now confined to maternal and domestic chores in Kensington, while he made these exciting new contacts in Fitzrovia.

Smith continued to work in his studio, but he could not ignore the newsboys' placards outside, the women flourishing white feathers and entreating him from posters WOMEN OF BRITAIN SAY – 'GO!' The news from France was increasingly grim. Amongst the thousands of dead, Britain had already lost one of its most promising young sculptors when Gaudier-Brzeska had been blown to pieces, then Isaac Rosenberg had been shot dead, and the young philosopher of Vorticism, T. E. Hulme, was killed before his monograph on Epstein could be produced.

All this must have played on Smith's patriotic conscience. He had brothers-in-law and a father-in-law who were professional military men; the *Studio* magazine was publishing lists of artists who had enlisted already, and at every Sickert 'at home' there were servicemen home on leave or about to leave for the Front. Kitchener's accusing eyes followed him whenever he ventured into the street. Even if he was already thirty-six and not very strong, there must surely be something he could do for his King and Country.

CHAPTER 9

War
1917–1919

One role for painters in the First World War was as War Artists. At first the Director of Propaganda, C. F. Masterman, used older academic artists such as Muirhead Bone and Francis Dodds, but soon fashionable society portraitists such as Lavery, Sargent and Orpen were called upon. Pay and conditions varied and some of the work was produced by artists who had actually served first as regular soldiers, such as Paul and John Nash, Stanley and Gilbert Spencer, Roberts, Nevinson, Kennington and Lewis. Others, Schwabe and Meninsky for example, were recruited specifically to draw events at home in England. Many of these were ex-Slade students and even Smith's tutors were used: the ageing Tonks drew on the Somme and in Russia, and recorded plastic surgery on face wounds, whilst Steer was sent to paint Dover Harbour but moaned about the wind, the vastness of the pier, and the irritating way boats kept moving about.[1]

There were several London exhibitions of these artists' impressions of the Front, most in 1917 and 1918 when Smith was already abroad, but he would surely have seen his Slade contemporary C. R. W. Nevinson's one-man show at the Leicester Galleries in 1916. By then Nevinson had adapted his Vorticist-Futurist style to depict the dehumanizing effect of a mechanized war. Paul Nash showed at the Goupil Gallery in July 1917, demonstrating his transformation from a fey Pre-Raphaelite into 'A messenger who will bring back word from the men who are fighting to those who want the war to go on for ever. Feeble, inarticulate, will be my message, but it will have a bitter truth, and may it burn their lousy souls.'[2]

Smith had no strings to pull, no London exhibitions and only a few nudes and flower pieces to show as evidence of his talents. He wanted to serve his country ('I should like the experience,' he wrote to Brooks) but it would have to be as a plain soldier. He tried to enlist, but predictably he was rejected as unfit by the Artists' Rifles and The Honourable Artillery Company, presumably on the grounds that he could not be trusted with a loaded rifle when he could barely see the target. His height was recorded as 5 feet 9 inches, which is odd because everyone I spoke to remembers him as being a tall man. His medical classification was C1, which meant fit only for garrison duty. He wrote to Brooks: 'It seems rather ridiculous that such fine material (!) should be allowed to leave a recruiting office for the lack of a worthless piece of board. I am not writing to the papers about it however.'[3] Nevertheless, he joined the Army Reserves in December 1915. Smith's two brothers, meantime, had been exempted on the grounds that making wire was a crucial part of the war effort. Harold was now a married man, but Arthur was to remain a bachelor until after the war. 'Dearest little Phyl' remained Smith's closest confidante and she served as a Red Cross nurse in Altrincham during this period.

Gwen gave birth to their second son, Christopher Dermot Salmond Smith, on 11 September 1916 at her parents' house in Somerset. Smith then moved his family to a cottage at Rustington in Sussex, but very soon after, on 6 November, the call came for Smith to report as a private to the Inns of Court Officer Training Corps. He spent a desolate winter training in Berkhampstead but must have been able to slip away occasionally to London, if Rothenstein's story is true:

The first morning he arrived on parade with the evidence showing too clearly in his face and bearing of the party (attended by members of 19 Fitzroy Street) at which he had spent the previous night. When his commanding officer told him to 'fall out', he dropped his rifle. The misery of his situation kindled in the mind of this pacific and almost pathologically shy young man the determination to become an officer. He applied for a commission. When asked if he had any experience in the control of men he answered 'Yes'. 'What sort of men?' 'Yorkshiremen,' said Matthew Smith. He was promptly gazetted second lieutenant.[4]

Had they known how inept he had been as a leader of men in his factory career they might have had second thoughts, but after the carnage in France the army was desperate for officers and Smith would just about do. He wrote, 'I feel sure I should fail, and the fact of failing would I suppose be a stigma,' but against the odds he somehow passed an examination for the first and only time in his career. He wrote to Gwen and Phyllis describing the gruelling marches in full pack, the night manoeuvres, the discomforts and the minor disasters of his daily life. 'In these first few days I often thought it would be a great relief to see you, and that it would make me feel less lost to everything. I am more accustomed and hardened to things now, it is indeed a hardening process.'[5]

He must also have had leisure moments, as we can see from this tetchy letter:

Porter annoyed me by coming in when I was doing my last and best canvas which I could not finish, being immensely struck by it and producing the next day a canvas founded on it absolutely, and the best thing he has done, and he can go on but I had to stop. Rather irritating, but I have suffered quite a lot from this sort of thing before. I should not have minded if *I* could have gone on and am really rather ashamed of myself for having let it bother me.[6]

All his life he was afraid of other artists stealing his hard-won ideas – though who else besides Porter could have thought them worth poaching at this stage is unclear. Fred Porter (1883–1944) was a New Zealander who had a studio at 8 Fitzroy Street before the war, so Smith was not entirely amongst strangers. Porter later became the Vice-President of the London Group and their friendship continued.

Then Temporary Second Lieutenant Smith received an official letter saying: 'In accordance with War Office Letter MSK 504 of the 5th of March 1917 you are attached for duty to No. 25 Labour Company Royal West Surrey Regiment at Lytton Grove, Putney SW.' Labour Companies were staffed by down-graded or over-aged men at this stage in the war. On the 17th he wrote from Putney to Phyllis: 'I am off tonight having been posted to the 25th Lb Co RWS . . . We go to Folkestone and Boulogne I hear . . . feel rather light-headed and empty.' This was his last chance to tell her where he was because of military censorship, and after that: 'It will be rather interesting and exciting.

Gwen is probably at my billet now packing she will have to leave at three. I am very glad to be going with this lot for many things principally because the officer commanding seems a good man and very approachable and heavens knows what the next one might be like . . . Keep an eye on little Gwenny.' First a short addendum: 'The pork pie was delicious.' Then a long PS about what was really on his mind: '. . . I am anxious to get Gwen a *Sunbeam* bike but have not been able to attend to the matter. They are beautiful cycles. I have often looked at them in a shop in Sloane Street.' He offers to send Phyllis a cheque to cover the expense and concludes: 'Afraid I am being rather a nuisance,' and adds on the back of the envelope '2 or 3 speed gear.'[7] These might have been fittingly diffident and unselfish last words to his family had he not survived, by the narrowest of margins, the hell which waited him at the Front.

At the beginning of May 1917 he had a hundred men under his command and was told to clear the battlefield of usable shells and other abandoned equipment, and later to bury the German dead. His first reaction to his task was unexpectedly matter-of-fact in one previously so sensitive:

We have got our new job . . . it is rather interesting . . . you can imagine we see a good deal . . . in one little place today we found 1200 boxes of Mills bombs. Strange to say the dud is the most dangerous of the lot . . . of course we find stacks of helmets, British and Boche, and many other things, some of them not too pleasant to come upon.[8]

But things got rapidly worse through the sodden summer and autumn of 1917 as the battles at Ypres and Passchendaele took their toll. In the Labour Corps he was not required to go over the parapet with a fixed bayonet and stumble his way through the machine-gun bullets and barbed wire of no man's land, but he was still doing an exposed and extremely dangerous job in appalling mud and squalid living conditions. It was not turning out to be the kind of adventure he had read about in his boys' books. His company suffered heavy shelling and gas attacks day and night as they buried the dead or struggled to lay rails for supplies. His army record says he was wounded first on 17 September 1917, though Phyllis had written in her diary for 14

September 'Matthew wounded in hand.' Then, on 29 September, Gwen was staying at the Smith holiday home in Llandudno when she received the following telegram redirected from Altrincham:

REGRET TO INFORM YOU 2ND LIEUT. M.A.B. SMITH LABOUR CORP ADMITTED 2 RED CROSS HOSPITAL ROUEN SEPT 27TH WITH GUNSHOT WOUND THIGH SEVERE FURTHER REPORTS WIRED IMMEDIATELY RECEIVED.

His field medical card records 'shrap. wd right thigh. Piece removed' so it is not clear exactly what hit him, though he later showed Alice Keene a jar containing the twisted piece of metal extracted from his wound. Nobody reported seeing him limp in later life. After this he was shipped back to recover in a London hospital until the beginning of December. He was home at Dunham Lawn with Gwen and the babies for Christmas but left again on 27 December, with orders to report for monthly check-ups, perhaps for his mental condition as much as his wound since it took him until the autumn to be passed fit for further service. During his convalescence he worked on and off in his London studio, or trawled the junk shops picking up broken objects to draw and books on Rodin, Delacroix and Gauguin to study. Hilma Brooks sent him a photograph of Gauguin's *Nevermore*, which Delius had now sold in London for 2,000 guineas, and he replied: 'The beauty of it touched me so profoundly so that I wanted to desert for the morning so that I might go for a walk and think about it.'[9]

Smith was made a full Lieutenant on 27 September 1918 and was sent on 6 November to spend the short remainder of the war working at a prisoner-of-war camp in Abbeville, northern France, 'where there are thousands and thousands of Huns' in a cage, he told Brooks. There he did some twenty-odd drawings of the German prisoners, the only works to survive from his years in the army. These show him using a much simpler linear manner than he had been taught at the Slade, learned from Matisse and reminiscent of Modigliani in the moon faces and almond eyes in these portraits. Smith was always a collector of trifles and one thing he found in the ruins of Abbeville was a worm-eaten limbless wooden figure which he used many times in later still lifes: of no aesthetic interest in itself it must have served as a personal *memento mori*.

23

From this Abbeville camp he applied to be a War Artist, since most of the artists he knew were doing this and he must have seen their works in the book *British Artists at the Front*, published and widely distributed in February 1918. He still lacked credibility with the art establishment and nothing came of it.[10] Anyway, by this time the scheme was being wound up and a huge exhibition (925 works) was being prepared of all the artists' contributions. This was finally opened at the Royal Academy in December 1919 when Smith would be home to see it.

By December 1918 he was in Paris waiting to be demobilized and there he was reunited with Alden Brooks. The American had risen to First Lieutenant in the French forces, in spite of his poor eyesight. He wrote of his experiences and had his *Battle of 1918* published in France in 1929, and later, retitled *As I Saw It*, in America. He introduced Smith to Roderic O'Conor – their first meeting – though Smith must have heard so much about him both in Pont Aven and Grez where O'Conor had preceded him, or from Maynard and Fry who were both his admirers. Brooks had known O'Conor since childhood, when he came to stay with Brooks senior in Grez.

Self portraits of this time show the Irishman as a gaunt-faced man with thick grey hair and a drooping moustache.[11] He was a solitary man, but one with strong opinions and a wide-ranging mind. He too had a private income but unlike Matthew felt no great desire to exhibit his work. He became the father-figure and guide Smith needed at this point (O'Conor was nearly twenty years older). Doubtless they visited his austere, book-crammed studio at 102 rue du Cherche-Midi to see his paintings, particularly the Brittany seascapes and the deliciously solid nudes of Renée Honta, O'Conor's model and mistress, and to admire his collection of works by such friends as Gauguin, Bonnard, Seguin, Segonzac, Rouault, Derain, Modigliani and Vlaminck. O'Conor was an eclectic painter, by turns Impressionist, Expressionist, Symbolist, Pre-Fauve, Intimist, Post-Impressionist or Synthetist, taking from each new French movement what he needed for his personal vision. He was essentially a daring colourist, one who simplified form and enjoyed the sensous handling of paint. It is easy to see why his works would appeal to Smith and why Smith would later refer to the Irishman as '*mon maître*'. This introduction by Alden Brooks proved to be an invaluable one.

The three friends went round Paris together to see the exhibitions and Brooks bought two Vlamincks and two Matisses, then took Smith to his apartment to show him the rest of his collection, and even sold Smith a flower piece, possibly by Utrillo. They also made a trip to Grez where the Brooks house had come through unscathed, since the German advance had stopped ten miles short of the village.

Smith was demobbed at last in March 1919. By now he was in his fortieth year, the father of two boys, and an artist who had painted only a very few substantial pictures. He was also severely depressed by the experiences he had undergone during those months in France and in no fit state to begin a new period of sustained work. Fortunately there were dividends from his inherited shares (much boosted by the wartime need for wire) to feed the growing family and this was supplemented when Dunham Lawn was sold in June 1919 and the money divided amongst the siblings.

Gwen and Matthew left the boys with a nurse in England and quickly returned to Paris to see a Matisse exhibition, and moved on to Grez for May and June 1919. John Lyman paid them a visit and Smith cheered him up, as Lyman wrote to his father: 'There is no-one who can do so much to revive a genial flame of enthusiasm in me as he. We wallow in art and humanities to the exclusion of everything else.'[12] On 20 May Brooks wrote in his diary:

Evening went for walk with Smith and Heseltine. Smith and I came back here and talked of our war adventures until late in the night, brandy, cigars, also much paint talk. Smith devoted to Cézanne and Matisse. Said Degas after movement in all his pictures and in that respect certainly a past master. I asked him if he wrote a diary, said when things were very hot 'I thought it was time to write something down.'[13]

Smith then painted his friend out of doors. After two days Brooks wrote:

It is coming on. He wanted to put in a yellow book in my hand, but decided not to, for fear it would look put in. Also blue water but it bothered him for the same reason, especially after he had read Nietzsche's Dreaded Eye in The Dawn of Day. Nietzsche 'always a blow below the belt.' Tried not to influence him in any way, yet we talked of many things and the same after supper – Hilma going to bed previously – until late at night on all manner of subjects from Rembrandt's influence on Maynard to our respective families.[14]

Nothing came of the portrait, but Brooks began a novel, *The Enchanted Land* (published in 1924), in which the central character, Dominique Prad, is modelled on Smith and his feelings, obviously derived from those intimate midnight conversations they both enjoyed so much. This Prad character regrets the swift passing of time in that hesitant, intermittent style of speech all Smith's friends remember and describe: 'Now I shall never paint . . . youth gone: an eternity of months wasted . . . and at thirty seven one is no longer a young man – all that first enthusiasm lost – maybe one's best vitality gone . . . And yet, even so, how to be sure that one has it in one to be a painter?'[15]

This account of the wounding of Prad must also be close to Smith's own experience at the Front:

. . . they had brought him back with a terrible wound in his side; and lying there in the dark of a first aid station, doubled up like a thing broken in two, half unconscious with pain, he had seen it all flit by again – not one redeeming feature – his whole life wasted – never known what life was – and now all over, ended, dying. 'Here,' said the voice, 'there's still some chance of saving this fellow; put him on the table.' Then, to wild spasms of pain as they lifted him into the light, he had tried to raise himself up on one elbow, look around, swear that, if it were true, he would never do anything else in future but live life, beautiful life, to the full, as it should be led.[16]

The sweetness of life must taste all the sweeter if one has choked on the muddy dregs of Ypres, and such an oath might explain some of Smith's later, seemingly selfish decisions, such as that to sacrifice family life in order to paint. The abominations he had seen in the burial squad he would put behind him – it was not within his capabilities to make art out of horror – and he would concentrate on the life-enhancing subjects soldiers would have dreamed of: the warm and welcoming bodies of women, fruit, flowers and empty sunlit landscapes unsullied by war. He would leave behind for ever khaki, grey, and all shades of mud, to wallow in the colours of flesh and blossoms. As an old man he made a broadcast in which he stated, 'I am attempting, only attempting, to insist that ugliness may exist as cruelty exists, but that an artist can make all things beautiful by his vision.'[17] It would seem that to make sensuous or erotic works a knowledge of evil is necessary, and a strong awareness of the inevitability that the flesh and all good things will perish. Smith had evidently sorted out some of his priorities as an artist and as a man during his convalescence.

Before he could put his resolution into practice Smith's health, mental and physical, collapsed and they returned to England, Gwen taking the boys away and Matthew incarcerating himself in Fitzroy Street. Rothenstein speculates that 'the immediate occasion of his breakdown may have been the sudden relaxation of the wartime tension that had given temporary cohesion to temperaments, coalitions and organisms of many kinds.'[18] No matter what the deeper cause, the effect was to make him shut himself up in solitary despair in his attic studio where he copied Ingres and painted watercolours based on black-and-white reproductions of Delacroix's illustrations to *Faust*. None survive – maybe he later destroyed them because they reminded him of this dismal time.

On top of his growing mental anguish Smith was having more eye trouble. Perhaps he followed the advice of Thomas Head Thomas who wrote on 12 July 1919: 'I know that, for the eyes, it is very important to wash them well everyday, because particles of dust and dirt adhere to the eye and irritate it, so I use Eau Borrigne . . . if you do the same I am sure you will do great benefit. It soothes the nerves.'[19]

The Fitzroy Street community was now depleted: Sickert returned to Dieppe in 1918, both Gore and Gilman were dead, whilst Derwent Lees suffered mental illness and would spend the rest of his life in an institution. Even those who had survived the war, such as the Old Slade firebrands Lewis, Roberts and Nevinson, came back subdued by the experience. 'Experimentation is waived,' said Lewis, 'the brave new world was a mirage – a snare and a delusion.' A return to unchallenging normality was needed now.

In spite of his mental problems Smith did produce some pictures, notably *The Little Seamstress*,[20] which is difficult to date with any precision. She is a sulky looking girl with a too long arm, painted and over-painted densely and tentatively in subdued colours on a large canvas. It was only rescued after he began to scrape it off because he could not resolve its many awkwardnesses. It contrasts sharply with the light-hearted *Dulcie* from before the war, and the darkening blues and purples presage those even more bruised and lowering ones to come in the next few years.

More successful is the small still life of *Apples on a Dish*, probably of 1919, where the fruit are seen in such close-up that the brown dish occupies the whole canvas except for tiny triangles at the corners. It reflects a knowledge of the greatest of apple painters, Cézanne, with perhaps hints of the Courbet exhibition he had seen in Paris in July, and shows Smith achieving volume by colour alone. Rothenstein enthused: 'These apples have an almost breathtaking nobility of form and, fused with it, a colour that is both audacious and delicately astringent.'[21]

Equally impressive is *Apple on a Blue Dish* of about 1919, which one writer sees as reflecting Smith's disturbed mind at this period:

It is almost as though the apple, thinly painted in yellow, turquoise, lilac and orange, and with its extraordinary 'nimbus' symbolised the last gleam of hope, when everything else is impregnated with dark and sombre hues; the dark ultramarine cloth, the dark green plates with their crimson haloes, and above all the claustrophobic strokes of the encroaching vermilion background.[22]

Clearly Smith needed to get outside his studio and take a holiday.

CHAPTER 10

Cornwall
1920–1922

Gwen usually managed the practicalities of family life and in June 1920 she organized a family holiday in Porthcothan, Cornwall, because, Smith told Brooks, he was not yet ready to resume 'the fancy Fitzroy life'.[1] Gwen must have hoped the rural peace would help heal his mind and body and that perhaps he would get back into his painting stride, since the south-west peninsula had been known since the 1880s as Britain's artistic equivalent of Brittany. There were two rival colonies at Newlyn and St Ives which modelled themselves on Concarneau and Pont Aven, and in them, wrote Smith, the painters 'cluster like limpets.' However, Smith had no interest now in the kind of rural realism perpetrated by Stanhope Forbes in Newlyn, and St Ives would have no reputation as a place for progressive work until the late 1930s. In the rainy summer of 1920 Smith was stuck in a seaside resort with two lively boys, a wife he was beginning to fall out of love with, and the frustrated urge to paint landscapes.

When the holiday was over he sent the family back to London and he stayed on. He showed no interest in tourist or historic Cornwall and never painted a harbour, ruined mine, menhir or fishing boat. Instead, he moved inland to St Columb Major, between Wadebridge and Truro, and three miles from the nearest station. It was a ribbon development with an old church and little else, its most interesting building being the ornate bank. It had nothing to offer that a thousand other English villages could not surpass, but it was peaceful and the lodgings with the Barnes family at Bank House were spacious and cheap. What Sickert called 'the august site motif' was never to be Smith's subject, but as he cycled round the small settlements and unspectacular farms of inland Cornwall he found them 'accidenté, amusing like a well-shuffled pack of cards,' and he started to paint.² A new and vigorous period of work began in which more than twenty canvases were completed. He stayed on alone working through the drizzling autumn and only rejoined his family in London for Christmas. He returned to Cornwall in the New Year of 1921 convinced he was, at last, 'getting somewhere.' Having settled down into a work rhythm he was then summoned back to London:

A telegram arrived from Mrs Epstein: would he please return at once, because Epstein was very ill and asking to see him. He took the train at once, only to find Epstein in the best of health working away with his habitual vitality and exuberant self confidence – just the qualities, in fact, which the shy, sensitive, and self-doubting Smith had always found daunting.³

Epstein had suffered a nervous breakdown during the war so Smith must have thought the request plausible, but what was Mrs Epstein up to? Had she broken under the strain of Jacob's infidelities? (She tried to shoot his mistress soon after.) Whatever her motives the episode broke Matthew's concentration and brought to an end the series of his most individual works so far. Like Coleridge interrupted by the person from Porlock he could no longer imagine his way back to the magic kingdom.

The first thing to strike one about these smallish landscapes which Smith produced around St Columb Major is their strangely foreboding colours: it is as if they had been painted by an artist wearing dark glasses. Black, purples, strong blues, murky reds and viridian predominate, with occasional shafts of vermilion or orange to relieve the gloom. White is absent, even as a lightening agent, and the ground no longer shows in chinks between the brush marks, though sometimes the deeper colours are thinned with turpentine. The skies are black, or of a blue or plum so deep they approach black – a lowering ominous effect John Piper was later to exploit in his Second World War pictures to express the nation's fears. Smith had no such public mood to convey, only his own private melancholy, though much later he told John Russell he denied such an interpretation: 'Nor did he ever heighten his colour or transpose it arbitrarily for expressive reasons . . . he claimed that even the reddest and most apparently anti-naturalistic of his Cornish landscapes were on the contrary a faithful representation of the conditions created by an unusually wet summer and autumn.'[4]

He admitted only changing the white walls of farmhouses into red or violet ones. Having visited the area myself in a wet autumn I find this difficult to believe and would rather trust the pictures than the artist, the tale and not the teller. Emile Zola declared, 'A work of art is a corner of Nature seen through a temperament'[5] and Smith's temperament at this time was evidently going through a very dark period indeed.

Russell sees in these works the obvious inspiration of Gauguin's South Sea pinky-purple pictures and the Fauves in the unreal range of colour, but also claims to detect traces of the Italian primitives – presumably in the naïve perspective, lack of chiaroscuro and rigid uncluttered designs of some of them.

It would be very interesting to know which of Roderic O'Conor's works Smith had seen when they met the year before, because there are design and colour echoes between an O'Conor work such as *The Path To Leazavan, Pont Aven* (c. 1884) and Smith's own *The West Road*.[6] The hot churned-up colours of O'Conor's Brittany coastal scenes might also have offered a reminder of the way colour could be heightened for emotional rather than representational ends – a lesson O'Conor had in turn learned from Gauguin.

Another artist who had assimilated Gauguin, Van Gogh and Matisse into his English vision was Spencer Gore. There are parallels in Smith's Cornish works with Gore's pictures of Camden Town and Letchworth in the purplish tones, the use of paths to lead the eye into the picture, the acidulous colours and the views from a window. But, essentially, these are not works derived from other artists' discoveries: they are painted under an emotional pressure which overrides all theories.

Whatever the trigger, these rich works do mark a major advance on the Fitzroy Street nudes in so far as drawing and painting are now fused and background and foreground are in the same style. At first there remains a firm foundation of design but now it is embodied in, and appears simultaneously with, the brushstrokes. In one view of St Columb parish church, *Cornish Church*, the colours appear in flat geometrical slices, getting smaller and more intricate towards the black sky, but with each red, purple, blue and green subtly differentiated, quite unlike the few strident primaries of the Fitzroy Street pictures. This was painted through the second-floor bedroom window of Bank House, and looking through it now one can see both how photographically accurate Smith's drawing was and how unreal the colours. In 1949 the poet Geoffrey Grigson saw this work glowing in a gallery window and admired how 'colour met colour with a straight edge, and together they become more active and melodiously irritant.'[7]

Similarly, two versions of *Steeple in Cornwall* are faithful outlines of a decorative five-foot-high brick pinnacle on the boundary wall of the back garden seen from the lounge. *Cornish Garden with Monkey-Puzzle Tree* shows the rest of the garden from the next window along. But the banal subject is not the point, it is in the strange colour harmonies where the breakthrough has been made.

24

Several of the works (*The Wet Road, Cornish Garden with Monkey-Puzzle Tree, A Winding Road, Cornish Church II* and *Cornish Landscape*) explore the device of offering the eye a curving path to follow around the picture space, and since the colours are all at full strength with no suggestion of fading into hazy blue horizons this is necessary to prevent them being only a carpet of gorgeous colours. In *Cornish Landscape*[8] there are only horizontal bands of variations on red, green and purple punctuated, off centre, by three vertical orange stripes and a yellow field. Smith was never interested in rendering space by illusionistic aerial perspective and later said, 'With me the background must always come forward.'

25, 26
27

In the drenched unpeopled landscapes of the south-west he appears to have found an 'objective correlative' (in T. S. Eliot's phrase), the formula through which he could channel his pent-up disquiet with his marriage, and the unresolved mental burdens he still carried from the war. Even though these works are unique in his *oeuvre* so far in documenting a place, they tell us very little about the literal appearance of Cornwall in a drenched autumn, but much more about the climate of Smith's inner landscape at the time. Most are undated but one might speculate that those with tighter structures came first and the ones with fevered flurries of strokes later as Smith's mental state deteriorated. They demonstrate Ruskin's 'pathetic fallacy', or the Romantic artist's morbid habit of ascribing his own human feelings to nature. Rothenstein likens them to the troubled pictures Constable painted after the death of his wife and said that, 'with their black oppressive skies and trance-livid fields, roads and trees, [they] were the products of a darkening mind, a mind engaged in a losing struggle to maintain its equilibrium.'[9] David Piper also felt their stifling power but thought there was in the earlier ones 'precisely too much control in design, a stringent reining-in for fear of running amok.'[10]

Around this time, 1920–21, Smith painted one more figure, a portrait of an unknown woman now called *The Black Dress*. This unsuccessfully attempts to use the suffocating purple-green-orange colour scale on the figure, applying each hue in parallel slashes which do nothing to describe the form. It has a broad unfinished quality and awkward composition as if Smith has tried to suppress any hint of prettiness – even the hand has a finger too many.[11]

These claustrophobic works were not seen in public until 1926, when Roger Fry commented on Smith's wilful interpretation of appearances in order to torture his own sensitive nerves: for evidently, 'his intention is neither to achieve dramatic expressiveness, although a certain almost melodramatic mood seems at times to result as an accidental by-product, nor to create decorative harmonies. He is clearly after some more intimate and significant interpretation of vision.'[12]

After Cornwall was spoiled for him by the Epstein fiasco Smith briefly visited Somerset and then 'fled' (Halliday's term) to Brittany, where 'he collapsed into a distracted melancholy'. Brooks took him on a visit to Maynard in Concarneau in the hope that old friends would cheer him up. In July and August 1921 he was in Gourin, forty kilometres inland from Pont Aven, where Maynard wrote to him hoping he felt better up in the hills. His eyes troubled him and he could not sleep. This turbulent state, in which he wandered from place to place without achieving anything of value in his work, lasted for about two years. Brooks described his travels as 'like a gnat upon the face of the waters.'

The whole Smith family were back together in their Grez house by October 1921 where the boys played with Alden Brooks's daughters throughout that winter. Brooks recalls Smith at this period, spoiling canvas after canvas and 'ever that recurring note of despair'. 'Absolutely worn out, my dear fellow, feeling perfectly rotten . . . should be in bed really.'[13] But even in bed he could not sleep because his eyes, his back and his mind all hurt. To encourage him Brooks bought the little 1912 landscape of *St-Jean-de-Luz*[14] and Smith was so overcome with gratitude that he threw in a still life of tomatoes for the same price.

Suddenly on 7 March 1922 Smith left his family in Grez and booked himself into the Clinique Valmont in Lausanne. This was run by the charismatic Swiss psychiatrist Dr Roger Vittoz (1863–1925), who was admired by William James and Conrad and a great favourite with the Bloomsbury literary set when they felt under stress. Lady Ottoline Morrell had been his patient in 1913, then recommended him to Julian Huxley who in turn advised T. S. Eliot to undergo treatment in November 1921. Whilst there Eliot annotated Vittoz's book *Traitement Des Psychoneuroses Par La Rééducation du Contrôle Cérébral* (2nd edition, Paris 1921), underlining '*aboulie*' or want of will.'[15] However, whilst in the clinic Eliot recovered enough will-power to complete *The Waste Land*. It may have been in Lausanne or a few months later back in London that Eliot and Smith became acquainted, because Eliot was later to claim he had known the painter as long as anyone in the art world.

What had Vittoz to offer all these exceptionally creative but anguished people? Basically he made them undergo a course of mental exercises which strengthened the Conscious Mind's control over the Unconscious. Ottoline Morrell wrote: 'Part of the treatment was the formation of the habit of eliminating unnecessary thoughts and worries from one's mind, and to do this one had to practice eliminating letters from words, or one number from a set of numbers.'[16] Huxley explained that

His method was to propose some simple subject on which to concentrate, such as visualising a circle or a square, or solving an easy mathematical problem, and to test the validity of my efforts with the side of his hand on my forehead, whereby he claimed that he could feel and estimate the special brain-pulse accompanying genuine concentration. Gradually more complex subjects for concentration were propounded and the exercises became easier to carry out. I thus got a little more control over my depression.'[17]

What was Smith suffering from exactly? Alice Keene, who knew him as well as anyone in later years, had this to say:

Smith worried more than his doctors and his friends about the state of his health, which was physically sound. He suffered from periods of debilitating nervous tension which came and went without him being able to discern the immediate cause. He would feel in the grip of unwelcome events: '. . . always what I want most to avoid always happens . . .' Most importantly for him, work would become impossible . . . He had a gift on the one hand of approaching near to people he loved. On the other hand he often felt persecuted by them.[18]

Around this time Smith's attitude towards his dead father changed. Vittoz was not a Freudian and Smith distrusted analysts of any kind, but from his reading, or some other source, he was somehow led to believe that his failures as a man and an artist were all due to his overpowering father's opposition. As suggested in earlier chapters this is somewhat unfair, since Smith offered his father very little convincing evidence of his potential as an artist. When Frederic died in 1914 his thirty-five-year-old son had not sold one picture nor shown any signs of being able to support himself by his painting. At the time of this Swiss therapy he was forty-two, had yet to realize his potential as an artist, and was still relying on his dead father's money to pay for his treatment. Frederic had been patient and supportive with allowances and Matthew's surviving letters to his father seem genuinely affectionate and grateful, so this realization of his father's guilt came years after his death. Ironically, the three artists who came to admire him most, Epstein, John and Bacon, all had much worse childhoods and dreadful fathers but they had few complaints. Whatever the truth might be, after this date Smith always bitterly told people of Frederic's meanness; of his opposition to a career in art; the restrictions he imposed, and his poor taste in painting.

After he came out of his therapy in summer 1922 Matthew's marriage was over: he and Gwen never lived together again, though this was his choice, not hers. The clinic had given him the time and privacy to sort out his priorities once more, and he had decided family life stifled his creativity. Gwen's loyal support now seemed bossily overbearing and her tactlessness an embarrassment. The remorse he felt for this desertion of a wife who still loved him was another burden he had to carry, though he tried to assuage it by sending her £60 every month and by never asking for a divorce. He wanted to pay the allowance through a bank, but so desperate was Gwen for his letters and the tenuous contact they still offered that she asked him to send it personally even if this meant some lean months when he forgot or delayed.

Matisse had behaved in a similarly steely way when he separated from his wife, and Smith told a friend approvingly how 'he continued, as usual, to work all day in his studio and would only drop in to some close friends to discuss his personal situation on his way home late in the afternoon. Matthew Smith absolved Matisse from all suspicion of callousness in the matter and simply gave him credit for great self-control and discipline.'[19] Some artists find it necessary to be ruthlessly single-minded because their art comes first.

Gwen and the boys waited in Grez for the whole of that summer hoping for Smith to join them, but instead he went from Switzerland to Lyons where Dr D'Espiney, the chief disciple of Vittoz, helped relieve his stress further. More focusings of the mind and senses were undertaken, moving through geometric shapes, curves and abstractions. D'Espiney believed he could record the psychic or electrical impulses such concentration gave off by use of microphones and an electrocardiogram.[20] Smith obviously believed Vittoz's regime worked for him and in future years whenever events were moving beyond his grasp he retreated to the Valmont Clinic to have his mind soothed and brought back under his control.

Finally, realizing he never would come back to her, Gwen gave up their house in Grez and took the boys back to England, first to a house in Pitt Street, Kensington, and then, when the lease ran out and Smith refused to renew it, to embark on an itinerant life in rented cottages around the south of England. With two boys under ten Gwen now had little chance of furthering her own artistic development for the next decade.

The family kept in touch by letter and Gwen ensured that the boys loved and respected their father, though their intermittent relationship puzzled the young Mark who asked, 'Isn't Daddy what you call a father-in-law?' Phyllis, Smith's sister, remained her friend, as did Gwen's Slade colleagues such as Edna Clark Hall. Gwen always wrote affectionately and hoped for a reconciliation, but Smith, once free, was determined he would remain so. They met periodically in London, but

Smith preferred it to be in public places such as restaurants with a third person present to keep the conversation from getting too personal, and later he occasionally returned for Christmas and family holidays. His brothers pretended to their own children that all was well with their aunt and uncle, since broken marriages and the kind of loose life Smith later led in Paris were too disgraceful to discuss.

Smith, now living temporarily in Lyons to be near his therapist, began to paint flowers and landscapes again in colours no longer so bruised and lowering, perhaps because his anguish was easing. *Lyonnais Flowers* (1922) is painted in a hail of juicy rhythmic brushstrokes reminiscent of the late works of the mentally disturbed Van Gogh, though now the rigid underpinning of structure in the Cornwall pictures has been loosed.[21] The landscape *Lyons* (1922) is also dashingly painted, rather in the Soutine manner, but is not a tranquil picture.[22] Louis MacNeice suggested once that writing poetry was a therapeutic activity and D'Espiney encouraged Matthew to return to painting for similar ends; Smith himself later spoke of each painting being a 'release'. The controlled frenzy of creation in which all other distractions were eliminated led to an exhausted calm and equilibrium he could perhaps achieve in no other way but sex. From now on there would always be a concentrated energy and speed in his attack which meant the painstaking exploration of form or subtle gradation of colour was not within his interest – grabbing the essence was all.

In 1922 Smith also made one rough and one more finished copy of El Greco's *The Despoiling of Christ*, which he saw in the Lyons museum. He may have come to respect the Spanish artist after hearing O'Conor praise him. This admiration stayed with Smith and in a 1946 broadcast he told an interviewer, 'People used to think El Greco a sombre painter, when actually he is a very great colourist.'[23]

At the end of 1922 he returned to London and a studio at 115 Charlotte Street, not very far away from his old one in Fitzroy Street. He had exhibited a few works with The London Group in summer 1920 and had been elected a member by that autumn, then shown again in the winter of 1922 and in 1923. He was now a middle-aged man, alone, insecure, and with no great reputation, though it seemed women were glad to comfort and mother him. Marjorie Lilly describes how a friend found him in the street, white and shaking from flu. She took him back to her studio and warmed him up with soup and received the reward of a still-life painting. After that he was a regular at their parties: 'Matthew took his pleasures seriously; between us we taught him the two-step . . . but he would not commit himself to the intricacies of the waltz.' Lilly also recalls:

On a short acquaintance no one would have suspected, from his mild and friendly exterior, the hidden fires within. Matthew Smith saw and heard all sorts of outrageous things without turning a hair but once, when he was confronted by a flashy and pretentious painting upon which he was called to pronounce a blessing, a sort of electric shock ran through him, his eyes blazed, the very hairs of his skin seemed to rise in protest, although the effect only lasted a few moments; he soon regained control of himself, turning his back on the offending object with a shudder. I realised then the connection which had often puzzled me before between this diffident, gentle man and his fiery, bold, colourful painting, and how much painting meant to him.[24]

By now it was clear that painting allowed him to channel his most powerful feelings and also offered a way of bringing them into some kind of resolution. If it caused him pain to paint, then it was even more painful not to do so. Now he needed a muse to transform those feelings into something positive and life-affirming.

CHAPTER 11

Paris Again
1922–1925

Bernard Meninsky (1891–1950) entered the Slade four years after Smith left it, but already before the war he was exhibiting at both the London Group and the New English Art Club. His one-man show of drawings of his wife and child in 1919 was very well received and Roger Fry took him under his wing. After this promising start, however, his wife left him for another man and then died in childbirth. Meninsky, who was always precariously balanced mentally, was left in a distressed state and had to give up his two infant boys to foster parents. In spite of his private troubles, Meninsky continued to paint his heavy limbed female nudes, often shown lolling in imaginary Arcadias. Later Smith, in his suspicious way, believed Meninsky had stolen some of the ideas for them from him.

These pictures must have impressed a young art student called Vera Cuningham who, together with her lifelong friend Eve Disher, called on Meninsky, perhaps with the hope he would give them both instruction in painting the figure. Soon, however, Vera was posing in the nude, cooking his meals and sharing his bed.

Matthew Smith visited Meninsky one day in the winter of 1922 and left the studio arm in arm with Vera. She was twenty-five and he forty-three, and this was both the beginning of a passionate love affair and Smith's great breakthrough as an artist.

Vera Irene Martin Walpole Cuningham's father was a civil engineer who had helped construct the Trans-Siberian railway and made enough money to buy an impressive house in Goff's Oak, Hertfordshire, in which to raise his son and four daughters. On her formidable mother's side there were Walpole ancestors and rumours of blue blood. Like other girls of her class Vera was educated at home by governesses. When her father lost his money in the Russian Revolution they all moved to a flat in Ladbroke Grove, together with the family parrot, Laura. Vera soon left home (or was perhaps turned out for bad behaviour), set up an attic studio in Margaret Street, near Oxford Circus, with Eve Disher and two other women friends, and attended Heatherleys and the Central School of Art for brief periods. When her father died Vera continued to look after her mother and, in spite of their thunderous rows, eventually inherited the remains of the estate when her mother died in 1950. Like Smith she always seems to have had a private income and not to have been dependent on sales.

Vera was a guffawing, red-haired, rosy-cheeked, plump-bodied, highly sexed young woman who was determined to become a professional artist. There was an exhibitionist strain in her which showed in her uninhibited table manners, her dress sense and her brutal comments on other artists' works. Meeting Smith and falling in love with him meant Vera had to put her artistic ambitions to one side for the moment, though in return she now had a war-hero father-figure who doted on her and had money to spend. Indeed, she probably had to suspend painting entirely because Matthew was eager for her to pose for him, clothed, nude, or in any state between. He had found and been kissed by the muse at last.

Matthew's first painting of his new mistress was *Woman Holding Daffodils*, painted in the spring of 1923 at 115 Charlotte Street and later sold to brother Harold for £30. They could not live together in London without exciting scandal, offending Vera's mother, or bumping into Gwen who was now living in Pitt Street, Kensington, so soon they left for Paris. There they occupied the second floor of 6 villa Brune in the 14th *arrondissement*, Montparnasse, then the favourite area for artists. This is a small house in a cul-de-sac off the rue des Plantes which in 1923 must have been leafier and quieter than it is today. It had a tiny garden at the back overlooking a deep railway cutting, now disused but then a busy commuter line. Beyond this was a maternity hospital, though both were determined not to call upon its services. Here Vera began to pose for the series of nudes which made Smith's reputation as one of Britain's foremost figurative artists: as Vera's biographer wrote, she had become like Rubens' Hélène Fourment, 'the splendid sitter desired both by the painter and the man.'[1]

Smith had now struggled for twenty-two years as a full-time artist but had painted only two significant groups of pictures: the Fitzroy Street nudes and flowers, and the Cornish landscapes. The first was too consciously willed and based on other men's theories, and the second too linked to a mood of deep depression and in colours that couldn't be adapted to work with the figure, especially a figure which aroused his passions as Vera's now did. Nothing currently happening in Paris offered a way forward so he would have to work out his own salvation from his own resources. Rothenstein describes Smith's breakthrough:

He grew certain that by his too close study and assimilation of Post-Impressionism, even of Cézanne and the Fauves, he had built himself what he described to me as a spiritual prison. His dissatisfaction became unbearable. Persuaded that the works of his first maturity were the products of this prison, he determined to renounce the attitudes and intellectual operations from which they sprang and to make a fresh start: to discover what it was that he had in him to paint and to search for the means to give it his own expression. Deeply despondent, he started all over again. But his renunciation was rewarded with a strange promptitude. Having cleared his mind of consciously held ideas and all doctrine, he shortly made the exhilarating discovery that he was able to paint, whether from the naked model or from fruit and flowers, with a fluency that he had never before known and that what now came from his brush was something that he recognised as uniquely his own and as what all the time he had wanted to do.[2]

Vittoz's lessons in eliminating the inessentials, and his own pressing feelings for Vera, together seem to have given him a purpose and a direction he had always lacked before.

In these new works the buxom body of Vera is invariably seen in close-up, which serves to stress the intimacy between the model and the artist, and hence between the spectator and the model, since we occupy his viewpoint. Unlike Picasso or Matisse, Smith never depicted himself contemplating the model, but his proprietorial presence is everywhere implied. An additional but more mundane reason for the model filling the whole canvas might be that the artist's myopia made it necessary for him to move close in order to keep both canvas and model in focus –

which would also explain their indeterminate backgrounds, bright unmodulated colours and bold suppression of detail. Degas, who was also very short-sighted, took a similar stance. The experts tell us that other colourists such as Dufy, Derain, Braque, Vlaminck, Kandinsky, and Matisse were similarly afflicted with myopia and needed correcting lenses – though Cézanne scorned to wear his. 'Take those vulgar things away,' he said. Perhaps myopics turn up the colour pitch in the way that deaf people turn up the volume.[3]

Apparently people with this condition may see objects at the red end of the spectrum in clearer definition than those at the blue end. Smith certainly painted these nudes with a 'hot' palette, favouring particularly a deep crimson, but this is more likely to be an instinctual choice to express his fervour and his masculinity. Goethe suggested that our response to colour is biologically based and that we see orange, red and yellow as enlivening and exciting: instinctively we see red as 'warm', drawing on our tactile experience of fire, sun and blood. For whatever reason, these nudes, like the late works of Renoir, are unrealistically ruddy in their flesh tones, as if pale Vera had lain too long in the sun. One critic thought these works 'suggest that a stout model has first been flogged alive, then left to bleed to death, slowly and luxuriously, on a pile of satin cushions,'[4] and when Wilson Steer saw them he is supposed to have commented slyly that Smith only painted in two colours: jam and marmalade.

Inspired as Smith was by Vera's solid corporeality on the bed before him he still could not paint her without being aware of other masters' treatment of the reclining female nude, as if the new canvas was already overlaid with ghostly forms. As Kenneth Clark pointed out, 'The naked human body was the central subject of art,' and since historically most artists and patrons have been heterosexual males this has meant the female body.[5] Smith's sketchbooks reveal copies of female nudes by Rubens, Velázquez, Rembrandt, Giorgione, Watteau, Leonardo, Raphael, Cranach, Titian, Veronese and Delacroix who had all set benchmarks which the nineteenth-century Salon painters had failed to reach with their pink sugar Venuses and titillating Nymphs.

Courbet, Manet, Degas, Lautrec and Renoir had reclaimed the discredited female figure for modern painting by putting her in contemporary situations. She was no longer a goddess lolling on a cloud but a woman who had just put aside her dress and corsets to attend to the rituals of the bath or bed. Degas said, 'Two centuries ago I would have painted *Susannah At Her Bath*, now I paint mere women in their tubs.'[6] Sickert had brought this modern type of reclining nude to the attention of the English painters, and artists such as Gertler and Stanley Spencer were to make it a key feature of their work, as did sculptors like Moore and Dobson, though the problem for all these artists was to see the old subject in a new way. Since Smith's time the nude has become a more problematic subject and the vehicle for all kinds of social, sexual and political messages and interpretations, but Smith had no programme in mind beyond prolonging his joyful arousal, his delectation in and appropriation of his beloved's flesh, in paint.

As Rothenstein suggests, the artificial poses and over-deliberation of Smith's Fitzroy Street works are now abandoned for an approach 'in which passion and intuition play the dominant parts, and in which the operations of the intellect count for little; the vision of an impassioned painter and an indifferent draughtsman.'[7] The passion is palpable and undeniably gives a sexual charge to many of these works in a way that was not present with the hired model in Fitzroy Street. There is a post-coital languor to the poses, and the closed curtains, the tumbled pillows and sheets add to this sense that he is capturing pleasures just past or about to come. We can almost smell this closed room. Not surprisingly, many of these recorded moments of intimacy he never wished to sell but kept by him for the rest of his life. Incidentally, Rothenstein's 'indifferent draughtsman' gibe was both untrue and beside the point for an artist who now thought in colour not line.

Reclining Nude No. 2 was once banned from an exhibition in Regina, Saskatchewan, as 'too intimate', yet it is difficult to find it, or any of the others, shocking. The poses are invariably discreet and dignified without being coy, with the loins often hidden by a pink or scarlet petticoat or by flowers – very different from Sickert's nudes where the woman sprawls, genitals exposed, across her grubby sheets. Smith, like Degas, seems to have been interested in dishabille, depicting stockings, camisoles, brassières and rather conventionally 'naughty' glimpses of Vera's toilette. Years later he said, 'I like a bit of drapery . . .

30

They always seem more nude that way . . . I always liked big girls – they have much more flowing lines, and I went in for curves.'[8] However, unlike Degas spying through the keyhole at his woman behaving like 'animals cleaning themselves,' Smith is present with his model's trust and approval; she lies passively to be admired, in no rush to don her clothes again. In Kenneth Clark's terms she is not naked but nude, 'balanced, prosperous, confident.'[9] Degas also favoured turning poses from the side or rear which express movement, his nudes rarely (except in the brothel monotypes) facing the viewer, whereas it is difficult to recall any back views, averted faces, or implied action other than a languorous roll, in the whole of Smith's oeuvre.

32

One can infer that Smith's main erotic focus in these and all his other nudes was the model's breasts, and the bigger they were the more he enjoyed painting them. He seemed to agree with Matisses's view that 'Every shape within the human body is convex. There is no concave line to be found in it.' Like other slightly built artists such as Etty, Renoir, Spencer and Gertler, Matthew liked his models hefty. This was the age of the androgyne sleek-legged flapper and Vera came nowhere near the ideal being promulgated on the covers of the English or French Vogue. Smith preferred his gentlemanly tweeds to the fashionable clothes of the Jazz Age, for which Vera was too sturdy, but Henry Green, the novelist, deduced from the paintings that neither she nor Smith cared a damn:

31

In his nudes those flaunting women so often stare us in the face with what seems to be contempt for the effect their chests might have on us. Arrogantly proud of their great soft thighs, they seem more conscious and disdainful of our peeping than the models of any other painter. Even when curled up in bed, eyes closed, they obviously pretend to ignore their audience. Or, sitting up, a rose impudently placed against a more than naked breast, the girl just looks past us, pouting.

Nearly always these models are big women and, if as often is, they are done asleep, and his colours suggest, as only Smith can, a great drowsy-hot afternoon, then has sleep portrayed on canvas ever been more secure or deeper? No, there is a sureness about these women which carries over to us that utter serenity which only great painting can impose.[10]

English critics made the assumption that these new canvases were largely the result of Smith's contact with the work of Matisse, but the differences between the two painters are by now more obvious than their affinities. Smith's settings for the Vera nudes are perfunctory and claustrophobic with dark voids opening behind the chair or bed, whereas Matisse's odalisques lie in sunlight under the open windows of fully furnished rooms in which we can even see the easel on which their image is emerging. 'I do not make a woman, I make a picture,' Matisse declared (though he still chose to make it of a woman, not a pile of rocks) and concerned himself with the dazzling interplay of patterns, elegant arabesques and flat areas of colour which lead the eye a merry dance round the whole canvas. Smith, on the other hand, directs us straight to the woman's body, makes us feel its weight and offers us the tactile pleasures of a loaded, caressing brush. He makes us see the link between the physicality of the paint itself and the body before him, in a way neither Ingres nor Matisse would have allowed themselves to do.

It seemed that as Smith became more expressionistic Matisse became less so. Some critics have detected a progressive withdrawal of Matisse's personality from his work, an ability to become 'aggressively cold' in order to distil the essence of the model's pose. The story goes that 'Matisse when asked whether he did not find himself sometimes seduced by the lure of the lovely girls who posed for him, replied that he could not find the time for such indulgence.'[11] Janet Hobhouse misses any sense of yearning in his nudes: 'It is as though his response, ecstatic though it is, were on a short circuit, as though it could move to the transcendent from the eye and intellect alone, bypassing the strictly physical and erotic, or as though Matisse's sensuality had something cold at its centre . . . He is like a Zen Buddhist in a brothel.'[12]

This is why John Russell could say with such conviction that

When it comes to the painting of the naked female figure, or of landscape, there is nothing whatever of Matisse in Matthew Smith's mature works: none of the delayed action sensuality, the nice calculation, the sweetness (often a mask for parsimony) in the choosing and refining of the original donnée. But important as it is to dismiss the legend of 'the latter day Fauve', there is of course no question at all that Matisse, at other times in his life, did contribute markedly both to Matthew Smith's subject matter and to his manner of presenting it. Over and over again, in still life, the use of a lapsed diagonal in composition, the placing of a pot or jug against a patterned cloth, and a reminiscence of serpentine, art nouveau rhythms in the ordering of the picture as a whole will remind us of Matisse, but with the difference that Matisse marks his transitions with a perceptible pause in space, a bar's rest in the sumptuous eye-music. With Matthew Smith there is none of this: heat calls to heat too insistently.[13]

Huysmans in 1881 had said the spectator of the unidealized realistic modern nude should be able to tell from 'the image of an undressed woman her nationality, and the historical period from which she comes, her social position, age, whether she was a virgin or not.'[14] Smith did not idealize Vera Cuningham, but neither are these 'naked portraits' in the way a later merciless painter of the realistic nude, Lucian Freud, uses that term of his models posed against paint rags or on beaten-up sofas. Nor does he emulate Stanley Spencer's eye, crawling like an ant over the body of Patricia Preece, and depicting every wrinkle, eyelash or pubic hair. Smith's figures are not of this order of literalness or character penetration and the face is no more expressive or detailed than Vera's massive knees or plump shoulders. He had little interest in what she was thinking and Vera is never allowed to sit up and challenge our gaze as Manet's Olympia does. Instead, Smith tried to embody in these works archetypal female qualities, rather as Moore was doing in wood and stone.

What makes Smith's nudes so modern and different from anything he had achieved before is not so much their subject but the way they now combine drawing with painting, so that the same broad wristy stroke of the laden brush both establishes a form and colours it. Typically, in such works as *Model à La Rose* or *Reclining Female Nude No. 1*,[15] these marks are in rapid zig-zags, or flurries of parallel dabs, with only here and there a sudden slashing curve in brown or red to establish a boundary. Nor has he attempted to smooth these marks away or make them imitate surface textures, which gives many of the works the lively feel of an *ébauche*, or first dashing in, of the whole composition. Others, such as *Standing Nude with Fan* (1925) are more considered and emerge from the paint as heavy and solid as a Maillol sculpture.

The colours, listed by Hendy as 'crimson and ultramarine, magenta and peacock, red gold and aquamarine'[16] are gorgeously orchestrated, the hot tones made hotter by sudden splashes of rich blue or green. The nearest English art had attained to this kind of chromatic sensuality previously was in the stained glass of our cathedrals and the poetry of

Keats, whilst the freedom of handling had not been seen since Hogarth's *Shrimp Girl* in the mid-eighteenth century.

35   During 1994 the Tate Gallery displayed Smith's *Model Turning* (1924) next to *The Bath* (1925) by one of the greatest French colourists, Pierre Bonnard. The similar backgrounds, appearances and nervy dispositions of both men are striking, but their art could not be further apart, as these two works demonstrate. Smith's Vera turns in her sleep and nearly falls from a tossed bed made up of blue and purple cushions with a near-black drape behind. No daylight penetrates this love-nest but the few colours are full strength, undiluted by white, and applied wet in wet. A crimson petticoat covers her thighs but one large breast is the focus of the whole picture. Her body is plump and brown and betrays those 'lineaments of gratified desire' that Blake wished to see in women: she is the cat who got the cream. No straight line appears amidst the riot of curves and it is obvious that the whole work must have been completed at full tilt, hit or miss, in one sitting.

The Bonnard by its side looks anaemic, cold and tentative. The colours are delicately applied in dabs, stains, rubs, glazes but every one qualified, so the white of the bath moves from warm to cool without any visible transition and the legs and water are made of touches of green, blue, purple, ochre and nameless tints between. 'The principal subject is the surface, which has its colour, its laws over and above those of the subject,' Bonnard declared, echoing Denis.[17] Bonnard's wife Marthe, his muse and gaoler, lies passive, like an oyster in a shell, or a corpse in formaldehyde, between the strong horizontals of her enamelled bath. This too is a painting of love, but one long domesticated, and with no suggestion that Bonnard will tear off his clothes and climb into the bath with her. It has been carefully composed, then painted slowly in the studio from drawings made many months, perhaps years, before. In direct contradiction to Smith, Bonnard believed 'Drawing is sensation. Colour is reasoning.'

Just before this picture was painted Bonnard was forced to choose between marrying his long-term mistress Marthe or a younger woman, Renée Monchaty, whom he also loved. He chose Marthe and Renée killed herself; some claim that he found her dead in her bath.[18] It is clear that Bonnard has edited out his inner turbulence in *The Bath* rather than given it free rein as Smith has done, for as he ruefully admitted, 'he who sings is not always happy.' He continued to depict Marthe as a young woman at her ablutions for years, even after she had died at the age of seventy-three. If parallels do exist between the nudes of Bonnard and Smith then it is amongst the early uninhibited ones of 1899–1900 (*Siesta, Indolence, Blue Nude*), showing Marthe sprawling on a tousled bed in a darkened room, rather than those where she has become bathed in water and light.

For most of the 1920s Smith and his mistress kept a base in Paris, though it was never quite a home, both valuing their independence too highly to settle for property, orthodox domesticity or parenthood. Vera would probably have married him if he had asked or been free to do so, but meanwhile, her friends say, she aborted several of his babies. Between sex, cooking and posing she also resumed painting and exhibited with the London Group in 1922, became a full member in 1927, and by 1929 had earned a solo exhibition at the Bloomsbury Gallery in London. Like Smith she showed with the Amis de Montparnasse and in the 1926 Salon des Indépendants. A collection of her satirical drawings, a kind of modernized Hogarth, called *Charlotte's Progress* was published in London in 1932 by Wishart. The undated but obviously early works reproduced in the only book about her are, unsurprisingly, influenced by Smith.[19] Such female nudes as *Rose Noir, Goddess* and the voluptuous *Olympia* show she had been watching as well as posing. Her combination of flowers and portraits in the red-toned freely brushed *Strawberry Blonde* is also close to Smith in technique and spirit. Nevertheless, in spite of Smith's later accusations, they are not imitations; she evolved her own tremulous drawing style and feathery ways of applying paint, and increasingly her own more imaginative subject matter. Smith might show more interest in her body than her mind, but the loss was his because she was no fool. He did not pose nude for her but she sketched him, did at least two oil portraits and a picture of his black hat and raincoat on a sofa entitled *La Visite De Joe*, Joe being her pet name for him.[20]

Things now looked very promising for Smith: he had an inspiring model, a rejuvenating sex life, a major breakthrough in his work, a settled routine with no responsibilities, and enough money to enable him to develop without pressure.

CHAPTER 12

The First Exhibition
1926–1928

Matthew Smith and Vera Cuningham did not spend all their time painting and posing, though Smith was certainly producing works faster and in greater numbers than ever before. They were, after all, in the capital of art and there were things to be seen. In spite of continuing conservatism in popular and official French taste, Paris still attracted foreign artists, critics, and writers, all eager to join the debates in the cafés along the boulevards of Saint-Michel and Montparnasse. However, Paris had changed since Smith first came. All the Impressionists were now dead, except Monet, and their once controversial art was well on the way to becoming the most accessible style in the history of painting, whilst Lepage-style Realism and Breton peasants had become irretrievably passé. No significant new movements were appearing and artists were still unravelling the implications of the great pre-war discoveries of Fauvism, Cubism and Surrealism. Travel was possible again and the main painters moved south: Bonnard divided his time between Paris and the Côte d'Azure; Dufy was in Venice or Nice; de Segonzac at Saint-Tropez; Matisse had a home in Nice, and Picasso had found the Riviera and begun a neo-classical phase. Only Braque and Derain were still in Paris, but Smith was too diffident to approach either.

Tourists, particularly Americans, were flooding in and changing the whole atmosphere and economy. Now it was the writers who took over the Paris cafés: Joyce, Hemingway, Eliot, Cocteau and Pound were around, but not within Smith's orbit. However, friends from before the war such as Brooks and Maynard were still there, and he could tour the galleries and cafés with them. Roderic O'Conor had stayed in Paris through the war and resisted the general post-war exodus to the sun and the south. He was still in the same studio in the rue du Cherche-Midi, now a vigorous man in his sixties, reticent usually, but generous with advice to younger artists who sought it such as Smith. The Irishman now had guru status with visiting intellectuals so that, Alden Brooks tells us, 'whenever art critics like Roger Fry and Clive Bell came to Paris their first care was to make a bee-line to O'Conor's studio and learn the latest and most informed art news.'[1] He then took them on a tour of the progressive galleries and dealers, all known to him both as an artist and as a buyer.

Both O'Conor and Smith tried the academic, but erotic, subject of Leda and the Swan, Smith making one version from Veronese on a screen and a second, very linear, almost comic rendering of Vera's amplitude in red on a pink ground on the reverse side. Perhaps he was remembering Duncan Grant's screens in the Omega Workshop before the war.[2] This became the background for many later still lifes. In 1936 Vera would make her own splendidly solid picture of the myth and show it at the Royal Academy.

O'Conor evidently thought enough of Smith's paintings to acquire one (*Nude on a Red Divan*) and to hang it alongside his originals by Gauguin, Modigliani, Bonnard, Rouault, Puy, Derain, Soutine, Cézanne, Marquet, Vlaminck and Van Gogh. In return he gave Smith his own 1916 *Reclining Nude*. Like Smith, O'Conor showed no interest in the more cerebral movements of Dadaism, Surrealism, Abstraction, or Analytic Cubism; instead both men relied on immediacy of response and rapidity of facture, working things out through the traditional genres of nude, still life and landscape. Neither looked later than the Post-Impressionists for inspiration. Smith must at this time have reconsidered Van Gogh's work in more detail, since no friend of O'Conor's could escape his long-established enthusiasm for the Dutchman – though neither artist aspired to make still lifes bear the symbolic weight Van Gogh expected his chairs, old boots or sunflowers to carry. Incidentally, back in London Tonks was still fighting his rearguard action: he declared in 1924, 'The Van Goghs at the Tate make me sick!'

36

It was not just Van Gogh's painting which Smith admired, but the man. For his birthday in 1928 brother Harold gave him some sort of joke blowpipe to shoot at cigarette packets and a volume of Van Gogh's letters. In his thank-you letter Matthew remarks: 'To me it is an inspired book and a Bible . . . If any modern should be canonised as a saint I think Vincent should be one of the very first on the list.'[3]

Through O'Conor Smith made the acquaintance of Manuel Ortiz de Zarate (1886-1946), a Chilean painter friend of Modigliani, Picasso, and Max Jacob, who was married to a Polish woman. Ortiz was 'one of the characters of Montparnasse, a boisterous chap who would conduct mock bullfights with Zawado at the Café Parnasse, nearly wrecking the establishment in the process.'[4]

He does not sound Smith's kind of person, but nevertheless in 1924 they, together with O'Conor and Vera, exhibited in a mixed show in a fashionable nightclub, the Monaco. This was organized by the Société des Amis de Montparnasse, of which Zarate was president. The 'Zawado' mentioned above was Jean Waclaw Zawado, a Pole who became a friend too and later in Aix painted Provençal landscapes alongside Smith. With these friends Smith sent works along to the Salon des Refusés, which was open to all comers.

Alden Brooks had kept on both his Paris flat in the rue Madame and the Grez residence. Although Smith no longer had a house in Grez he spent odd weeks at the hotel there through the 1920s, often dining with the Brooks, though it is not clear if he took Vera with him. He was beginning to be rather reluctant to introduce her, fearing, perhaps, to have her stolen from him in the way he had taken her from Meninsky, or that she would begin to assert her own place in the artistic community. They both returned to London frequently, though discreetly to separate addresses, and exhibited there through the decade. For example, Smith showed with the London Group in April 1923 and asked around £20 for his Vera nudes, which was about the same price Fry, Meninsky, Vanessa Bell and Paul Nash were charging for their works.

After two years of stifling intimacy both Vera and Matthew began to come up for air. That they were not always together is shown by this anecdote set some time before 1926 from Adrian Daintrey:

So I was sitting dateless at about eight o'clock on the evening of Christmas day in a café with a bare acquaintance, an American remittance man when, flitting in and out of the orbit of the lights, appeared another unmistakable Englishman, of middle age, quietly dressed, a soft hat with the brim pulled down all the way round, slim, slightly round shouldered and spectacled. His manner was abstracted. Whom or what was he seeking? It appeared no one and nothing. For after a few gyrations my companion had called the name 'Matthew Smith' and the moth was firmly pinned down at our table. He, like us, was uninvited for Christmas dinner. After a drink or two we three set off together to a restaurant near the Bourse. The American did all the talking, neither Matthew Smith nor I getting a word in edgeways.[5]

Smith then befriended the young Daintrey who, though he had reservations about the 'unrelieved, dull redness of the canvases' in Smith's studio, nevertheless found him completely devoid of pose or conceit. Smith kindly pointed out to Daintrey that in Paris 'sooner or later you have to decide whether to live for the night or the day.'

News of Smith's new work and manner filtered back to London. Roger Fry went over and bought an O'Conor and a Smith for the Contemporary Art Society and spread the word back in London that Smith had made great progress, particularly with his nudes.

At last Smith had accumulated enough works for a one-man exhibition – a move the dealer Freddy Mayor had been urging him to make for over two years. This took place at the Mayor Gallery in Sackville Street, from 7 to 28 April 1926. At forty-six he was finally launched. Twenty-four works were on display and besides the recent nudes and four Cornish landscapes he included his copy of Ingres' *Madame Rivière*, and a study after Delacroix, presumably to impress the London critics with his French credentials. Prices were from 15 to a top 70 guineas for the magnificent picture of Vera, *Femme du Cirque* of 1926.[6]

Richard Wyndham wrote this account of the event:

Matthew Smith was present at his private view (he has attended none since) but few bothered to hush their voices when expressing their disgust at the pictures on the walls. For who could have recognised the artist in the timid myopic slightly stooping figure whose afternoon consisted in being tugged from one side of the narrow room to the other by his two small boys up for the day from school? Who could have believed that here was the creator of these turgid nudes that still lived, still tempted, though conceived in tones of crimson so deep that the highest light of the cheek bone or breast held the richness of pigeon's blood: or these landscapes seen with such ferocity of ownership that one would hardly have dared walk the dark roads without the artist by one's side. Few thought of buying, and, of those few, painters predominated: Epstein, Augustus John.[7]

This gives a false impression: the works did sell and their power was acknowledged by the surprised critics. Anthony Bertram in *The Saturday Review* wrote of Rabelaisian, Fieldingesque, even Shakespearean, vigour amounting almost to brutality, and how 'these rich and lustrous canvases, glowing from the walls like vast Limoges enamels, heavy with the sense of form and colour, bound together with a relentless and powerful rhythm, demand that we shall look at them and be ashamed about some of the pleasant things that have taken us in before.'[8] Another influential critic, P. G. Konody in *The Observer*, thought the paintings vivid and impetuous but 'Mr Smith is too aggressively daring to "go down" with the general public, though in his brilliant handling of the human form he is, apart from the arbitrary colour, quite a realist, without any kind of distortion or extravagance.'[9]

The single portrait on show, of A. T. Cholerton (a new friend Smith had made in Paris and who would play a greater part in his later life) was much praised by Fry for its 'Rembrandtesque salience of relief' and more generally,

one sees that it is upon colour that he lays the task of situating the planes in the spatial and plastic construction. Upon colour, too, he relies to achieve the suggestion of chiaroscuro. In all this he is pushing to the furthest limits the essentially modern view of the functional as opposed to the ornamental role played by colour in pictorial design . . . What surprises one in those pictures where his method has become completely successful, where the colour functions entirely, is the intensity which it gives to the plastic relief. This seems, in fact, to be more completely and clearly suggested to the imagination that it could be by vehement oppositions of light and shade. The need for large divisions in which to develop the transitions of any given colour area impels him to design in a few simple and broadly related volumes.[10]

Perhaps Fry's reservations about Smith's 'tendency to define his volumes with too uniformly rounded, too insensitive a contour' was a veiled reference to Vera's blatant breasts and haunches, though it accurately predicted faults in Smith's later works. Gwen's reaction to them is not recorded, but she could no longer have any doubts that Smith had left her for a younger woman who inspired him to paint in a way she had never done. He had finally and reluctantly admitted Vera's existence to her in late 1924.

Fry's praise apparently made Sickert very resentful of Smith, though it is hard to see why, unless he thought his former protégé had been recruited into the Bloomsbury coterie. Rothenstein says, 'The following year Matthew Smith said to Sickert: "I've sent you a card for my show. But you needn't go; it's only complimentary." "You may be sure," answered Sickert, "that my visit won't be complimentary." After this encounter they rarely met again.' Smith also offended Fry by refusing his invitation to join the London Artists' Association, apparently because his privately held view was that Fry was too slippery an art politician to trust. 'Fry's response was to cut him in the street.'[11] Smith was not good at art politics and he never became a clubbable painter.

The reviews generally reflected people's astonishment at his juicy full-blooded colour, contrasted with what they were used to in muddy Sickert or the pallid landscapes of Nash or Nicholson. Critics were forced to mint new similes; for example, The Times critic who admired Smith's taste for 'colour and plenty of it' later revealed: 'The comparison that comes to mind, however, is that of the superior effect when a military band plays music really composed for the military band to that produced by crooning in a maudlin way over matter for a string quartet.'[12] But Smith rather resented this kind of reaction, and complained: 'People always talk about my colour, but I like to think I have other qualities – for instance, composition, form, and I hope, sometimes line.'

Vera Cuningham eventually rebelled against having to pose from the moment she woke up, and then being expected to fit in the cooking, shopping, washing and other chores. She began to paint more and pose less after about 1925. Whilst the artistic careers of Smith and his mistress continued to develop in Paris, that of his wife seemed stalled. Gwen's lifestyle and domestic burdens left her little time to develop her own painting, though she is known to have done several pastels of the boys, none of which survives. Her Slade friends had now dispersed: Gwen John was settled permanently in Paris and becoming so reclusive that when Gwen visited she refused to see her, while Ida Nettleship had long ago married Augustus John, abandoned art, accepted a ménage à trois, and died after giving birth to her fifth son. Only Edna Clark Hall (née Waugh) still continued to paint in England, though her husband was so brutally discouraging she produced little. At least she provided a refuge and a sympathetic audience for Gwen in her Essex house and her Gray's Inn studio.

The two Smith boys became boarders at Wellington School and, unlike their father, began to excel at sports and to thrive on the public school regime. But once they were off Gwen's hands more pressures came from her father, now a widower in his nineties, living at Whaddon Hall, Bruton, Somerset. She went to nurse him for long periods, and while Matthew sympathized with her, he did little beyond sending the monthly allowance, though it was often delayed when he forgot. In return she kept a steady stream of missives flowing across the Channel telling of the boys' exploits, her tax problems, her frustrated attempts to paint, and enclosing school reports, socks, hankies, chocolate, books of Japanese prints and blotting paper. Smith sent news of friends in Grez, stamps for the boys, and endless moans about his colds, insomnia, and difficulties with his dentists, oculists and work. Neither mentioned Vera or anything of the deeper feelings which kept them apart.

Then, in the winter of 1926, at the age of forty-nine, Gwen cast off her ties and decided she would become a student again. She went to Paris, booked into the Hotel Odessa and enlisted in the atelier of André Lhôte (1885–1962), one of the minor, more decorative Cubists but an outstanding teacher. Only one nude survives from this time but it is solid enough to show that Gwen still had the skills which had so impressed Tonks and her fellow students.[13] She exhibited six works in a mixed show at the Warren Gallery in autumn 1927, for which Augustus John wrote the catalogue introduction. He commented to Smith: 'She has a lot of talent, which of course we all knew,' which praise Smith passed on to Gwen in a letter and added his own. The roles were now reversed and it was Gwen who needed boosting. Smith always seems to have had the highest respect for his wife's talents but did little to help her realize them through those difficult years when she was bringing up two boys in rented accommodation. He wrote to say it was a pity she was doing only 'a little sowing and no reaping.'[14] It is not known if they met in Paris but Smith moved to Sickert's favourite town, Dieppe, for six months in 1926 in order to paint harbour scenes and flowers. In summer 1927 Gwen went on holiday to Le Pouldu, near Pont Aven, but perversely Smith had by then returned to London – it seemed he felt uneasy even being in the same country as his wife.

Smith was always attractive to women with love to give, but he also had a gift for friendships with highly intelligent men. Around 1923 he met Francis Halliday, then a young bachelor of about thirty, who had spent the war in Military Intelligence. He taught German at Manchester University, but had a taste for art and Left Bank living which he was happy to share with Smith. Halliday's close friend from student days was Alfred Thornton Cholerton (Chol), who was also an ex-colleague in Military Intelligence, a Fellow of King's College, Cambridge (where he had known Fry), and a man of much learning and humour. Chol was married at this time to a French wife and had a property in the Pyrenees, but the marriage ended in 1926 and Chol departed for Moscow to cover the show trials and later the war as a *Daily Telegraph* journalist. Before then the three friends enjoyed bachelor sprees in France and London, one in Chartres being particularly memorable. Both these men would play significant roles in Smith's future life.

Another new and distinctly glamorous acquaintance of Smith's from this period was Alvaro Guevara (1894–1951), who had been a pampered child prodigy in his native Valparaiso before moving to Bradford to study textiles, and then on to the Slade in 1913. He was rich, talented, a champion boxer, dandy, poet, opium smoker and bisexual. Society hostesses fought for his favours and Sickert, Fry, John, and D. H. Lawrence had all been impressed by his painting.

Smith continued to slip away to Grez when he tired of Paris or Vera and there he made a second bungled attempt to paint Alden Brooks's portrait, as the sitter recorded in November 1929:

After a long while spent nibbling ginger snaps ... 'Feeling old, must eat something,' and interjecting odd and end remarks ... 'Picture dealers at present seem to be vying with each other to see who can be the biggest shits' . . . he persuaded me I was looking bad, so we gave it up. Then I offered him a Modigliani caryatid drawing for a canvas of trees he had slashed and thrown away. Then he went out to a meal. That evening he was ill and I had to take care of him, we ate in his studio but no posing. Next day when I went round to see how he was, he was all dressed, bags packed, off to London. He roared over the Modigliani drawing. He said I was a damned fool to have him take it for a picture he had slashed and thrown away. I said he was a damned fool to have taken it. Found him a taxi and said goodbye.[15]

Modigliani's self-destructive life had ended in 1920, and with him died a wild Parisian bohemianism that was not be resurrected. Smith must have seen him selling drawings for drinks in the Montparnasse cafés and become interested in his work. Brooks gives another insight into Smith's enthusiasm for Modigliani at this time:

Furthermore, if copies are an indication, what of the splendid copy Smith made of a Modigliani of mine, called 'Germaine', a picture that to my mind outdid the original, and this is in a purely luscious Smith way of its own? Another picture that he gave me. And a picture that with the original was stolen from me during the German occupation of Grez.'[16]

Modigliani, like Smith, painted his close-up nudes in a hot terracotta colour and worked at terrific speed in one trance-like sitting, but there the similarities end. The Italian artist distorted, flattened, simplified and sweetened more than Smith, working towards a sinuous outline and a smooth surface, the figures' decorative poise disturbed only by realistic touches, such as the pubic and armpit hairs, and their challenging gazes aimed at the spectator.

Brooks acquired other works from Smith, but not easily:

He told me: 'I really can't have you buying up all my best pictures. Just as soon as I do anything half way respectable, along you come and buy it and I have nothing left to show anyone else. And some day I must have a show of my pictures in London.' But I got even with him. When my book came out, he wired me from London, 'Send me ten copies of your book, my expense;' and I wired back, 'No. Can't have you buying up all my books.'[17]

Smith was always paranoid about his pictures disappearing into private hands, even those of close friends such as Halliday or Epstein, or of a new enthusiast, Dudley Wallis, Director of the Whitworth Art

Gallery in Manchester. He desperately wanted the works to be seen and appreciated, but resented selling them since each had cost him so much travail. By now, however, Smith had become highly collectable and the buyers were clamouring.

CHAPTER 13

Growing Fame
1928–1932

Though he spent more time in France than in England during the 1920s Smith was still a frequent visitor to the London art scene and one given increasing respect within it. He exhibited every year of the decade with the London Group and was represented in the English section at the 1930 Carnegie International Exhibition in America. When in London he lived at Charlotte Street and after 1928 at 78 Grove End Road (where Gwen was forbidden to visit) and painted in 8 Fitzroy Street or, when Vera was willing to sit for him, at her nearby flat in Maida Vale.

It was not difficult to keep in touch with old friends: all he had to do was turn up at the Café Royal in Piccadilly on Friday night where Augustus John would be holding court. When this rendezvous was closed for rebuilding in 1928 it left the intelligentsia temporarily without a home. John was now a Royal Academician and had failed to fulfil the amazing promise he had shown at the Slade, though he was still a formidable presence in the pubs and restaurants and a tireless seducer of women. He bought Smith's pictures and boosted his reputation wherever he could. For example, he wrote in *Vogue* in his florid way:

French influences are inevitably to be noticed in his work, but the fulness of form which characterises so many of his figures has a distinct relationship with Indian and Persian drawings. With a cataract of emotional sensibility he casts upon the canvas a pageant of grandiose and voluptuous form and sumptuous colour, which are nonetheless controlled by an ordered design and a thoroughly learned command of technique. This makes him one of the most brilliant figures in modern painting.[1]

John, more than most, could appreciate that these works were about a man looking at a desirable woman: 'He sits apart and converts what to other men are the ever-partial triumphs of passion into permanent monuments of profound sensory emotion.'

Smith's other artist admirer, Epstein, moved in 1928 to 18 Hyde Park Gate with his wife but maintained his new love and model, Kathleen Garman, in another establishment nearby. She too became a good friend to Smith, later recalling his 'dry humour which was like the exquisitely dry champagne he always served when he invited one to "tea".'² Epstein filled both places with his growing collection of Matthew Smiths, including one of the greatest of the Vera nudes, *Woman With A Fan* (1925), called by Hendy 'one of the masterpieces of English painting: a heavy-weight champion, a tremendous monument of glowing flesh. Few English painters have achieved form so near to that of true sculpture.'³

Epstein's wife was a collector, too, and wrote to Smith after seeing one exhibition with a ridiculously high offer: 'Will you sell me the picture you have at the London Group for 250 guineas? . . . I will pay you 250 guineas on the word of a Scots woman.' The picture she described as 'red smoulding flowers in front of a darker background and pears yellow in front and greener at the back'.⁴

By now the two artists, Matt and Jake as they called each other, were also linked together in the public's narrow mind. Epstein recounts in his autobiography how Smith 'overheard a man saying to a woman in front of a Bond Street dealer's window which showed a flower painting of his: "These fellows Epstein and Smith ought to be in jail!" which is not quite so extreme as the man who left an exhibition of Epstein's drawings telling the gallery owner, "I should like to take Epstein out to a butcher's shop and have his hands chopped off."⁵ Was it their lack of 'finish', uninhibited use of materials, their disregard for the idealized Royal Academy figure, or, more likely, their shared love of the female body which so offended the prudes? There was certainly something disturbingly carnal about both of them to the prurient English mind.

At this time Epstein was undergoing vicious attacks on his sculptures *Night* and *Day* for the London Underground. He defended himself with more force than Smith was ever called upon to do, but in terms that

Smith would have approved of. The *Sunday Times* critic, Frank Rutter, said of Smith's nudes, 'in his rather haphazard choice of types, Mr Smith is liable to be accused of cultivating ugliness.'[6] Similarly Epstein had been accused of a 'cult of ugliness' and replied, 'Nobody seeks for ugliness. I am not sure that anyone seeks for beauty. The artist seeks to express himself, and if he is sufficiently an artist he finds beauty in his way of expressing himself. But he does not set out "to seek for beauty." That is not how beauty is found.'[7]

By the second half of the 1920s Smith needed to employ alternative models because Vera found posing tedious and wished to get on with her own work. His portrait of her entitled *Madame Ennui* of 1925 conveys this growing feeling succinctly.[8]

The title is presumably a deliberate echo of Sickert's best known work, *Ennui*, which shows a couple in a room totally bored with each other and with life. By 1929 Vera had a London flat which she shared with Lisa Hewitt, Secretary to the Ballet Rambert. Lisa posed for some of Vera's own nudes and acted as a peacemaker between the couple, who were increasingly getting on each other's nerves. Around this time Vera was ill, probably following another abortion, but Smith helped nurse her back to her usual vigour and appetite. In Paris they had given up villa Brune and Smith had moved alone to 10 passage Noirot about a mile away: he kept it as his Paris base until 1932 and painted some of his best nudes there, though Vera was no longer the model. Today the street has been buried under hideous tenements.

However, if her posing was now intermittent and Vera and Smith lived apart, they still took frequent holidays together, especially now that he had a racy convertible Citroën car, nicknamed Modestine after Stevenson's companion in *Travels With a Donkey*. In it they criss-crossed France whilst Smith's erratic and nervous driving contributed to a growing fund of Modestine anecdotes amongst his friends: for example, he complained to Phyllis that the car 'had leapt backwards into a shop,' and on another occasion it was so entangled in a tree the tree had to be felled. Vera and Matthew visited Siena, Venice and Florence in 1927, Cornwall in 1928, and Dieppe in spring 1929. To the Hotel Aguado, where they were staying in Dieppe, came the young and precocious painter Christopher Wood who wrote a postcard to his friend Ben Nicholson: 'Matthew Smith lives downstairs. We are dining with him tomorrow. He is like a charming mouse.'[9] Later in summer 1929 they went to Wensleydale in Yorkshire (scene of a number of landscapes), and in 1930 they went on a Van Gogh pilgrimage to Arles   37 as well as to the Auvergne and Puy de Dôme. From all of these places he wrote to Gwen and the boys, never hinting he was not alone.

Sometimes they were accompanied on their British tours by Vera's Green Amazon Parakeet, Laura, one of a succession of such birds, all with the same name. Vera posed in Smith's Grove End lodgings wearing her slip and holding her bird on her knee in *Girl with Parrot* (1929).   38 There were other pictures of this bird and once when it was shown one of them it bit Smith in the cheek.

Smith was also developing flower and fruit paintings alongside the nudes during these years. His colours and forms had always evoked fruity comparisons: those tartly coloured nudes of Fitzroy Street with lemons, peppers, limes; the Cornish landscapes with the sullen purples of damsons or aubergines, and then the Vera nudes which provoked thoughts of peaches, melons, nectarines, all that was rounded, smooth and juicy. As with the nudes details are suppressed – the flower species is often unclear – as the artist goes all out for colour and paint quality. Philip Hendy later saw the continuity from the nudes to the table-top works: 'As a flower painter he is unique. I can think of no other painter who had used flowers and fruit to express such a variety of ecstasy, from cool delight to passionate orgy.'[10] Hendy evoked Chardin, Cézanne,   49 Renoir and Matisse as Smith's only rivals in this sensual apprehension of things. Smith wrote to his sister Phyllis: 'Of course flower pieces do in a way make an easier appeal and although there may be very similar qualities in the other things many people are slower to realise them.'[11]

In December 1927 Smith held another one-man exhibition, at the Reid and Lefevre Gallery in King Street. The prices of the thirty works on show had now taken off, so that for example the wonderfully free *Model à la Rose* (1924) which had originally been priced at £30 now sold for £150. The critics were on the whole respectful and treated him as an established major English painter, rather than an imitation French one as they had tended to previously. 'One of the greatest contemporary artists this country is lucky to claim,' wrote the *New Statesman* critic, the works 'equal any the European galleries can show,' and he noted how in mixed shows Smith's power killed his neighbours stone dead.[12] Konody in *The Observer* was also quick to claim him for the glory of England: 'I doubt if among the younger generation of independent English painters there is an artist who owes less to French influence than Mr Matthew Smith.'[13] Only the writer in the *Morning Post* was snide: he found a reclining nude of Vera 'a trifle masculine' and claimed, 'Mr Matthew Smith is finding out the fatuity of affectation. Hitherto his pictures might have been designed to decorate an abbatoir, so gory was their colour.'[14]

The 1920s were wonderful years for Smith. By the end of them he was acknowledged as a master among his contemporaries. Even his drawings, which the critics had initially seen as his weakness, were now praised. His sketchbooks show him to be an inveterate doodler – jugs, parrots, flowers, cafés, fruit, cats, swans, horses, trees, boats, streets, and friends, all crowd his pages in ink, pencil and watercolour, though many are very slight as if he had lost interest half-way through. A series of pencil sketches of a bored Vera in her bloomers and stockings were commended by William Gaunt in *Drawing and Design* in the following terms:

He can draw, and draw beautifully, with a very simple firm outline. His drawing is quite natural and spontaneous, and yet it is precise in its rendering of things seen. He gives the effect of solidity without resorting to patches of shade to indicate masses . . . they are drawings without adventitious attraction – depending on pure quality of line – which suggests dimension. They are like so many modern drawings, austere and sculptural in feeling.[15]

He had certainly shed everything Tonks had taught him about the systematic analysis of form at the Slade and forged a simpler, almost naïve graphic style which evoked comparisons with Matisse, though without his relentless pursuit of essences. A juxtaposition of any of these drawings of Vera with the red chalk portrait he had done of Gwen in 1908 demonstrates how radical his new beginning had been: it represented a shift from the Victorian to the modern.

Further signs of his new status in England were the purchase of *Peonies* by the Tate Gallery and the offer by Dudley Tooth to act as his dealer. Until now Smith had sold direct to patrons or through mixed exhibitions in the Victorian manner, but the twentieth-century artist needed a dealer, one-man shows, and later the support of government institutions such as the Arts Council and British Council to spread his reputation nationally and internationally. Tooth arranged a full-scale Smith retrospective at his gallery in New Bond Street for the month 16 October to 16 November 1929 – just in time for the Wall Street crash and the Depression.

P. G. Konody's reactions to the retrospective were representative: 'If I were asked whom I consider the outstanding personality in modern British art, I would unhesitatingly pronounce the name of Matthew Smith.' Konody confesses to having reservations about individual works, but overall, 'his is the most significant – perhaps the only significant – contribution made by England to the modern movement in painting.' This is because he shows no French influence, being a self-made, indeed self-taught, improviser. He points out to the prissy that Smith's heightened colour 'raises his interpretation of the nude to an abstract and purely aesthetic plane and imposes silence on the prurient who will prefer to reserve their sniggers for the naked sirens exposing their fleshy charms of the official academies and Paris salons.'

Chauvinistic as much of this might be, Konody does point to the crucial breakthrough that Smith had made:

The forms, as it were, grow out of the pigment itself. The brush stroke has a constructive function. It varies in direction, in density, in size, in energy. Drawing and painting, in a word, are but a single operation in which colour plays so vital a part that a translation of these pictures into black and white becomes almost meaningless.[16]

One reviewer amused Smith by calling him 'the son of a marmalade manufacturer' and another referred to his father's book of poems as *A Chest of Violets*.[17] A further reminder of his father came in a letter from an old family friend who was very rude about the ugly nudes on display and then wondered what puritanical Frederic would have thought of them: 'He would have gone off at the deep end – but when he heard all the plaudits of the highbrows I think his pride would have been tickled and he would probably have turned round and broadcast to the world that he taught you all you know! He looked upon the "spotlight" as his perquisite.'[18]

Meanwhile the painter these critics were anxious to claim for the national school had slipped away back to Paris for the winter, and to the Auvergne with Vera for the spring of 1930.

The growing interest in bright colour as an end in itself amongst modern French artists meant they were keen to find places to paint that were themselves full of colour. Gauguin had searched in Tahiti (in 1930 Matisse went there too) but less adventurous artists realized they were available nearer home in the south of France. Many English artists followed, including Augustus John and Smith. He took Vera Cuningham to visit Arles in October 1930. From there Van Gogh had written to his brother Theo in 1886: 'Not only in Africa but from Arles onward you are bound to find beautiful contrasts of red and green, of blue and orange, of sulphur and lilac. And all true colourists must come to this, must admit there is another kind of colour than that of the north.'[19]

Smith had now made this discovery for himself and was converted both to the southern landscape and to the easy way of life. He was also fancy-free to enjoy it because he no longer took Vera with him on holidays: the break was final, though it seems not to have been too acrimonious. Alice Keene tells a poignant story:

While he was away in Paris they had promised to write to each other every day. Feeling unable to carry this out, as he was already interested in someone else, he sent her instead a little package of violets, which were her favourite flowers. The post was much swifter than now, but on this occasion it was delayed and the flowers arrived dead.[20]

It had been an intense intimacy from which both gained as individuals and artists. Alden Brooks attempted to put Smith's debt to Vera in perspective after both were dead and when Francis Halliday was contemplating writing a biography of Smith:

As for 'MS's passion for VC' and its effects upon him, you may be right. Still, how enduring is a passion, and this in a continuing masterful way? And I do know that at the end of their association Matthew's complaint was that she was living upon him, imitating him too much and well, for any continuance. So while there may be no bad taste in saying that Vera Cuningham was the dominating influence upon Matthew Smith, that it was she who truly made him, a chief objector to such a remark might be Matthew Smith himself. Indeed it might make him turn in his grave.[21]

Smith suffered another severe bout of mental distress, possibly brought on by his confused love affairs and the break with Vera, and in spring 1930 he retreated once more to Lyons for treatment under Dr D'Espiney. From there he wrote to Brooks: 'I have passed through every nuance of torture so far down here but that was inevitable . . . I have repaved Lyons with my footprints.'[22]

When he had recovered, Smith desperately needed a new woman to cosset and inspire him. One of Epstein's favourite models was a Kashmiri woman named Sunita Peerboy (or Peerbhoy) who had left her husband and fled to England with her son Enver and sister Anita. She had worked in a circus and sold erotica from a stall at the Wembley International Exhibition of 1924 before the three of them moved into the Epstein household for the next six years. Sunita was fond of alcohol and none too reliable but she and Enver modelled for the sculptor's ethereal *Madonna and Child*. Smith evidently drew her as early as 1924 and may even have introduced her to Epstein, but his paintings of her both nude and in colourful saris date from 1930 to early 1933 and were done at 10 passage Noirot. Both artists slept with her though this caused no tensions between them, since love was not involved. Sunita sat for both figures in Smith's *The Two Sisters* (1931) and several more nudes where her distinctive colouring, thick midriff and pointed breasts can be recognized. A couple of years later Sunita returned to India and disappeared in mysterious circumstances.

Another plump young red-haired model, every ounce as voluptuous as Vera, appeared at this time in passage Noirot, though she has not been identified and it is not known if she is the one who first replaced Vera in his affections. The most famous image of her, entitled *Jeune Femme* (1930), has one breast bared and a red rose lodged in her cleavage.[23] She appears again wearing only a red petticoat, lying prone in *Siesta* (1931) and supine in *Model Waking* (1931).[24] She obviously rejuvenated Smith to produce nudes every bit as erotically charged as those of Vera a decade before. The coloured drapes which divide the

40

42

43

space behind her still play on the same sumptuous harmonies of crimson against greens and blues, deep purples against yellows, and amongst these the cream of her flesh stands out deliciously. The former overall redness has cooled down now and there are subtler plays with pinks and lavenders, but the brushwork still moulds the forms, like a potter's fingers shaping clay, as vigorously as ever.

Smith, aware of the poet's enjoinment to 'gather ye rosebuds while ye may', liked to pose his women with blossoms between their breasts or in their naked laps, as we have seen. This soon became his trademark, and eventually a cliché. It comes as no surprise, therefore, that when he comes to paint flowers themselves as still lifes this fleshy quality is carried over, for example in *Pale Pink Roses* (1929),[25] *Dahlias* (1933) and the Tate Gallery's *Peaches* (1937). Even though flowers and fruit will stay motionless longer than young women he still painted them in a fever of concentration. For example, of *Peaches* Smith said, 'It was painted *premier coup* on white canvas, probably in about two hours. No previous studies at a time when things were going well.'[26]

Around 1930–35 Picasso was also producing still lifes full of rounded forms which were coded portraits of the body of his mistress Marie-Thérèse Walter. Picasso's work often changed style as his relationships with women changed – sometimes sadistically destructive, sometimes tender, sometimes lustful, sometimes making them weep uncontrollably. Smith's own affairs did not always run smoothly, but the mood of his pictures did: they celebrate only the good days when the women co-operated, passive as nectarines, and allowed themselves to be worshipped in paint. He called the paintings 'moments of liberation' but Smith's darker moods, unlike Picasso's, had to find their outlets elsewhere.

Henry Green gives something of the flavour of these middle period nudes, choosing one for which Sunita was probably the model:

To take only one picture, the *Nude With Pearl Necklace* from 1931. With what loving brutality has Smith painted the model's belly and that thick strong wrist. How proudly she lies, how superb her bent right knee. How gaily she lies and how little she cares! And that right breast walloping to the couch! The happy fling of her necklace, to the right as well, is all humour and gaiety, while her face (and surely Smith is one of the very few modern painters to fit the right face to his nudes) her face holds just the expression of what must have been the mood in that studio more than twenty years ago, a situation that is now fixed for ever.[27]

Sometimes these uninhibited works of Smith's proved too pagan for thin-blooded critics back in the London drizzle. Reviewers still made sneering remarks about his taste for women who were not conventionally pretty ('His physical types are clearly chosen for painter's reasons') and protested against the vigour of his brushwork because 'there is an aesthetical as well as a moral obligation not to "do violence" to anyone or anything.'[28] Frank Rutter of the *Sunday Times* stung Smith by commenting how his nudes

have offended many observers by the coarseness of the forms of the models selected, but in these recent paintings Mr Smith is far less aggressive in his choice of models. His two portraits *Jeune Femme* and *Girl Holding A Yellow Rose* are reasonably attractive in subject as well as in treatment, and his sense of form is not the less well displayed because it is exercised on more refined models.[29]

Rutter also published a popular survey of modern art in which he wrote: 'Mr Smith also paints landscapes and figure subjects, the last being influenced by Rouault and tending to be characterised by a choice of massive, coarse-looking women for models. Like Rouault, Matthew Smith on these occasions is apt to let his power and force degenerate into brutality.'[30] After several attacks in this vein Smith wrote: 'I long for Rutter to be told that my representation of women is sane, and healthy, a state usually unattractive to "refined taste" I admit, also that they are derived from Rubens and Delacroix, with an eye on Courbet, Ingres, and perhaps Renoir, and not from the prostitutes of Rouault.'[31]

Rutter later tried to place Smith amongst his contemporaries in a way he thought a Yorkshireman like Matthew might appreciate. He considered 'Steer, Sickert and Augustus John the obvious three to lead an England painting eleven, while . . . Grant, Gertler, Matthew Smith, Stanley and Gilbert Spencer, Wadsworth and Paul Nash were fairly safe, with Sutherland perhaps as spare man, and Vanessa Bell as an odd woman.'[32]

Smith's acceptance as a first-team player was confirmed when in 1934 the Tate bought his *Cyclamen* and two years later paid £250 for *Model Turning*, one of the best nudes of Vera. Some people were even agitating to have Smith accepted into the establishment of British painting, the *Manchester Guardian* suggesting he was the man to replace Orpen (who had died) as an Academician. Winston Churchill himself chided the Academy for not showing Smith, but nothing came of it, Smith being too modern for that establishment and probably too close to the uppity Epstein whom they turned down three times between 1929 and 1932.

44 Early in the decade Smith painted his third self-portrait, subsequently donated by its owner, Alden Brooks, to the National Portrait Gallery. This shows only his head, turning left, away from the light. It is boldly painted in orange and brown against a dirty green background, but is hardly flattering: the mouth is downturned and his mole's eyes peer through the round spectacles with suspicion. Compared to the more considered portraits on the walls around it by such conventional contemporaries as Frampton, Carrington, Lamb, Vanessa Bell, Roberts, Proctor and Laura Knight it looks dashed off, but the likeness is convincing and the paint surface lively. Smith had reason to look more confident than he did since his reputation in England (though not in France) was now well established and would climb through the decade. Brooks even caught him wondering about posterity: 'Smith, as we stood in the Rue de la Gaieté before a tailor's dummy representing Foujita, "I wonder if I shall ever be as celebrated as that."'[33] Few now remember this Japanese painter (1886–1968) of pallid nudes and cats, so Smith's wish came true.

Smith's friend Halliday was still around, and in April 1932 he married Mary, a rich lady with an interest in collecting paintings, especially Smith's. When the Halliday children, Elizabeth and Christopher, were born in 1933 and 1935 Smith became godfather to the boy. The Hallidays soon moved to Wales where Francis taught German at Swansea University and where their home in the Gower Peninsula became one of Smith's bolt-holes from this time onwards. Their mutual friend Cholerton was still in Russia, where he had taken a new wife and had a daughter, Katerina. It would not be until after the Second World War that he played any more part in Smith's life.

The year 1932 was a hectic one for Smith and taxed his ability to keep all the parts of his life in separate compartments. He had a major exhibition at Tooths, a visit to Burgundy with Alden Brooks, a trip back to England in the company of Brooks and Augustus John, a stay in Hereford with Vera Cuningham and an autumn holiday at Le Pouldu in Brittany with Gwen and the boys. There he found the sixteen-year-old Dermot showed some aptitude for painting and later Matthew wrote to Gwen:

I really thought when I had this success (horrid word) things would be easier possibly, with regard to the pleasure of doing one's job and producing but certainly things have not been any easier certainly still more difficult and I have always the feeling that my talent is being wasted which I really feel is exactly what you probably feel about yourself. Perhaps our Dermot will have long years of really developing his talent in a more happy way. He will certainly have sympathy from his parents.[34]

All this attention would have made any other artist happy, but self-doubt was so much part of his nature that Smith could never believe praise was truly meant. He confided to Gwen as his fame grew:

People come up to me sometimes and exclaim 'you are very successful now': this I neither like very much nor feel to be true. I feel in most ways a very unsuccessful artist and being generally. But with just the right ingredients of life I might be a successful artist, almost. I mean for myself, by this I mean the producer of a large amount of fairly successful work and by this sparing myself much very real pain.[35]

CHAPTER 14

Southern France
1933–1936

Smith was now as happy as his neurotic nature would ever allow him to be, but Gwen was not. Her mother was dead but her ailing father had lingered on at Whaddon House, where Smith reluctantly joined the family for the Christmases of 1930 and 1931. Briefly Gwen had tried to escape these ties by taking a job as a cook-companion to a temperamental old lady in Rustington – a village of happy memories from the beginning of their marriage. Smith was sympathetic to her plight but determined there would be no reconciliation and that he could not afford to help her buy a cottage. Fortunately, the death of her father gave Gwen the money she needed to buy Ship House in the village of Burnham Overy Staithe on the north Norfolk coast. At last, in 1933, she had a permanent home to which the boys could return in the holidays and where they could indulge their passion for sailing. Smith joined them in the summer that year, but soon left to drive Vera round Scotland. On his return to London he rented two rooms at 7 Clarendon Gardens, where he rarely stayed but accumulated canvases and clutter for the next twenty years.

Gwen, meanwhile, settled down to becoming the village eccentric, painting outdoors in all weathers and wearing unconventional hats and clothes, bathing each morning in the sea and dancing in the rain. She too now had a car which she drove erratically and without any sense of direction. For a time she took lodgers but Smith put a stop to that when he found he was paying income tax on her takings. She was now free to paint but wrote to Smith's sister Phyllis 'my inner energy artistically doesn't seem to be there – old age I suppose.'¹ She was then fifty-seven years old but it was the beginning of her most sustained twenty years of work. The few paintings of hers that I have seen are competent academic works of considerable charm. Alison Thomas, who has seen more, describes them thus:

Gwen uses colour in an ordered, structural way to describe the objects and scenes she paints. It is but one of several formal elements which for Gwen must be fully resolved when creating a picture. Thus along with her subtle yet rich tonal harmonies we may also admire her strength of drawing and finely controlled composition balance. There is always a prevailing sense of control in Gwen's paintings based on a thoughtful observation of her subject.[2]

In other words, she displayed none of Matthew's exuberant spontaneity or his characteristically bold touch and colour, but had developed her own orthodox style based on her years at the Slade and her time as Whistler's pupil.

Smith's sons continued to write to 'Dear Dear Daddy', at first from boarding school where they were happy collecting stamps, playing games and complaining about the food, and later from the Royal Air Force College, Cranwell, about their training as fighter pilots, cross-country running, football, and fast cars. Mark eventually graduated as the youngest pilot officer in the RAF. Several of their letters pleaded for Matthew to come home for a family Christmas, but he usually resisted and sent lavish presents instead. One undated letter from Dermot says Uncle Harold had given them two guineas each 'And a nice man with an occasional golden hair brushed over a bald head sent us a large case of wines and spirits which we all like very much.' Another from Mark sends 'hearty congratulations to Mummy on her silver wedding', which must have rung rather hollow for Gwen.

In 1935 Mark joined No 33 Bomber Squadron in Egypt and passed the time with sports, stunt flying, sailing his own boat and flying around to Cairo, Aqaba, Jerusalem ('a terrible hole') and Tel Aviv ('beastly Jews'). 'Life is perfectly marvellous,' he reported. Smith was proud of them and sincerely loved them, but their hearty enthusiasms were not his and he had taken no part in moulding their characters. 'Mark and Dermot really are a charming couple,' he wrote to Gwen after spending Christmas 1937 at home with them, 'thank you for producing them.'

He could never be responsible to, or for, other people and on the whole was happier seeing his sons occasionally in England, and then retreating to his own self-centred life in the south of France.

By October 1932 he was first in Arles and then in Aix-en-Provence and moaning to Phyllis about his cold and how badly work was going. He was also in trouble with his tax and therefore could only spare his nephews two shillings each for Christmas.

If Arles meant Van Gogh, and Nice implied Matisse, Cagnes Renoir, and Le Cannet Bonnard, then any painter who went to Aix and saw Mont Sainte-Victoire rising on the eastern outskirts knew he was treading Cézanne's territory. Every twentieth-century artist, critic and historian has had to come to terms with the heritage of this grouchy recluse, and because Cézanne did not leave behind a coherent theory each has been able to take from his work what they wished to find there. Matisse, for example, said, 'Cézanne, you see, is a sort of God of painting,' and was inspired by Cézanne's colour, whilst Picasso admired his analysis of form.

Cézanne disliked Gauguin's sinuously outlined decorations because the line does not exist in nature, and he rebuked Bernard for being 'an intellectual stuffed by the memory of the museums, who does not look at nature enough – and that is the great thing, to make oneself free of the school and indeed of all schools.' One should try 'to see like a man who has just been born.' Cézanne was a revolutionary, but paradoxically one with a reverence for the past who wanted to 'do Poussin over again from Nature'. Yet how to make from transient nature something permanent enough to justify its place alongside the masters in the Louvre? 'To see nature directly consists of sifting out the character of one's subject. To paint something does not mean making a servile copy of it. It means seizing a single harmony out of all the interconnections one has observed; transposing these into a formal series with its own validity by means of working them up according to a new and original logic,' he declared.[3] It was not all logical thinking but also involved 'realizing one's sensations' in front of nature by the use of colour – which must have struck a chord within Smith, as it had with the Fauves. Cézanne found this could be done either with enormous deliberation in oils ('He never made a mark that was not long considered' Bernard reported), or in thin swishes of watercolour which barely stained the paper and dried almost instantly in the Midi sun. Smith studied Cézanne's use of both media intently, but he lacked the Frenchman's dogged temperament.

Smith painted his own view of Cézanne's mountain in 1932. His 47 version, done in one sitting while the mistral blew, is full of wristy scribbles of thin paint to indicate trees and grass and the orange soil, coarse horizontal scrubbings of a cool dilute blue for the sky and a denser warm grey for the bulk of the mountain. He must have had no more than eight or nine pigments on his palette, whereas Cézanne customarily used up to nineteen. It is typical in its gestural freedom and the refusal to push towards a deeper exploration of individual forms of trees or rocks or mountain. If we contrast this painting with just one of Cézanne's sixty or so views of the same mountain, the Courtauld's version of 1886–8, with its *repoussoir* tree derived from Poussin and its methodical play of horizontal and vertical, cool patches against warm, curves of branch against line of mountain, regularized brushstrokes ('*taches colorées*'), paint of consistent strength and thickness from foreground to horizon, then here all is classical order and deliberation – 'everything has to mesh', said Cézanne. Beside the methodical carpentry of Cézanne's work Smith's looks jerry-built.

After the small-scale fields and short horizons of Pont Aven, Grez and Cornwall these long rolling vistas of Provence provided a new challenge. Smith worked *en plein air* and scribbled opaque paint on to his white canvas in a race against his own failing staying power and tired eyes. This is not the sunny Provence tourists come in search of, but one tinged with melancholy or made slightly ominous by an approaching storm or night. Compared to the Cornish works, however, they are 48 optimistic and realistic in colour. It is also noticeable that he never includes a car, telegraph pole, railway or any sign of modernity in his unpeopled vistas because, like Cézanne, he had no interest in the Impressionists' determination to record the transient effects of modern life.

Over the next few years Smith worked on landscapes at Cagnes, Vence, Fréjus and Aix, giving them a wilder northern slant, nearer to Rubens than the French landscape tradition of Claude, Poussin, Corot, or the

Matisse of *Le Bonheur de Vivre*. There is too much cloud in the sky and too much agitation in the paint for nymphs to loll around here. Cézanne's bathers did not inspire him to try to integrate the nude and landscape, neither did he emulate the blonde light that Derain and Matisse had painted at Collioure, nor attempt the Riviera high-life subjects of Dufy – in fact, several works look very similar to the dark Yorkshire landscapes he painted on his English holidays, perhaps because, as Constable observed, 'A man sees nothing in nature but what he knows.' If Smith failed to see Provence with French eyes, he also did little to further the traditional English view of landscape, being too generalized, lacking in nostalgia, and showing no interest in 'the spirit of place'.

In late 1933 Smith found another place to his liking: Cagnes-sur-Mer, between Nice and Cannes, once the home of Renoir and the inspiration of Soutine, and he spent a good deal of time there until 1936. At first he was unsettled and work went badly, but he refused to join his family for Christmas 1934 on the grounds that 'it is absolutely necessary to stay if I am to take myself seriously as an artist. To leave now means that I have gone through a great deal down here for nothing and then going through a similar time again all for nothing probably and so on until there is no more time to go through'.[4]

Smith lived for almost two years at the exclusive Hôtel Le Cagnard, set on a hill above the town with views towards Cap d'Antibes. At intervals he continued his restless excursions in Modestine around France, and returned to London for a successful exhibition in April 1934 at Tooth's, where he sold £1,000 worth of pictures (but the gallery took one third in commission, which he resented). The critics were generous, though the *Sunday Times* critic thought Smith overworked the red-blue combinations: 'Regimental colours are all very well in their place, but we can easily grow tired of seeing Guards' ties in the background of pictures.'[5]

Smith charmed the landlady's youngest olive-skinned and darkly beautiful daughter, Christiane de Mauberg, into posing for him in a studio near the hotel. Of the works he did with her co-operation his own favourite was *Lady with a Rose* (1934) which stayed with him until he died.[6] There are several other tender works of her holding roses, with eyes modestly downcast, and an arm or hand across her bare breasts. He thought her '*moitié Raphael, moitié Gauguin.*' She was very much in love with Smith, and he with her, but her strong piety probably prevented her from sleeping with him. The consequent tensions built up until finally he left for Aix in February 1936, though she visited him there and in Paris, and passionate letters in French flew between them. Smith made a small plaster nude of her, presumably from imagination, and it became a regular feature of his still lifes from then on. After the war, to Smith's horror, she became a nun in the enclosed order of the Poor Clares in Avignon.

When Smith left Cagnes for Aix in 1936, admitting he could no longer compete with Christiane's God, he moved into the Hôtel Moderne, then into a seventeenth-century farmhouse, the Villa Maria in the estate of the Château Noir, where Cézanne had once rented a studio from the Tessier family (who still own it). This overgrown farmhouse and scatter of cottages is set in dense woods on the outskirts of Aix and is ideal for a painter who wished to work undisturbed. In the same year he also rented a studio-flat in Paris at 18 villa Seurat, a desirable little cul-de-sac off the rue de la Tombe Issoire, Montparnasse. This he kept on for only two years, though it must have served its purpose as a place of assignation with Christiane and others, and a base from which to check the latest developments in the Paris galleries. The Lithuanian Expressionist Chaim Soutine (1893–1943) and his German mistress Gerda Groth also lived there at this time but there is no record of their meeting.[7] Henry Miller had a flat upstairs where he entertained Anaïs Nin and was visited by Lawrence Durrell. Miller's only recorded comment on Smith is how alike the two of them looked. Hans Reichel, another artist, also had a studio in the building and the sculptress Chana Orloff worked a few doors away.[8]

From villa Seurat he could visit Grez where the Brookses still lived and where Jelka Delius was now a widow. When she played him a recording of Delius's music and showed him the composer's death mask Smith burst into tears. In 1936 Eric Fenby produced his biography of the composer and Smith wrote to congratulate him: 'Without you Delius would never have been presented to the world as he was and no one can deny that his curious character was worth immortalising.' He added the supreme compliment, 'I think it is a courageous book and worthy of a Yorkshireman!'[9]

In Aix, as in Pont Aven, Grez-sur-Loing and Cagnes, Smith found a ready-made community of well-heeled English-speaking exiles, together with a group of Cézanne-worshipping painters of all nationalities – including his Polish friend Zawado, who had moved down from Paris to his Domaine d'Orcel. Amongst them was a young diamond heiress from South Africa called Iris Michaelis and her artist brother Cecil, then in his early twenties but already the owner of L'Harmas, a picturesque estate where Smith became a frequent visitor. Later, when she became Mrs Hughes, Iris would prove to be a generous patron and hostess back in England. Other now forgotten artists in this group were Harry Morton Colville, a Scot called Laurens, Marchutz a German lithographer, Francis Tailleux, and local collectors and enthusiasts such as Dr Casse and two civil servants, Mahout and Nicholas. There was no 'school' of Aix and a certain contempt for Picasso's protean genius seemed to be the only shared belief. After market or a day at their easels these expatriates gathered round the marble-topped tables in the Café des Deux Garçons where once Cézanne and Zola had met, or they sat outside in the shade of the plane trees to watch the passing crowds on the Cours Mirabeau.

When he left their company Smith always sneaked off so no one would know where his studio was, according to Mrs Hughes, and very few saw his works. He lived 'in all the hotels in Aix,' he told Brooks, and changed his original Château Noir studio for one at 3 rue de 4 Septembre, then within two years added another at 17 rue Alpheron just to keep them guessing. He collected his mail from various hotels and cafés and insisted Tooth's gave nothing away since: 'What is the use of my reducing the habit of avoiding people to a fine art, if you do not aid and abet me?'[10]

Augustus John was one who knew how to find his friend as he occasionally passed through, trailing his family, en route to his own Provençal villa. The John daughters were charmed by Matthew's old-fashioned courtesy, as all women were. Occasionally the expatriate group went off on excursions in Cecil's Rolls-Royce to see the bullfights at Nîmes or Arles, which Smith seemed to enjoy, though never felt moved, as Picasso did, to make them a subject for his art. Overall Smith was living the kind of extravagant and hedonistic expatriate existence during these years in Aix that he had not known before and was rarely to achieve again.

To this community of artists the news came in 1934 that Roger Fry had died aged sixty-seven. He had dominated the English art community since 1910, influencing how people thought about art and how they made it. His Francophilia and disregard for English art had skewed the whole history and development of British modernism and, without his advocacy of Cézanne, Smith would probably not have settled in Aix. He wrote to Gwen: 'I nearly went to Fry's funeral, but *not* quite! I think it was partly on account of all the people I should meet if I said so.'[11] Tonks's valediction was, 'It was as if (for English art) a Mussolini, a Hitler or a Stalin had passed away.' Tonks himself died three years later and Smith was just as dismissive in his comments on his former teacher. Fry's successor as grand panjandrum of English art was Herbert Read, a defender of both Abstraction and Surrealism and so unlikely to be immediately sympathetic to Smith's need to work in direct response to the model or landscape in front of him.

From Aix Smith periodically journeyed back to England to see his family, to keep in touch with old friends and to exhibit at Tooth's. Russell told a story of Smith taking his most recent Aix landscapes through French customs: 'They are mine you know,' said Smith, hoping to cut the episode short. '*Dans tous les cas, Monsieur*,' said the official, '*il n'y a pas une fortune dedans*.'[12] The English patrons took a different view, particularly of the November 1936 exhibition at Tooth's which sold out and had the critics writing enthusiastically: the *Telegraph* reviewer, for example, now saw him as 'the most exciting of British post-war painters'.[13] The Tate bought *Model Turning* on this occasion and Kenneth Clark, a rising star in the art establishment, acquired two for his own collection.

On his London visits Smith met his brothers for drinks and chaff about the old days and went on the town with Augustus John and Epstein. The sculptor was still the most controversial artist in Britain and during the 1930s his *Genesis, Ecce Homo, Consummatum Est* and *Adam* had all aroused storms of abuse. He had further entangled his already knotty private life with another illegitimate child by one of his models. The long-suffering Mrs Epstein, now over sixty, strapped a cushion under her dress and pretended it was hers. She wrote the next year to Smith about his coming visit and how her husband was thinking 'of the baby son I had in Sept 1934', but Matthew was not to be fooled by such pitiful stratagems.

In 1936 Epstein had begun obsessively to paint flowers in water-colour and it is clear they owed much of their free-flowing power to Smith's example, a fact Epstein freely acknowledged by saying to him 'There's a lot of Matthew Smith on show here,' but Smith was not flattered, only speechless with fury, thinking his ideas had been stolen. In December Epstein followed an exhibition of Smith's at Tooth's with a display of his large brilliantly coloured works and sold every one. The *Telegraph* critic wrote, 'He has filled with explosive energy the most fatigued sector of contemporary art, the flower piece in watercolour,' praise which should rightly have been Smith's and both artists knew it.

CHAPTER 15

Aix-En-Provence
1937–1939

Smith continued his travels from his base in Aix to Paris, Saint-Tropez, the Var, and back to Grez to see the Brooks. On all these travels his mind was less on painting or scenery than on the various young women who served his meals or shared his railway carriage or, on one occasion, offered him a lift he was too nervous to accept and regretted missing the rest of his life. He told friends stories of how he had fallen instantly in love with many such women, but had usually been too indecisive and tongue-tied to approach them directly. Less respectable women he had no such qualms about. According to one family member there was an occasion when he telegraphed his brothers in London to come quickly as he was in dire trouble. They dashed across the Channel and traced the address he had given them, only to find it was a brothel and that Matthew was being kept prisoner until his bills were paid.[1]

There were also less fleeting encounters with women to occupy his mind. Rothenstein recalled:

As so often his talk turned to France. 'I started to speak French too late ever to speak it well; I speak fluently but badly – fluently but badly,' he repeated in his voice like a muffled echo. I said that I supposed the only way to learn it really well later in life was to live with a Frenchwoman. 'I did that,' he said; 'she was a delightful woman. Many Frenchwomen are, but you must either avoid politics or agree with them.'[2]

In Aix he had fallen in love again. In 1937 he met first Pierre and then Marion Monay, Swiss residents who had a very open marriage (Harry Morton Colville was Matthew's predecessor as her lover) and who seem to have invited Smith to share their flat at 23 rue de 4 Septembre and enter into a *ménage à trois* – hence the reference to living with a 'Frenchwoman'. Pierre was an artist and Cézanne enthusiast, then aged about forty, who helped Matthew through a difficult encounter with the traffic police. Marion was about thirty-six or seven and famous for her plump good looks, her blond hair (*'fait de soleil'* said Smith) and her chic dress sense, though she had lost a breast through cancer in the early 1930s. They were childless. Iris Hughes reminisced about this period:

52

One evening, we were invited to dine at the house of a Swiss painter called Monay. . . and his beautiful wife who we believed to be Matthew's mistress – after dinner the ladies were taken upstairs to the loo – and there in the bedroom above the bed was a very fine painting of Madame Monay in the nude! I must confess it rather shook me, I was only about nineteen at the time and felt surprised that the husband did not mind – to the contrary I think he found it an honour to have this painting by a famous artist.[3]

This nude does not survive, nor do others of her, perhaps destroyed or deliberately misdated by Smith in an attempt at discretion, or disposed of by Marion herself before she finally returned to her respectable Swiss background. The unattainable Christiane was forgotten in Matthew's new passion for the very willing Marion, and his letters to her occasionally reached heights he had not attained since courting Gwen: *'Votre dernier lettre est si si precieuse chérie si precieuse terriblement c'est comme si ton coeur vien pres de mois et je suis rempli de une joie inquiétant. C'est comme la joie du'un enfant quand une oiseaux perche dans sa main.'*[4] More usually he wrote of his colds, sore eyes, insomnia, how 'my brain is hurting', and the irritation of visitors and exhibitions. When in London he wrote to her before rising from his bed each morning, inspired by the scent from her handkerchief.

In spite of this ardour he was also painting another local Aixian called Aniése Moreau. She and her dark-haired sister Marie both slept with the artist and sat for him between 1936 and 1940, Aniése usually nude or semi-nude, her jacket open to show her breasts. Her short yellow hair, striking looks, slim figure, fashionable clothes and absurd hats make her instantly recognizable, as do the simpler compositions, range of saturated yellows against pale blues, rather slick paint and sometimes insensitive red outlines he used to depict her. Faults which

53

had appeared intermittently before now became more glaring. The anatomy, especially of hands and arms, is perfunctory, as if he lost interest and after looking at one hand let the other go as a mere smudge. These are brassy superficial works when compared to those earlier ones of Vera, flirtatious rather than voluptuously sensual. They do not represent an advance but in a way they are more French than ever before, with something of the obvious charms of Dufy, or even Boucher. Sometimes the woman sat together as in *The Two Sisters* (an idea perhaps derived from Courbet), and on one occasion Aniése fell asleep while posing and the furious Smith, who hated to have his trance of concentration broken, filled her with black coffee before subsequent sittings.

54

Smith continued to moan about how difficult work was and how much he had to destroy, but this was a fertile time. His nudes may not have progressed but he was having breakthroughs with his landscapes and a series of large still lifes composed round the clay figure he had made of Christiane when he could have her in no other way. These explore very daring, often upright compositions, for example *Still Life with Clay Figure III* of 1938[5] and have less agitated brushwork than the figures. He had obviously been looking at Cézanne again. Fruit and flower works also burgeoned during these fecund years.

In art, several turbulent regroupings and significant exhibitions took place in the 1930s which even Smith in his Aix paradise must have noted, perhaps with some alarm, since none of them endorsed the kind of art he was producing. The Surrealists, most of them immigrants to France, had international exhibitions in London in 1936 and Paris in 1938. Similarly abstraction was growing on French soil, fertilized by such foreigners as Mondrian, Kandinsky, and Brancusi. Even the feeble but popular French Neo-Romanticism was mostly powered by Russians. Native French art was still carried forward by Matisse's heroic generation, now middle aged or old, who had made their major breakthroughs before the First World War, but the long-term future of the Ecole de Paris that Smith knew looked increasingly doubtful as a new war approached.

Back home art was also moving into territories which Smith had no interest in exploring. The Euston Road School had been formed in the autumn of 1937 by artists who claimed to be 'Objective Realists' following an aesthetic of close observation. Its characteristics were subdued colours, drab subjects and a painstaking method of measurement and paint application. It was an attempt to return to traditional English, rather than French, values and to spread art beyond the élite few, but it was disbanded by summer 1939. However, William Coldstream was to go on to inculcate its style into his Slade students from 1949 onwards.

Paul Nash and his wife visited Smith on the Riviera and risked their necks by accepting a tour in Modestine. No doubt he told Smith about his ideas for Unit One, a grouping of the English avant-garde, but Smith would not have felt much empathy with this mixture of near-surrealists and semi-abstractionists. Another creative nucleus was in Hampstead where Herbert Read's 'Nest of Gentle Artists' were all moving towards a kind of painting 'without upholstery'. Nicholson and Hepworth had been invited as equals to join the Paris based Abstract-Création Group in 1933 and the same year Nicholson had made his first *White Relief*. Nicholson had taken over the 7 and 5 Society and in 1935 they held the first all-abstract exhibition in Britain. *Axis* magazine was launched in 1935 to discuss abstract art and Read and Kenneth Clark locked horns in *The Listener* over the relative merits of abstraction and figuration. This group round Read looked to Mondrian, Braque, Arp, Hélion and Brancusi, who represented a cooler line of Parisian modernism than the hedonistic Matisse-led one that Smith had followed. There would be no roly-poly half-nudes in petticoats from these Hampstead ascetics nor any vulgar colours such as brown, purple, green or orange, because white was now the colour which represented all things modern.

Some of these new cliques rejected Bell's 'significant form' theories and took a political stance as well as an artistic one. While Smith had been living the life of an epicure in the south of France events in other parts of Europe had taken a distinctly nasty turn. These were the years of the Depression, hunger marches, the rise of Fascism in Germany, Italy and Britain, the persecution of Jews in Germany, show trials and purges in Russia and the Spanish Civil War, all leading inexorably to a second World War. In response British painters and sculptors set up the Artists' International Association in 1933 with its slogan 'conservative in art, radical in politics,' and followed the Russians' lead into Socialist Realism painting. Behind this politicization of poetry, prose, painting, sculpture and drama was a belief that art could change society for the better by participating in the analysis of its problems and by suggesting solutions. When war came there was a terrible disillusionment for, as Auden wrote home from the safety of New York:

> Art in intention is mimesis
> But, realised, the resemblance ceases;
> Art is not life, and cannot be
> A midwife to society.
> For art is a fait accompli.
> ('New Year Letter', 1940)

Some artists had always known that. Matisse and Bonnard for example, whose contribution to these austere times was to celebrate those physical things which made life worth living – food, wine, sunlight, flowers and beautiful young flesh. After all, this guilt-free hedonism was one of France's great contributions to the world's art. Smith was obviously of this celebratory school of thought, though he never felt the need to justify himself in words. We have no recorded reaction by him to any of the dire events of the 1930s or indeed to political crises of any other period, except that in the 1950s he suggested that if we were going to have an atom bomb we ought to have the best, and then drop it on the Russians. His political vision, like his eyesight, was myopic, but that does not lessen his stature as an artist.

When the war forced Smith to return reluctantly to England he was doomed to find himself out of touch with all these new ideas and younger artists, though not with his own generation of enlightened patrons. Between March 1928 and July 1938 Tooth's had sold 189 paintings to such collectors as Dudley Wallis, Angus Wilson, Charles Laughton, Victor Gollancz, Michael Sadler, Kenneth Clark, J. B. Priestley and assorted lords and ladies. His studio book also lists sales to Arnold Bennett, Maynard Keynes, Duncan Grant, Jacob Kremer, and Hugh Walpole. Epstein, John, Brooks and Halliday continued to buy or beg directly from Smith.

In 1937 the Exposition Universelle was held in Paris where the most remarkable works were by Spaniards: murals by Miró, an artist Smith had once met through Brooks, and *Guernica* by Picasso. Smith can have hardly failed to see *Guernica*, though neither the political theme nor the dismembered forms could be related to his own work. In July of the same year Hitler organized his *Entartete Kunst* exhibition in Munich to mock art made by such decadents as Picasso with his African-influenced forms, and all Marxists, Jews, Abstractionists, Expressionists and non-Aryans. In the same month an exhibition entitled *The Entente Cordiale* was shown at the Lefevre Gallery as a riposte and to emphasize British solidarity with our French neighbours in the impending troubles. Smith was shown alongside the painters he felt most admiration for: Bonnard, Braque, Derain, Friesz, Matisse, Rouault, Utrillo, Vuillard and Segonzac. By now he could hold his own in such exalted company and was considered every bit as worthy as the other senior English contributors such as Bell, Grant, John, Lewis, Nash, Sickert, Steer and Wadsworth.

At the same time Smith showed work in Paris at the Galérie Bing alongside Sickert and Christopher Wood (with a catalogue preface by de Segonzac) – though with war looming it was not the best time to attract the French connoisseurs. Further afield he had twenty-three works on display (alongside those of Nash, Spencer, Wood, Epstein, Anderson and Blair Hughes-Stanton) at the British pavilion in the 1938 Venice Biennale – though critical response seems to have been just as muted as it had been in Paris.[6]

Smith's friendship with Epstein still held firm. In spite of his sales of flower paintings and portrait busts, by 1939 the sculptor was in financial trouble. He had a bitter choice between selling his collection of African carvings from which he drew so much sculptural inspiration, or his Matthew Smiths which gave him so much sensuous pleasure. Reluctantly he decided to sell twenty-eight Smiths through the Leicester Galleries (Tooth's, as Smith's agents, were indignant). Smith returned for a chilly family Christmas in Norfolk and then, in spite of a heavy cold, he helped Epstein hang the exhibition for the January opening. Half were sold on the first day at around £150 each, so Epstein's debts were met.

The *Times* critic, who had a clear image of his readership, explained to them: 'The general effect of this exhibition is like nothing so much as that of a generous Burgundy, full, deep, warm, and fragrant, and to be taken in grateful gulps'.[7] Other writers thought that Titian and Veronese would have enjoyed the show and that 'Wagnerian' best summed it up.

By February Smith was back with Marion and stayed until mid-August when he left Aix for a trip to Geneva to see some old masterpieces on loan from the Prado. He drove there in Modestine with the Monays as passengers. Whilst in Switzerland his old nervous paralysis returned severely enough for him to go into hospital and then to retreat once more to the Clinique Valmont for a total of six weeks, where the Monays were his only visitors. Cataracts were also diagnosed in each eye ('cheerful *n'est pas*' he wrote to Brooks) and he confided that he thought he was not going to recover from his 'never ending tensions' – not the least of which were his worries about his sons, both now pilots in the war that was declared whilst he was convalescing. He decided he must take a duty trip home for Christmas.

He narrowly missed Mark, who had been on leave but left for Aden just before Christmas on a daredevil solo trip in a plane he had bought for £60. He refuelled at Italian bases en route, Gwen's brother Jack having pulled strings on his behalf. Smith had food poisoning in London, then struggled back to a snow-covered Aix and the warm arms of Marion by late January 1940, and worked on in spite of the late spring, painful eyes, and the worsening news through his letter box. This came thick and fast.

First in April he reported to Halliday: 'I had the sad news a week or two ago that Roderic O'Conor had died. His wife sent me a line . . . I feel it very much I had known him and admired him and failed to write to him which is sad now'.[8] They had lost touch after 1933 when O'Conor had at last married Renée and left Paris for village life in Maine-et-Loire.

Mark wrote from Egypt to his father: 'I haven't heard from Dermot lately. I think it is nearly time he shot somebody down and got a DFC. Do you see any war where you are? . . . I have been trying to persuade Mama that all this war work she is trying to do is nonsense. She and you have done your stuff by producing cannon-fodder in the shape of Mark and Dermot.'[9] Such bravado seemed to be tempting the gods.

In mid-May Dermot was flying off Holland when he was shot through the left forearm and right shoulder, and had two broken ribs. He managed to land the plane and did indeed receive the DFC. Gwen wrote to him on 31 May, 'Daddy wants to come home but says if the war comes to Aix it will look bad if he leaves which makes one feel he has real ties there!'[10]

Then on 2 June a telegram informed Smith that Mark had been killed in a flying accident in Aden (some accounts say while stunt flying). Smith could stay in Marion's embrace no longer. He left his rolled-up canvases with the Monays, took a plane from Marseille to Paris on 5 June but ineptly arrived too late to catch his London flight the next morning. After two days of frustrating bureaucracy he was helped by the diplomat Donald Maclean on to another plane and back to London on 8 June. On the 14th the Germans marched into Paris.

CHAPTER 16

Another War
1940–41

Back in London news filtered through, often by the most circuitous route, of those Smith had left behind in France. He received letters from the Monays via the USA and Portugal and his sad but passionate replies were routed through Geneva. None of the news was good. He was difficult to reach by letter since he was constantly on the move round various seedy hotels and studios across London, interspersing these with visits outside London to Harold in Cheshire, Phyllis in Watford, the Hugheses in Hertfordshire, Michaelises in Oxfordshire, Hallidays in Wales and the Johns in Hampshire, where at each place he was fussed over and given decent meals. He also visited Gwen and wrote to his sister about Mark's death: 'Our loss is a perpetual grief a really quite unbearable wound and of course still worse for Gwen even than for me though of course she appears very brave about it as of course she would be.'[1] This was written from Oxford where he had retreated, miserable and weary, to a nursing home to have a hernia operation. However, Gwen told Phyllis, 'He looks very well, is feeling well, really, *Quite Happy*'.[2]

In London Matthew narrowly escaped being blown up when a Sloane Square hotel he was staying in was bombed and he saw the nearby Underground gaping open and many injured pulled from the wreckage. His pre-war paintings remained locked up in the store at 7 Clarendon Gardens and he would wake in a cold sweat fearing they had been bombed to smithereens; yet there seemed little point in setting up an easel to make more when he felt restlessly compelled to move on every few weeks.

When the bombing began the London art world almost disappeared. The public collections were sent out of the capital for safe storage, though the National Gallery put on *British Painting since Whistler* in 1940 and included six of Smith's works. Soon the art schools were evacuated, and two-thirds of the commercial galleries closed. No foreign works entered the country and so English painters were thrown back on their own resources. Nevertheless, a few galleries did keep their doors open (the Leicester, Lefevre and Zwemmer galleries for example) and continued to show living painters, including Smith. Eventually London was left as the only free and semi-functioning art centre in Europe.

Kenneth Clark was now the biggest fish in this very reduced pond, having been appointed Fry's literary executor, Surveyor of the King's Pictures, and Director of the National Gallery at the age of twenty-nine, so that his powers of patronage were enormous. When a War Artists Advisory Committee was set up under Clark's chairmanship he appointed only those painters he wanted to keep working and protected from danger. He explained in *The Studio*:

The War Artists collection cannot be completely representative of modern British art, because it cannot include those pure painters who are interested solely in putting down their feelings about shapes and colours, and not in facts, drama, and human emotions generally. For this reason it contains no work by such distinguished painters as Matthew Smith, Frances Hodgkins, Ethel Walker, Ivon Hitchens, Ben Nicholson and Victor Pasmore. It would be a pleasure to see the names of these fine painters among those of the War Artists, but it is very doubtful if they would do as good work on war subjects as they are continuing to do on the subjects which they have made their own.[3]

In Smith's case it was a reasonable decision because the anecdotal or tragic were beyond his scope. Clark bought several of Smith's works for his own collection, including the superb *Peaches* of 1935, but more to give encouragement than from real enthusiasm. Later he sold them with the comment that Smith could now get on without his support.

Alden Brooks had left Grez and gone to write in Hollywood and it was from there that he wrote to Smith offering his condolences on Mark's death, and expressing his disgust at French collaboration with the Germans. He was anxious for the USA to join in the fight for

European freedom but feared 'Communist propaganda has made sixty percent of our youth pink rabbits.'[4]

Early in 1941 Dermot was sent by the RAF to Washington to recover from his wounds and to try to help persuade the Americans to join the war. Brooks went to meet him and reported that Dermot was 'splendidly fit . . . and quite on the crest of the wave', and he was enthusiastic about American cars, women and food. Brooks was shocked to see how like a wraith Smith looked in the photograph Dermot carried with him and to cheer him up recalled happier times in France: 'How often I look back at it, seeing us sitting together, now in a café at Sens, now by the sea in Brittany, or your trying to paint in the wind at Doelan, or the sailing hotel at Quimperlé, or another hotel at Toulon and a morning exit, and how much more.' He reported that his own house in Grez had been pillaged by the Germans who had looted his paintings, including a landscape by Smith and his wife's copy of Gauguin's *Nevermore*.[5]

Another friend trying to cheer Smith was Augustus John. His sister Gwen had died in September 1939 in Dieppe after many years of solitary self-neglect, but Augustus was still in robust form and back in the critics' good books after 112 of his drawings had been displayed at the National Gallery in November 1940. His rambling autobiography was appearing in instalments in *Horizon* magazine; Lilian Browse and Rothenstein were both preparing books on him; and in June 1942 the old reprobate was raised to the Order of Merit (the fact that he was not married to Dorelia, the mother of some of his children, apparently barred him from being presented at the Palace for a knighthood). Augustus's twenty-five-year-old daughter Vivien, who had met Smith in Aix, wrote inviting him to join 'the tiny tots' at Fryern – they'd even got some black market food to offer as a bribe. 'Dear Matthew our thoughts are not alike, but we really ought to meet more often – Dear Matthew I'm sure I'm giving you a wrong impression but when I like somebody I like them to know it, at least I can't keep it an interesting secret.'[6]

Another young person who now came into his life in late autumn 1941, and was destined to take over a large part of it, was Mary Keene. 64 At this time she was aged twenty, slim, blonde, pale, with a distinctive long nose, and a refined accent that had only recently been acquired.

She had just married Ralph (Bunny) Keene who was double her age, and they lived at 1 Selwood Place, off the Fulham Road. Keene had worked for Tooth's and had written a perceptive article praising Smith as early as 1934,[7] but now he had moved into film-making.

Mary, young as she was, had an eventful past. She was born in Limehouse to a penurious and violent widow, spent some time in an orphanage, and at the age of eleven was run over by a lorry and lost her right foot and had to be fitted with a metal one. This contraption never seemed to inhibit her in any way nor to diminish her attraction for men. She was sent to a 'cripple school' and taught nothing that would help her earn a living or run a household. Her teens were spent in extreme poverty working in various London sweatshops and then on one occasion acting as a model at Cedric Morris's art school in Dedham, where she met and perhaps posed for Lucian Freud. She drifted into the literary-arty world of Soho where the poet Ruthven Todd declared her to be 'the most beautiful girl I ever saw.' Then in 1939 at age seventeen she had a love affair with the poet Louis MacNeice and soon after became the lover of the novelist Henry Yorke (who wrote under the name Henry Green).[8] Both men were then in their thirties and it is clear that Mary, who had never known the love of a father, preferred older creative men.

One of Bunny Keene's friends was Dick Wyndham, a journalist and painter who invited them all to his house at Tickeridge Mill in Sussex, where Smith drew Mary and taught her to ride a bicycle. Wyndham then wrote an admiring but inaccurate article on Smith for the August 1942 edition of *Horizon* magazine and reproduced a fine portrait of Mary bundled up in two sweaters and a coat.[9] The Dylan Thomases were Mary's friends too, particularly Caitlin who, like so many others, had been pounced on by Augustus John whilst posing. The same may have happened to Mary who also sat for him.

It is not clear how or where Mary first met Smith but a letter of early 1942 is already addressing him as 'Darlingest Matthew.' In spite of her minimal education she was an avid reader and had literary ambitions as well as toying with the idea of film and stage work. She introduced Smith to Henry Green who quickly became his friend, and Smith in turn introduced her to Dermot, though she soon made it clear she preferred the distinguished father to the callow son. From now on her letters came in a torrent, telling Smith of her illnesses, dreams, clothes, invitations, visits to operas and concerts, boredom, debts, and thanks for all the cheques and flowers he kept sending her. He hoarded these letters, and one day she would inherit them all back again.

The emotion passing between them became a strong bond, but at times it felt more like a shackle: both Mary Keene and Matthew Smith seemed to lack a protective skin, and as time went on every little setback or slight was like a terrible wound to be brooded over, scratched at and enlarged. They were lonely people with too much time on their hands in which to mull over imagined injustices or magnify slights into major crises. The letters are full of reproaches and protestations of love, apologies and accusations, misunderstandings and devastating insights. They became inextricably bound together by ties of love and hate, unable to part but unable ever to live together. 'He knows not what it is to burn/Who can his flame in words express,' Smith wrote to her.[10] And again, 'you are a sensitive plant and there are only little bits here and there of this world that are made or near enough made for you, but that is partly why some of us love you so much.'[11] Not all his friends did love her, and several were resentful of the demands this girl now made on his time and attention.

If Mary was now his main amorous interest he was still intermittently in touch with an old one. Vera Cuningham had returned from France to a flat at 47 Heath Street, opposite Hampstead tube station. She was still painting and still unmarried, though she had lovers, one being the painter Denis Matthews. As part of her war effort she had volunteered as an air-raid warden, patrolling the unlit streets for £2 5s per week to enforce the blackout. Smith wrote to her with a cheque, saying, 'I do admire you for what you are doing I must say. I would rather like to see you strolling round of a night with your thumb stuck in your belt and looking rather awe-inspiring in your tin hat!'[12] She also organized the Civil Defence Artists Association in an empty gallery, making many painters squirm with her scathing and tactless judgements.

Other links with Smith's past were to be found on his forays into Fitzrovia, now the wartime meeting place for artistic and literary London, as well as being the market place for sex of all persuasions.

This area round Charlotte Street, which encompassed his old haunts in Fitzroy Street as well as Soho and its pubs, cafés, restaurants and drinking clubs, attracted those who needed company to help them through the drab days and hideous nights. He would go with Augustus John and encounter former models such as Betty May or the artist Nina Hamnett, now both in alcoholic decline. Smith could indulge his taste for the disreputable here, though he never succumbed, as so many did, to that combination of drink, talk and wishful thinking that the poet Tambimuttu called 'Sohoitis'. Smith always seemed able to pull himself back from whatever threatened to overwhelm him as a man and to return to his work. But the next blow almost pushed him over the edge.

On his return from America Dermot had been made a squadron leader and posted to Wales. From his base he would fly over the Hallidays' home and waggle his wings in greeting. One day he told a fledgling pilot to follow him up in order to demonstrate the tricks of combat, but once in the air he spotted a German plane, gave chase and was last seen by the novice going down in flames ten miles off the coast of Ireland. Gwen's brother Jack, now very senior in the RAF, turned up at Matthew's hotel just before Christmas 1941 to announce that Dermot had been killed on 22 December. His body was not recovered, though his camera full of undeveloped film was returned to his father, and an official letter sent to Gwen at a hotel on the Cromwell Road where she had moved in order to work in wartime censorship.

Smith's relationship with Gwen had continued to be tense and even though they now had this tragedy in common they could not share it. He shirked spending the following bleak Christmas with her even though she lived so near, because 'I fear Christmas is always the date that I most dread in the year, and I behave like an ostrich until the last moments when out comes my head and I make frantic and futile efforts and feel so sad and tormented about it all.'[13] Instead he spent the time with his brother Arthur and she with Jack. Later, on behalf of them both, he presented a wonderful still life of 1936 to the Tate in memory of their two sons, though he would contribute nothing towards the memorial Gwen set up in her local parish church.

Smith wrote to Halliday of Dermot: 'I am full of so many remorses . . . He really was the apple of my eye and it does seem incredible that

that apparently joyous and colourful boy should have gone for ever.'[14] He also told Cecil Beaton there was no one in the whole world who could put so much relish and enjoyment into the word 'delicious' as Dermot. Evidently the religion of Smith's childhood offered no consolations. The Hallidays took him to Wales 'and used to plant him in the mornings in a deck chair by the sea. When they went back to collect him in the afternoons they would find him as they left him, slumped in his chair in the same position.'[15]

During one of these 1942 stays with the Hallidays he painted two small ($11\frac{1}{2}$ x $8\frac{1}{2}$ in.) panels of Francis and Mary. These are vigorously brushed in with hot reds and ochres relieved only by Mary's deep blue dress, but they look like trial runs for more finished works which were never completed. The Hallidays also encouraged him to paint the landscape round Abermule, but he found it then, and on subsequent visits, too complex and lacking in the wide vistas he had come to love in France. Their son Christopher remembers how he and his sister were kept quiet and away from their distinguished guest, though Smith would probably have preferred their lively company to that of his paintbox at this depressing time.

Death must have been constantly on Smith's mind during the early years of the war. Apart from the death of his sons he saw the carnage in the London blitz and people he had known in the art world began to die off. Tonks had gone in 1937; Brown in 1941; Steer died blind and Sickert gaga in 1942. His own health continued to be robust in spite of his heavy smoking, drinking, lack of exercise apart from walking the streets, and rackety bachelor lifestyle, and yet most of his letters begin with complaints about how low he is feeling or of his latest cold, stomach upset or eye soreness. Dr Herbert, who at this time became his doctor and would remain so for the rest of his life, seemed to find nothing serious to worry about: Smith swallowed his placebos and pills and paid his fees in paintings. The problem was not with his body but his numbed mind. He could no longer flee to the Valmont Clinic for therapy and his anxious friends realized that the only way he could retain his sanity was to return to painting. And the only way that could be brought about would be for him to receive the inspiring attentions of one or more beautiful young women.

56

CHAPTER 17

A Slow Revival
1942–1944

Other friends besides the Hallidays were trying to get Smith involved in art again. Epstein invited Matthew down to his cottage in Epping Forest to sketch with him and to listen to a proposal. *Let There Be Sculpture*, Epstein's autobiography, had been published at the end of 1940 and he had taken the opportunity to speak his mind about English critics and architects, so once more he was under attack. He was also broke as usual and convinced that there was a conspiracy against him, which there probably was. Taking part in a joint show was something Smith could do to show solidarity with his besieged friend, so this was arranged at Temple Newsam House, an Elizabethan mansion near Leeds, in 1942. Matthew had forty-four pre-war oils in this exhibition and the two friends' expressionistic styles in oils and clay complemented each other nicely. The next year Hepworth and Paul Nash were paired as exhibitors at Temple Newsam, which provided a marked contrast in styles and temperaments to the Smith–Epstein show. Simultaneously Tooth's organized an exhibition of Smith's works at Lefevre's since their own gallery had been bombed, and this was a great success with a public cut off from colour and France. Eric Newton welcomed it as 'a warm big hearted gesture, like sunshine on bare flesh' after the dour and prickly works of the younger Neo-Romantic artists.[1]

Smith, Epstein and John, all now in their sixties, were becoming the Grand Old Men of English art and rather out of sympathy with what was happening within the introverted younger generation. Sutherland, Nash and Piper had turned to the English countryside and saw it through the lenses of our own Romantic landscape tradition rather than

through the French. This seemed an appropriate celebration of English-
ness when the nation's very existence was in the balance, or as Cyril
Connolly put it: 'At the moment civilization is on the operating table
and we sit in the waiting room'. Still younger painters such as Vaughan,
Minton, Ayrton, Craxton, Colquhoun and MacBryde had followed and
put their own interpretations on what became known as English Neo-
Romanticism. Their works were moon-haunted, full of ruins, deserted
streets or skeletal trees and totally at odds with anything Smith, John or
Epstein would have painted. If there were any vestiges of the pre-war
School of Paris in these austere works then they derived from Picasso
rather than from Matisse.[2]

Mary Keene continued to dominate Matthew's amorous thoughts   63
and early in 1943 he hired a cottage from Ida, the wife of the wood-
engraver Blair Hughes-Stanton (who was then a prisoner of war), in
Stratford St Mary in East Anglia. To this he invited Mary, but between
them they reduced the exquisitely restored cottage to such squalor that
they were ejected with legal retribution threatened for the damage and
missing items. He fled leaving behind his palette, pyjamas and bicycle,
but later expressed surprise to Ida that she should have been 'so
bourgeois' as to be upset by damage to mere material possessions. Smith
was not used to alarums like this, but would have to bear more from
Mary in the years to come. He seems at this time to have been amicably
sharing Mary's favours with Henry Yorke, both with the connivance of
Bunny Keene, who was having his own affairs, and of Yorke's wife Dig.

Before the war Dermot had begun to move in rather fast company
and had met in the so-called 'Chelsea Set' the daughter of the Marquess   57
Townsend, Lady Elizabeth White. She was already unhappily married
to Sir Richard White but fell in love with Dermot, who must have
introduced her to his father, because after Dermot's death she became
Smith's second most frequent sitter during the war years after Mary
Keene. A cousin of hers, Lauretta Hope-Nicholson, also sat for her
portrait, and the two women appeared, arms round each other, in a
double work of 1941, his third to be called *The Two Sisters*.[3] Elizabeth   55
later divorced, published a book of poems dedicated to the memory of
Dermot, took to drink and suffered an early death.

These pictures of Elizabeth and Lauretta are not silkily ingratiating society portraits in the Sargent or Ingres manner, or remotely like those in the Royal Academy annual exhibition, though they are of well-bred women famous for their beauty. They lack the obvious charm of female portraits by Renoir, Matisse, Bonnard or Dufy, or, nearer home, of Augustus John. There is no attempt to flatter, or slavishly imitate the glossy surfaces of their skin or clothes or hair, or to deck them with symbolic jewels or gowns – though flowers are still stock accessories. There is something riskily intimate about such portrait painting: both participants have to consent to the exposure and scrutiny and have to live with the results – and some hated them. To Matthew's credit he was more concerned to make a painting than an academic likeness. Other names which have been attached to the many paintings of women from this period are Henry Yorke's niece Josephine Lowry-Corry, Jacqueline Fothergill, Mavis Wheeler (wife of Sir Mortimer Wheeler and mistress of Augustus John) and a beautiful girl called Lucy who posed for some outstanding nudes.

Several sitters seemed to have wanted to comfort him in his melancholy, to feed him and tell him to put another cardigan on. He was self-absorbed, grouchy and a complainer at times but he attracted, at all periods of his life, intelligent women who perhaps sensed a mystery, a vulnerability which needed protecting, a suffering that needed cool hands and warm lips to soothe it away. Of course Smith enjoyed this coddling, but then invariably saw things in sexual terms and wanted more than comfort, and often received it. It seemed that before long he was coming out of his depression, saved by the two things which mattered most to him: his work and attractive young women.

Smith also portrayed his brother Arthur's pretty daughter, Phoebe, in several works entitled *Young Actress*. Phoebe was a chorus girl in London musicals and this gave Smith entry to several theatrical parties where he could sit quietly admiring the actresses. One of his portraits of her was bought by the Tate and after his death Mary Keene gave another to his native Halifax. Later Phoebe's mother attacked Smith for never painting her or Arthur. 'This embarrassed me dreadfully and I came away almost suicidal,' he wrote to Mary, but he stubbornly refused to paint people who did not arouse his interest.[4]

58

59

Another young woman who tracked him down, this time to a flat in Motcomb Street, was the actress Valerie Hobson. She remembers that in the middle of the war she bought a small nude from an exhibition and was introduced to the artist. He invited her to tea, and so began another long friendship. She was then married to Anthony Havelock Allan and all three of them would go to Brighton together and stroll with linked arms along the pier. She was just beginning to acquire fame as an actress and Smith, with his love of all things theatrical, was fascinated by her show business connections as well as her glamour. She sat for perhaps eight or nine oils over the years and many drawings, posing in a variety of poorly furnished and cramped studios. She recalls that he worked fast, silently, and always by artificial light. From a woman's point of view she found him colourless to look at but with exquisite manners, delicate hands and a vivid laugh. He was not articulate, a slow hesitant speaker, but a good listener, genuinely interested in people and their problems – for example he was extremely caring over Valerie's handicapped son and her elderly mother.

60

Mary Keene did not approve of these rivals for Smith's time and admiration. Augustus John encountered her in a highly-strung state 'with a yellow face and magenta lips . . . she shouldn't take so much whisky,' he wrote to Matthew.[5] She was jealous of the other women Smith painted and perhaps slept with, such as Simone Renwick: 'Saw that Simone on Saturday which depressed me for 2 days, there is something so raw and animal about her which is rather horrible I think, and the dreadful complete lack of gentleness and tenderness. You may perhaps think I am biased. I thought the canvas of her very good.'[6] This Simone would keep up an impassioned correspondence with Smith long after she had married and left England.

Another young person who came into Smith's orbit and stayed for life was Roald Dahl. He had come back in July 1941 from flying for the RAF in North Africa, invalided home after a bad crash, and now had money and time to spare. Strolling round the drab streets he had come across a few of Smith's works glowing in the Bond Street dealers' windows and decided he had enough cash to buy one, and if possible he would like to meet the artist. He was directed to a cheap hotel in Fulham Road, but Smith had moved on, as he had also from a boarding house in Edith Grove. 'I remember him well. Quiet as a mouse. He only stayed a few days then he scuttled away,' the landlady told Dahl. From there he followed Smith's trail through numerous seedy lodgings until he found him at the Hamilton House Hotel near Hyde Park Corner, then much run down. Eventually he found the right room with one of the Brandenburg Concertos wheezing through the door from a tinny gramophone. Smith answered his knock 'like a small frightened animal out of its hole.'

'I . . . well . . . I really only came here to tell you how much I like your pictures,' I said, because that was all I had to say. I did not realise then that he had not long before lost both his sons in the RAF, and that the shock of suddenly seeing a young man standing outside his door in full RAF uniform with wings on his chest must have been tremendous. It bowled him over. 'Come in,' he said, 'Do come in.' He was in stockinged feet and there were holes in both socks. He began talking very fast. The hands fluttered, the words tumbled out in a nervous torrent. 'I'm sorry I'm in such a mess. Everything's in a mess. Oh, what an awful mess. Where are you going to sit? I can't do things properly. I can't do anything properly these days. I don't know what's the matter with me. How nice to see you. How good of you to come . . .'[7]

And so Smith, then sixty-two, began a friendship with the twenty-five year old Dahl who was in many ways much more worldly-wise than he was. Dahl, like Dermot before him, was posted to Washington in winter 1941 to act as an Assistant Air Attaché at the Embassy, but on his return Smith painted his portrait which the sitter said 'took two or three sessions of about an hour and a half each, during which Smith worked at furious speed, only stopping to "fuss" at the end of each session.'

61   This might be taken as an example of the kind of portrait Smith did best. It was painted in a fury of concentration – his sitters all agree they were not allowed to chat or move an eyelash until the end of the sittings, when Smith collapsed exhausted. The composition was worked out broadly on a white primed canvas in charcoal or more usually thin turpsy paint (often crimson) which could be wiped and corrected: once satisfied with this Smith worked at a gallop, standing well back from the sitter. There was no analysis of character, and even getting a likeness was a hit or miss affair (Gwen was better at this). Dahl's portrait is typical in being half-length, right-facing with the light falling from the

36 *Nude on a Red Divan*, 1923–4
37 *Yorkshire Landscape*, 1926

38 *Laura the Parrot*, 1928
39 *Nude, c.* 1925
40 *The Red Sari, c.* 1931

41 *Still Life with Blue Jug and Date Box, c.* 1925

42 *The Two Sisters*, 1931
43 *Model Waking*, 1931

44 *Self Portrait*, 1932
45 Christiane de Mauberg, date unknown
46 *Nude with Necklace*, c. 1931

47 *Mont Sainte-Victoire*, 1932
48 *Evening Landscape near Aix*, date unknown

49 *Peaches*, 1935
50 *Portrait of Christiane*, 1934–6

51 *Vase of Flowers with Apple*, no date

52 *Marion Monay*, 1939

53 *Nude with Yellow Roses (Aniése Moreau)*, 1936–7

54 *The Two Sisters*, 1936–7
55 *The Two Sisters*, c. 1941

56 *Francis Halliday*, 1942
57 *Elizabeth White Holding a Rose*, 1942–5
58 *Young Actress (Phoebe)*, 1943
59 *Young Girl with Arms Folded (Phoebe)*, c. 1943

60 *Valerie Hobson, c.* 1951

61 *Roald Dahl, c.* 1944

62 *Augustus John,* 1944

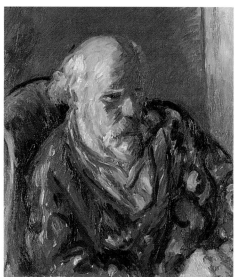

64 Mary Keene

63 *Mary Keene, c.* 1950

65 *Peaches in a Striped Dish*, 1950
66 *Fruit in a Blue Dish*, 1950–55

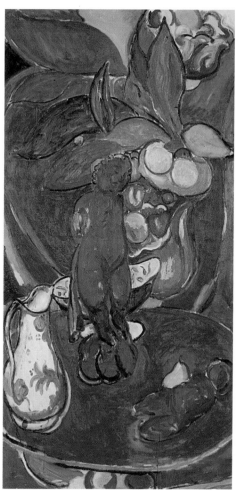

67 *Patricia Neal*, 1954
68 *Cathleen Mann*, 1952
69 *Large Decoration I, c.* 1952–3

70 Matthew Smith in his Yeoman's Row studio, 1956

left and the background made shallow by a draped cloth behind the head. It is a painting first and a portrait second: there are full-blooded colours, vigorous slashes and scribbles of fluid paint from which form solidifies, a strong simple composition and all detail is subdued to the minimum. Given this method it is not surprising that sometimes the paintings went wrong and the wet colours became muddy under his flying brushes. Sometimes, too, he failed to find fresh ways of sitting a model in a chair or supporting a cheek on a palm and the result looks routine and tired. He would wait a few weeks before looking at them afresh and if they could not be rescued he destroyed them ruthlessly by slashing them with a knife. He did not paint over spoiled canvases as many painters have to do to save money.

Cecil Beaton admired Smith's 'meaty great nudes and violently sensuous still lifes' and was surprised when they met to find a 'whisp of a man' with frail and trembling hands, rather than the Hercules he had expected. Over lunch Smith moaned about all the miserable places he had lived in, then unexpectedly opened up about his working methods:

'Work in progress is so difficult to discuss,' he said. 'What I am doing now may be experimental; it is different from the stuff I did in France before the war – the colours less vivid. Changes of life, light and environment influence my work, and emotional crises bring about tremendous reactions. Now,' he complained, 'I am completely knocked off my perch without that piece of material which I always use for my backgrounds. I came across it accidentally many years ago when I was lying on a bed; and it's been the background for all my paintings ever since; that, and a screen I designed. Now I am stranded without the piece of material and the screen; they are in France, and God knows if I shall ever see them again. I look everywhere, but I can't find anything that compares. Just occasionally in life one sees some colour combination that pleases – three colours hung up in a shop – that one would never have thought of. But, oh! What one has to contend with during a war! The difficulty of getting the right quality paint! My people have written to say they are closing down, so I've ordered a great quantity of Venetian or Titian yellow. It's lovely for skies; for white – it's yellow so pale that it looks transparent. I paint while the paint is wet; a picture is finished for me once the paints dry, but that means an appalling amount of concentration while the picture is in progress. I paint my picture at one sitting, and get so exhausted that sometimes for three days afterwards I'm ill in bed, racked by appalling pains, and then when I get up and find the picture is no good I become so depressed that I wonder if it is all worthwhile.'[8]

Beaton then persuaded Smith to be photographed 'in the late-Victorian manner with cloak and stick; and, although he knew that in the results he would be "over-hatted", he wore the large felt trilby which comes down on to his nose like a candle snuffer.'

Smith was now looking his age, thin and stooped, but both Dahl and Valerie Hobson could not but remark that his pursuit of young women, whether waitresses or duchesses, was still obsessional. Dahl thought him too shy to approach them, and this perhaps explained why he went about with worldly younger men such as Halliday, or Dahl himself, or favoured the company of such womanizers as John and Epstein, neither of whom could be called bashful or slow to make their interests known.

Prostitutes, on the other hand, did the approaching themselves: one pair, judging him by his expensive clothes to be at least a bank manager, threatened to shout out of his window and expose him, but he merely laughed. Once he was robbed by a woman he had taken back to his flat, and on another occasion whilst riding on a bus he thrust a note of assignation into a pretty woman's hand only to have an entirely different and plainer woman turn up at his door next day. He cheerfully told these stories against himself to his friends, carefully cultivating the reputation for blundering helplessness he had acquired in his youth.

In spite of all these friends and acquaintances Smith was a lonely man during the war years, often dining alone and brooding for days in his poky little lodgings. He ate at the restaurant in his block of flats and on occasions he ventured out to dine at the Athenaeum Club, the Queen's Restaurant or more often at the refurbished Café Royal, 'the resort of the lonely' as Smith described it, where the much younger John Rothenstein, since 1938 Director of the Tate Gallery, would sometimes meet him for a good gossip, and other artists such as John, Epstein, Charles Ginner or Edward le Bas might join them.

The clearest impression was of a melancholy man of about sixty, very pale, wearing a grey check suit of rather formal cut, who read the menu from very near through thick-lensed spectacles, who spoke in an even voice so quiet that it seemed to come from far away, who repeated sentences to which he wished to give emphasis twice over, in precisely similar tones.[9]

Rothenstein felt privileged to be Smith's confidant on these occasions, even though Smith whinged remorselessly about his studios or his sufferings at the hands of women. Moreover, 'although well-read, his intellect was neither wide-ranging nor profound, and he was not a wit.' He revealed 'the courage of a nature constitutionally timid and without a vestige of aggressive impulse, and the benevolence that did not tempt him – except to avoid inflicting gratuitous pain – to refrain from expressing his own strong convictions about anything other than questions concerning himself.'[10] These meetings followed a pattern:

He was a hypochondriac, but a hypochondriac with a difference. I became accustomed to hearing him, barely audible over the telephone, explaining that he felt extremely unwell and wouldn't be able to drink anything, needed urgently to get to bed early, but he would be very happy, provided I understood all this, if we could have some dinner together. At first I was astonished at the way the evening would end, but soon came to accept it as characteristic that well after midnight and after a luxurious dinner with a good deal to drink, and after we had decided to return to our homes, he should order two double brandies and then suddenly remember, for example, that some actress had invited him to a party to which he would thereupon decide to go, expressing his regret that I did not feel 'up' to coming with him.[11]

Others also remember Smith as an enthusiastic party-goer with the stamina to take him through to dawn, when he might leave by taxi with some new young woman on his arm. Apart from his chivalrous charm and his relish for the company of women, one wonders if Smith's money and the possibility of having a portrait done might also have been factors contributing to his popularity on these occasions. Whatever the reason it was clear that Matthew had largely regained his appetite, both for work and for company.

CHAPTER 18

A Book and a Return
1944–1947

The public were thirsty for art, as for music and literature, during the austere war years and one response to this need was a series on English painters published by Penguin Books at two shillings and sixpence each. Kenneth Clark advised on the artists and writers and paired Matthew Smith with Philip Hendy, the curator of his Leeds exhibition with Epstein. Other artists in the series were Piper, Jones, Burra, Moore, Grant, Sutherland, Nash and Pasmore, so he was in distinguished company. Hendy's 1944 book might be seen as an attempt to assess Smith's achievements in mid-career and to place him in his niche. It began by giving with one hand and taking away with the other:

Among the English painters of his generation, the generation which is now in full maturity, it is Matthew Smith alone who seems to me to have a place in the European tradition. It is not a place in the van. He is not great with the warm humanism of a Bonnard or with the clear and varied brilliance of a Matisse; he does not pour out inventions from the overflowing cornucopia of a Picasso. He is, on the contrary, a man with a small repertoire of subjects, in which he propounds what is almost a single, rather narrow theme. Yet the theme is a fundamental one, and his very ability to make a vital art out of a limited material shows that its principles are the grand essential principles of the Continental school. Paris has, in fact, been his capital, and Provence his province.[1]

Hendy depicts a dour struggle upwards from the grey twilight of Halifax to a place in the sun of France and a position in the second stream of the School of Paris. He also began the pseudo-psychological theory which came to annoy Smith so much: 'Some men in their persons and their lives are just like their art, which seems to be only an extension of their personality. Smith is of the opposite kind. Spare and shy and self-deprecatory, he puts into his painting, I should say, the things which nature has not given him. His art is complementary to himself.'[2]

Perhaps this is a way of saying his works are bold and extrovert, but if this is also a hint that their eroticism is a sublimation of a frustrated sexual drive then Hendy could not have known the artist well: at this level the works were surely yet another way of caressing and possessing his women and commemorating his intimacy with them – this is why he never sold many of them. These were the very things which nature *had* given him and the canvases were his notes of thanks.

Hendy explains that the works are full of instinct and passion, largeness of scale, audacity of simplification and forceful composition, though a lack of intellectual control leads to their unevenness and their patches of insensitive form and colour. For these faults Hendy prescribes more lessons from the same French teachers:

If he does not become complacent from the excessive praise which falls to the outstanding man in a country of many collectors and few artists; if instead he links himself more closely with the Continental tradition by studying its science and its greater carefulness of form; then out of his exceptional instinct for colour, out of his fire and courage and bigness of vision new developments will come.[3]

It was a generous evaluation overall, but also a good demonstration of how some critics had been brainwashed by Fry into disparaging their own English tradition and looking to France for its salvation.

Smith's main reaction to the book was odd: he seemed to want his father portrayed in it as the villain he had outwitted in becoming an artist. 'He complained bitterly to me and on several occasions,' wrote Rothenstein, 'that his family's opposition to his becoming a painter had been ignored (although he had made, he said, a special point of it in talking to Philip Hendy), as well as the disastrous and lifelong effect of the consequent friction upon his nerves.'[4] When Rothenstein came to write about Smith later he gave Matthew's version of events full credence, and in my opinion too much emphasis. It is a stereotype in every artist's biography that they have to overcome early opposition, and perhaps Smith was unconsciously trying to conform to this formula.[5] Smith was also rightly disgruntled that Hendy had attributed his depth of colour to the use of glazing (i.e. floating one layer of thin colour over another which then shows through), a technique he never used since it needs time for the lower layers to dry and Smith could not wait in his haste to wrestle his vision down on to the canvas.

Reactions to the book were favourable though muted, but one reviewer thought Smith did not deserve Hendy's encomium for his colour: 'All critics agree that Mr Smith is a modest man, but some of them have encouraged him to exploit a pretentious manner . . . quality in paint is not obtained by lumping it on straight from the tube, the result is invariably poor and greasy.'[6]

One of the pictures in Hendy's book, *Young Actress* (1943), a portrait of Smith's niece Phoebe, had been bought by the Tate. Matthew then asked the Director, Rothenstein, if he could re-touch it.

At last permission was obtained from the Trustees, and one morning in January 1944 he arrived at the Gallery with a very small paintbox and I left him to make a minute rectification – 'only a sixteenth of an inch, you know, only a sixteenth', he explained – on his very broadly, almost coarsely painted canvas. Two hours later I rejoined him and found that after anguished debate with himself he had decided that, after all, no rectification was needed. These two distressing hours, however, were not vainly spent: his doubts were resolved, and I have rarely known him more cheerful than he was at lunch that afternoon at the Café Royal.[7]

In the same year as the book, in May 1944, Mary Keene had a daughter, Alice, and soon after she parted from, and eventually divorced, Ralph Keene, who continued to pay her a small allowance until he remarried and had a new family. To avoid the London bombing she took the baby to the Johns' place at Fryern, near Fordingbridge, Hampshire, earning her lodgings by posing for Augustus, who did at least one superb pencil portrait of her, now in her daughter's possession. She wangled an invitation for Smith, who stayed from August to late October, and the two of them raided the larder and crept into each other's bedrooms after the Johns were safely asleep. Smith reported from there to Halliday, 'My life its usual muddled state, the studios in London both since the spring practically unworkable.'[8] He had been in the Hamilton House Hotel and had moved from one bedroom to another just before his original room was blasted by a bomb. It had been bombed again after he left so now he was trying, without success, to buy a cottage at Bishop's Stortford.

Augustus kept his guest occupied by painting his portrait and inviting Smith to do the same for him. Smith did three paintings in fact, one of them amongst his best, stressing the bare-chested, big belt-buckled, fiery-faced machismo of his host.[9] It is expressionistic in the fierceness of its handling and colour: 'Another haemorrhage from Matthew; all the same he will be a portrait painter yet' was John's verdict. Another showed John in his pyjama jacket and dressing gown, looking hung- 62 over. John returned the compliment with one of his best works, which is now in the Tate Gallery: it is more traditionally painted and acutely penetrating of his sitter's nervous tension. Smith reported on John's effort to Brooks with a mixture of pride and modesty 'but I did not think his so good!! but then think of the model I had and the model he had.'[10]

Mary and the baby moved on from Fryern to stay with the Dylan Thomases in Wales, narrowly escaping injury when an ex-soldier ran amok with a gun after hearing about Dylan's amorous overtures to his wife. Meanwhile Smith returned to London and another lodging in Wilbraham Place. His eyes had been bad all this year: at one point he had to read Brooks's new book on Shakespeare 'with it against my forehead' using one eye at a time because they hurt so much.[11] Even though the Battle of Britain had been won by the RAF, London was still unsafe because the Germans were launching doodlebugs and then rockets across the Channel. However, with the D-Day landings in June the tide of war had begun to turn for the Allies.

By now the conflict had inspired a considerable body of work by British artists, much of it in the Neo-Romantic mode and all of it ignoring the nude as a subject. Smith and Moore showed several works alongside these younger painters in the Lefevre Gallery during April 1945. For once Smith's bravura did not overwhelm his fellow exhibitors because, as if from nowhere, there appeared Francis Bacon's *Three Studies for Figures at the Base of a Crucifixion* (1944), which had nothing to do with the traditional Christian icon but everything to do with the painter's own view of the body as a sack of meat with various orifices, the most horrific of which was the screaming mouth ('Of course we are meat, we are potential carcasses', said Bacon). The break with antiquity and Renaissance idealism was now complete. The picture's nihilistic disgust had no precedent in English art but signalled that Smith's reverent and sensuous approach to the body was going to be severely questioned from now on. Smith's reaction to his own sufferings and those of his country was to turn his back on events, to escape into the consolations of the senses and to affirm in his paintings that what we lived for was the beauty of young women's breasts, the presence of our friends and the few cherished possessions we could assemble on a table-top. It was an affirmation he had earned his right to make at Ypres – a harder lesson than anything Bacon had yet endured in his self-indulgent young life. But such optimism was not going to win Smith many followers amongst the younger artists in the post-war years.

If Smith did not extend his subject range during these disturbing times then he made some technical advances. When the Hughes family invited him to their gracious old house at Pelham Furneaux, Hertfordshire, he drew Iris and the children in pastel and tried watercolour landscapes. He also teased their neighbour, Henry Moore, about his devotion to Picasso. For the summer of 1945 he rented a cottage nearby in Stocking Furneaux and Mary and Halliday visited. He quickly became a fluent, fluid painter of watercolour landscapes and flowers, leaving lots of white paper and keeping the colours bright and unsullied, the very speed of the medium seeming to suit his impetuous attack. Obviously he had studied Cézanne, but there is a sweep and boldness to them that is all Smith's own.

Mary Keene was now set up with her child in a flat at 15 Cheyne Place, Chelsea, for which Smith paid the rent. Henry Yorke paid for her divorce and Vera Cuningham was persuaded to donate some spare furniture. Later Mary sub-let a room to a friend, Kathleen Kavanagh, who in turn sat for Smith's nudes when he needed a change from Mary. In 1944 on Mary's advice Smith moved into 762 Chelsea Cloisters, a narrow one-room cell high in an enormous block of flats in Sloane Avenue, South Kensington, which held about 1,400 other residents. He would make it his main London base for the rest of his life. Rothenstein thought it 'a flat that might have been devised expressly to exasperate. Another might have had no choice, but Matthew was a rich man.' On the other hand, it was so small there was no danger of Mary or any other woman thinking she could move in to share it and he could not be expected to entertain more than one person at a time. He still had his studio at Clarendon Gardens and would continue to have a series of others, possibly as a way of throwing his lady friends off his trail and having a different place in which to meet each new partner. He was never to make himself a home, but on the other hand he was never without several picture-crammed properties on the go at once. As he said, 'I've never really *left* any place.'

Post-war London was not a good place to be for someone who, like Smith, loved good food, wine, stylish clothes and sunshine. Great areas of the capital were in rubble after the bombing, including his old haunts in Fitzroy Street. Food rationing was to last until 1954, clothing required coupons, petrol and domestic fuel were in short supply and no restaurant could serve a meal costing more than five shillings until 1950. Fitzrovia still offered cheap sex and alcohol to those poets, painters, and drifters who wanted to escape their cold bed-sitters and find companionship, but it was poor comfort to someone who had known the hedonism of pre-war Paris and Provence. To sustain him in the drabness of London Brooks sent him shirts, vitamin pills, socks and food parcels ('like being at school' said Smith) and wrote from California, where he had bought a hacienda in the mountains and a beach house at Malibu, that he was nostalgic for Paris and Grez but that the lotus-eater's life of sun and cheap alcohol had sapped his will to travel. He invited Smith to Hollywood because 'it would put ten years on your life. Not only the climate, but for the ten thousand virtually naked lovely women walking the beaches and the streets to brighten those poor tired eyes of yours.'[12]

Churchill, the politician Smith most admired, was ousted by the British voters in the first peacetime elections. Smith wrote about it to Henry Yorke who, besides being a successful novelist, was the managing director of the family firm in Birmingham and enjoyed an affluent lifestyle in Knightsbridge: 'People like us have no doubt to be beggared before the new world can start, I quite see that, we are being told it in one form or another every day, the trouble is that we are likely to be taken at our face value rather than at our real. Justly we should be *raised up* and given extra marmalade.'[13]

Smith now needed to get away from London with its bombed-out shabbiness and emotional entanglements and to go back to his beloved France to pick up his pre-war canvases. He had also received a letter from Marion, now safely in Switzerland, which brought back all the feelings he had suppressed during their long separation. He heard that the Monays had endured privations in Aix and all Marion's lovely hair had fallen out as a consequence – though fortunately it grew again.

Somehow he evaded the £25 travel allowance and set off in late summer 1946 to Paris, which was full of Americans – tourists, writers, GIs, Marshall Plan bureaucrats, all dollar-rich in a city as dingy as London. From there Smith saw Ortiz off to the USA with tears in his eyes and later heard from Brooks that he had died of cancer. Another Grez friend, Lloyd Osbourne, also died in California around this time.

Paris had its rationing and austerities, strikes and political turmoil, but at least it had escaped bombing. Art shows had continued under the Nazi censors, providing that exhibits were middle-of-the-road, figurative, and unpolitical, but now there were recriminations against collaborators, including painters Smith admired such as Derain, Despiau, Vlaminck, Van Dongen, Friesz and de Segonzac, who had naïvely accepted a free trip to Germany in 1941. As Simone de Beauvoir wrote, 'The war was over; it remained on our hands like a great unwanted corpse, and there was no place on earth to bury it.'[14] But, in a brave bid to recapture Paris's pre-eminence in the world of progressive art, a Picasso show was held at the 1944 Salon d'Automne only weeks after the liberation. The following year Matisse was given the same honour.

The British art establishment was quick to resume its connections with French painting and held popular exhibitions of Picasso and Matisse at the Victoria and Albert Museum in December 1945, and of Braque and Rouault at the Tate in 1946. Internationally, too, critics were keen to bend the knee as the painting prizes at the Venice Biennale went to Braque in 1948, Matisse in 1950 and Dufy in 1952.

All these artists were now old men who had made their major

discoveries before the First World War. Cyril Connolly asked Henry Kahnweiler, Picasso's dealer, to tell his *Horizon* readers about the newest Parisian stars and received the blunt answer, 'In my opinion no painter of importance has appeared since 1940.'[15] There were younger painters such as Wols, Hélion, Gruber, Mathieu, Bram Van Velde, Riopelle, Fautrier, Hartung and Buffet working through their war experiences in a variety of styles from psychotic scribbles to hard-edged abstraction, but none were of the first rank and from now on modern painting would happen elsewhere. Only Giacometti's etiolated figures and Dubuffet's 'Art Brut' seemed to have something new to say which Picasso and Matisse had not said better before. None of this 'miserabi-list' stuff would have appealed to Smith, and Bram Van Velde's declaration that 'Only men who are sick can be artists . . . I paint my misery' would have baffled him.

Smith was to return to Paris and the south of France every year between 1946 and his death, except for 1948 and 1957, but it is impossible to imagine the now aged Smith sitting in the cafés of Saint-Germain-des-Prés reading *Les Temps Modernes* and *Le Deuxième Sexe* or discussing existentialism and the Theatre of Cruelty. He was already alarmed by the return of a Labour government in England and would have no sympathy for the French intellectuals' grovelling abasement before Stalin. He found his old haunts 'sadly changed' and Smith was now increasingly out of step and out of touch with artistic developments at home and in France. The war had wrenched English art in new directions and left him isolated, though respected. He no longer had a studio in Paris, and now O'Conor was dead and Brooks was in the USA there were no friends with whom he could chew over the latest ideas. Clive Bell encountered him there in June 1947 still seeking out Anglophone company to relieve his solitude.

Although he had books on traditional Japanese and Indian art in his library, in effect Smith did not look outside France for inspiration and showed no curiosity about modern developments elsewhere. As Rothenstein observed, after hearing that Smith had dined with Hemingway in Paris and found him 'neither forthcoming nor attractive', he could never imagine Smith in the USA, 'a world far beyond the range of his natural sympathies.'[16] Non-Latin Europe was of little interest to him, nor did he show any curiosity about African art, though he must have seen plenty of it in Epstein's collection. Rothenstein recalled:

On one particular evening he [Smith] spoke of the supremacy of French painting, of his confidence in its continuing supremacy, and of the bracing effect for a painter of living in France. His belief in its future derived from his reverence for the older painters, Matisse especially, for I never heard him praise or even refer to the work of any painter of a later generation. 'Who,' I asked him, 'are the successors of Matisse, Braque and Rouault?' He evaded my question, even when I pressed for an answer.[17]

From the disappointments of Paris the depressed Smith went for another recuperative stay at the Valmont Clinic in Switzerland, then on to see the Monays, only to find they were in the process of setting up an art gallery in Lully. He wrote guiltily to Mary of the plentiful food, wine and tobacco he was consuming and drew his ham lunch for her. He stayed for seven weeks, learned from an optician that his cataracts were still thickening, got poisoned by mushrooms, and slowly realized that his relationship with Marion could not be revived on the old terms. He wrote to Dig Yorke: 'Even though it is pleasant for a time to live other people's lives, one suddenly realises that it must not continue and one begins to fumble for the emergency exit, but at the moment all the exits are lost in interminable corridors.'[18]

Marion went back to Aix with Smith in November to uncover his hidden canvases but left him for Switzerland and her husband at Christmas. He was also shocked to hear that his other great pre-war love, Christiane, had entered a convent. He wrote to Mary, 'As far as the world is concerned she might as well be dead, they never come out at all. I never answered her last letter to me.'[19] So there was more guilt and regret to carry around. He had to sell his car to raise money and there were frustrations in finding places to work. Twenty-seven of the canvases he had just recovered went astray on a train and were stuck for three months in customs.

However, by March 1947 he was settled in the Hôtel Nègre Coste at Aix, in touch with Guevara and his wild wife Meraud Guinness ('Meraud being Meraud Beauty is Truth etc') who lent him her flat to work in and then turfed him out after a month when she needed it herself. Smith reported to Halliday that 'Aix is astonishingly the same at least superficially the one change one can see is that one eats better if one can pay for it. In the past I always considered it to have the worst cuisine in France.' But, 'lately I have felt the chances of retrieving my sanity were slight and I do not really mean this as a joke . . . in a nutshell things have gone badly with me here whereas with a little luck they might have gone fairly well. That's the humour of it.'[20] He cracked his ribs in a fall, contracted pneumonia and was down to 8 stone 5lbs. Worst of all he no longer felt loved or at home in Aix, even though many of his friends were drifting back.

Mary Keene must have been terrified that she had lost her hold on Smith when he stayed abroad these ten months in 1946–7. Mary's affair with Henry Yorke was now over (though he remained a generous friend), as were one or two more, and presumably Smith forgave her these as she in turn forgave him his trespasses – though both remained jealous and possessive. Finally he wrote to Mary: 'It may seem strange to you that I am longing to be back in London. Maybe it is just a criminal instinct to give oneself up. But I think it is something else really that is of course this longing to see you and feel that life is real again.'[21]

Once Smith was back in London and after his pictures were released from their three-month hold-up in customs Tooth's showed his pre-war work, priced between £200 and £735, which sold well in spite of the depressed market. This elicited the most perceptive criticism he had received since the days of Fry, and again it was from a painter-writer, Patrick Heron. He saw progress in the still lifes:

But if his impulsive brush is used sometimes to register the single object too summarily, too much in terms dictated by a rapid apprehension of the whole subject so that the same scribble of colour that evokes the pear also to some extent suppresses it, obscuring as well as creating its form, that is increasingly a feature of the past. Matthew Smith's still-life series at Tooth's have a gigantic calm and clarity. His objects no longer lurch into one another, or sway in a crowd towards a corner of the canvas, blown by the gale of the painter's passion. Each stands free of its neighbour; fully created, in space; yet detached, aloof and refined to the point of being almost a symbol of itself.

Heron thought the portraits less resolved than the rotund, more abstracted, nudes:

In the faces Matthew Smith descends to his most naturalistic: he lacks Matisse's intellectual power and cannot reduce face and figure to the economical terms of his own best design. On the other hand, he can't rid himself of the linear to the extent of forcing a harder and clearer form, built plastically; for this would involve the tonal modulation he has so rarely attempted, as well, perhaps, as a resort to differentiated planes – another kind of expression he has never bothered much about.

And of the landscapes:

We might notice that Matthew Smith's idiom precludes all detailed comment: what the fat, volume-evoking swirls leave unsaid cannot be added; the afterthought of a leaf or two on a bush, or an extra accent of drawing, these are impossible. Such detail must be supplied by the spectator (as it would have to be with Cézanne, but not with Renoir). As for the drawing, the drawing's all in the paint and the paint is all colour. There is no paint here which is not drawing; and none which is not operative colour. What other definitions has fine painting?[22]

Soon after this they were introduced and Smith, delighted to have been noticed by the younger generation at last (Heron was twenty-seven), leapt to his feet, spilling sherry down his waistcoat and exclaimed, 'It is the first time anyone has written something that means anything to me.'[23]

CHAPTER 19

Late Maturity
1948–1950

Unusually, Smith spent 1948 solely in England, visiting Iris Hughes in Hertfordshire and painting other friends such as Henry Yorke. From spring to autumn he rented Dick Wyndham's house at Tickerage and stayed on even after Dick had been killed by a sniper in Jerusalem, where he had been sent as a reporter by *The Sunday Times.* Mary was now set up in a flat at 9 Drayton Court near the Fulham Road, and was trying to make a career as an actress, but she found time to visit Smith in the country and have her portrait painted. The real actress, Valerie Hobson, also came to be painted and comforted for the disintegration of her marriage, but at different times because Mary was jealous.[1]

In spite of his remoteness from many of the newer fashionable art movements Smith was awarded a CBE in the January Honours List of 1949 for his contribution to British Art. Arthur and Gwen went with him to the Palace in July but she offended protocol by loudly admiring the Queen's sapphires. Frederic Smith would have been proud, and his brothers certainly were. They themselves had done very little that was creative with their lives and had long been bought out of the family firm so they could give their full attention to golf, horse racing and enjoying life on a private income, with none of Matthew's burden of guilt. Roald Dahl, always a harsh judge, thought they were both 'twirps.' Arthur had helped to establish the Hansdown Club with private drinking facilities near Sloane Square, which became one of Matthew's favourite rendezvous with his brothers. His sister Phyllis now had two sons and Matthew monitored their progress through letters, but his oldest sibling, Hilda, had died in 1938. It seemed that it was the family clown, Matthew, after all, who had inherited his father's creativity and driving will to succeed.

In early 1949 Smith had a highly successful show of fifteen of his pre-war pictures at the Mayor gallery, which did £10,000 of business in the first two days. He spent some of the proceeds on a return to Paris in April. Eardly Knollys regretted that 'our most distinguished painter' never had large-scale commissions since he painted in the grand manner. This is true but it was never on a big canvas, perhaps because his 'one-wet' method was unsuited to large-scale projects, or his endurance ran out. Knollys also made the observation: 'He paints only three subjects – still lifes with flowers and fruit, female models, country landscapes. His exotic tastes restrict the list still more. No withered daisy, no weedy spinster or deserted moorland, stands a chance of attracting his brush.'[2] Maybe, but other painters had worked with less (Morandi, Modigliani, Utrillo, Ivon Hitchens). It is not so much that his subjects are limited but that his manner is: Smith's chromatic volume is constantly turned up fortissimo, every colour full strength, every brushstroke fully laden, every form vigorously modelled so that in the end they are not placid works to live with. Another critic wrote of 'a kind of rapturous vulgarity' which was only saved by his 'fastidious respect for paint . . . As statements about the weight and construction of the nude, the complex lie of the land, the shape of a pear or a vase, his pictures are often puerile and the later ones tend to become more so. But without that deliberate rejection he could never achieve his sonorous intensity of colour.'[3] Smith often failed in his endeavours and such defeats made him wretched, but he never compromised or took further steps along 'the Fake and Fudge road' he had identified in Whitby in 1907. He kept to the straight and narrow, guided only by the need to grapple with subjects in a way that allowed him 'to release something from my interior life.'

Later in the year *Picture Post* ran an article ironically entitled 'The Wild Man of Art', with photographs of Smith in his cluttered studio muffled up in tweeds and scarf painting in front of a little electric fire.[4] By the time it was published he was touring Brittany with the Brookses, who were back in France to see how their properties had survived the war.

If he preferred to scuttle off to France at every opportunity and so openly admired its art, could he have any relevance to post-war British art? Some critics thought not. In 1946 Michael Ayrton, spokesman for younger Neo-Romantic followers of Sutherland and Nash, rejoiced that we were at last shaking off France's grip and returning to 'the main streams or characteristics of the British genius.' These he defined as 'the lyrical, the satiric, the mystical, the romantic and the preoccupation with linear rhythms.'[5] Smith was not thought to embody any of these. Robin Ironside's popular 1948 book *Painting Since 1939* also regretted Fry's Francophiliac influence on British art and his overstress on plastic values. Had we been directed to Chagall, Rouault or Chirico rather than Cézanne and the Fauves our development might have been different and more in tune with our native temper. At the time of writing the British genius was reasserting itself in Neo-Romanticism, Ironside claimed, and only Duncan Grant and Smith survived with any dignity from the era of Fry: 'The work of both painters is historically related to the aspirations of the beginning of the century, and preserves its circumscribed appeal – and may have confirmed its repute – amid the diffuse, figurative currents of thought and sensation that have animated more recent developments.'[6]

The new force in the London art world, Herbert Read, published his *Contemporary British Art* and similarly set out to demonstrate the patriotic thesis that our art was essentially northern European rather than French, and was consequently introspective and personal in mood and Expressionist in manner. The 'relatively polite Fauvism' of Smith and his interest in paint rather than ideas did not fit this theory, even though 'there is an element of plastic violence, of rich saturation in reds and blacks, which make his technique superficially similar to the techniques of the Expressionists; but though this might be attributed to the artist's Nordic sensibility (Matthew Smith is a Yorkshireman), it is no doubt unconscious.'[7] Interestingly, Read reproduced, without comment, Ivon Hitchens's *Reclining Nude* (1947), which clearly showed that someone else had taken his inspiration from Matisse and was also pursuing colour researches in the field of voluptuous, but unparticularized, figure painting. Landscapes were Hitchens's main concern, but the few nudes he painted showed he might well have been Smith's rival had he persisted with them.

By now Smith was well paid in money if not in critical praise for his work, and able to indulge his generous impulses. He was godfather to many of his friends' children and receiving numerous thank-you letters addressed to 'Uncle Matthew' for cheques, his gifts of pictures, and from the older ones gratitude for taking them out to swanky restaurants. He gave the youths advice on good tailors and how to tip, and made the girls feel like ladies with his attentiveness and impeccable manners.

London life now had its routines. On weekdays Mary would walk Alice to school and then go on to Chelsea Cloisters to get Smith up and to drink coffee with him. The relationship was not always easy and friends referred to her as his 'hair shirt.' As she said in one letter: 'Dearest darling . . . there is so much between us that neither of us understands and which we cannot think about and which leaves a perpetual anxious brooding.'[8] The relationship was not always this tense however, and Alice Keene remembers numerous family jokes and sayings which grew up and made them roar with laughter. Mary was demanding, temperamental and resentful of other women, and Gwen, who still hoped vainly for a reconciliation, was in turn understandably jealous of Mary, though she painted her portrait ('She's made you look ordinary,' Smith said of it) and would telephone for Mary's advice on what to buy him for Christmas or birthdays.

When Smith was away Mary maintained a stream of letters all about her money troubles, Alice's progress, illnesses, dreams, visits to the theatre (she had occasional walk-on parts), her reading (Pater, Flaubert, Rousseau, Pound, Eliot), and in return he sent earrings, drawings, books, a watch, chocolates, skirts and frequent cheques. It seems to have been an emotionally exhausting relationship that neither could do without, but though Smith ranged far and wide in his travels and his affections, he always returned to her. During one of his many trips abroad she let herself into his cluttered room in The Cloisters and found swarming cockroaches. Mary reported that the housekeeper admitted that Smith's was the worst-kept room in the whole block but protested 'she didn't dare touch anything for fear of upsetting you etc. Of course with these artists, they never *see* anything, they live in the clouds but we all love him here.'[9]

In October 1949 this *modus vivendi* was severely disrupted when Mary gave birth to a daughter. Smith, feeling trapped by her claim that he was the father, did not want her to go through with the pregnancy (though he would offer no practical help) and denied paternity on the grounds that he was now, at seventy, infertile though not impotent. Mary probably still had other lovers, just as he did, but genuinely believed the child to be Smith's and was deeply hurt by his rejection of it and her. The unfortunate baby girl had a heart defect and only survived six days. A shaken Smith collected Mary from the hospital on the day of its death and took her back to sleep at The Cloisters, but they failed to reconcile their differences and Mary left distraught. The goodbye letter she wrote elicited a savagely cruel reply in which he pointed out that even though she had some of his canvases in her flat she had no legal rights to them: 'I think it would really be better all round if you could put them all back into my possession. Probably one of the reasons for helping in the matter is your insistence that we do not see each other any more i.e. a general winding up. Matthew. I would prefer to live and even laugh sometimes paint also perhaps. M.S.'[10] The hysterical Mary then threw all his works into a taxi, dumped them in the tiny entrance to his flat and went off to sink into the deepest misery.

Smith too was profoundly unhappy but determined he was in the right. Dahl found him so paralysed he could not clear his returned pictures from the hallway. He wrote to Brooks in February, 'By the way get it right out of your mind that that child had anything to do with me, anyway the poor child died and you might think this was proof but it was not.'[11] He was not enjoying his freedom from Mary and his guilty conscience spoiled his sleep and ruined his digestion. It may have been at this unhappy period that he made a plasticine bust of Mary, only his second sculpture, after the one he made of Christiane when he realized he could not keep her. Making an image was still, for him, a way of holding on to those he loved.

Somehow Henry Yorke reconciled them and the edgy relationship continued with Mary trapped by her financial dependence and Smith by his guilt. He escaped abroad as often as he could. Each inflicted cruelties on the other at times, yet both wrote letters tenderly solicitous about the other's comfort and health and happiness. Alice Keene admits: 'The relationship between Matthew Smith and Mary Keene was happy only in moments. It was difficult for her to define. She was not his mistress, nor his daughter, nor his granddaughter. They loved each other and were mutually dependent, and yet independence was very important to both of them.'[12] Mary knew how to make Smith feel blameworthy and his letters are full of pleas for forgiveness, but away from her he did much as he liked and told her only what he wanted her to hear – just as he had always done with Gwen.

When Dylan Thomas died in 1953 Mary went to Laugharne to comfort his widow and help look after the Thomas children, but Caitlin proved a handful and insulted people in the pub. Smith bought a primitive holiday cottage, The Lakes, nearby so Mary and Alice could be independent of Caitlin. Mary later wrote to Smith: 'When I was in Wales and often since I have thought about affairs between us, realising that we have our roles and that it is when we try to get out of them that troubles begin and we suffer (PS I mean we make the mistake of being passionate for instance).'[13] After the baby's death Mary became increasingly religious, more reclusive, and for the next ten years concentrated on writing her semi-autobiographical novel, *Mrs Donald*. Smith encouraged her: 'I am intensely interested in your writing half my heart is in it!' he protested when she thought he was not interested enough. In spite of Smith's support and the advocacy of Henry Yorke this work did not find a publisher until 1983, two years after Mary died of cancer.[14] It is a strange work, written in a sub-Virginia Woolf prose, full of family violence and child abuse mixed with religiosity and sexuality which in some undefined way relates to Mary Keene's own experiences as a child, lover and mother. There is a romantic character called Louis, which must refer to MacNeice, but little that could be related directly to her relationship with Matthew Smith.

In spite of these emotional upheavals Smith still managed to work and exhibit. There were two new patrons in England after the war: the Arts Council, whose art section was chaired by Kenneth Clark and administered by the formidable Lilian Somerville, and the British Council, headed by Herbert Read; the former to promote English art at home and the latter abroad. The Arts Council came to own three Smiths and the British Council ten, all of them good. In 1950 Smith was chosen by a committee, which included Hendy and Rothenstein, to represent British painting at the recently revived Venice Biennale, alongside Constable and the sculptor Barbara Hepworth.

Moore had won the sculpture prize in 1948 and Turner had represented our painting, so British art was riding high on the Continent. However, in 1950 the reviewers concentrated on Constable and neither living artist made the impact they deserved, Hepworth being seen as sub-Moore and the critics claiming that Italian light killed the colours in the twenty-six Smiths on show. Eric Newton, never a Smith enthusiast, put it brutally:

Matthew Smith . . . speaks much the same language as a hundred other artists in adjacent pavilions. We English think of him as exceptionally courageous, but courage such as his is not uncommon in France and Italy. And since his weakest point is the basic structure of his pictures he seems, to foreign eyes, outmatched by a dozen of his contemporaries both in colour and design.[15]

Certainly Sutherland, who followed in 1952, was much more to Italian taste, as were the young sculptors whose 'geometry of fear' constructions made rounded nudes seem a thing of the past. Then Bacon's and Freud's menacing figures and Nicholson's abstracts in 1954 surprised all those Continentals who thought Britain had no modern art. Smith had no more big foreign shows after this flop.

Roald Dahl's biographer tells us that Dahl spent several weekends during these years in Paris with Smith 'cruising the galleries by day and the red-light districts by night.'[16] Dahl was learning how to buy good works and was steadily acquiring Smith's own, often as gifts. He introduced Smith to one of his own rich patrons, Charles Marsh, and soon Smith was painting Marsh's teenage daughter Diana. She wrote to him from Jamaica in 1950: 'You seem to believe that sitting for you is an unendurable hardship, and that I was undergoing more or less of a marathon at the studio. If you will search your memory you will recall that I spent more time resting and eating the delicious chocolates you gave me than sitting.'[17] The Marshes collected his work and continued to invite Smith to their Jamaica home each winter, but he never made the trip.

For about a year Smith rented a studio in Clareville Grove from one of Gwen's young nieces, Penelope Salmond, who had trained at the Royal College but gave up art to become a nun. He put in lights and electricity but eventually tired of it. Then in 1950 Dahl persuaded Smith to take a studio at Amersham, near Dahl's own property at Great Missenden. Poppet John, Augustus's daughter, came and made the curtains for him and Dahl stored fifty-four works whilst the move was made, trying perhaps to keep them out of the hands of Dudley Tooth, whom he nicknamed Dog's Tooth and unjustly regarded as avaricious and an inadequate publicist for his friend's reputation. Something went wrong at this point and Smith accused Dahl of sharp practice and of stealing one of his paintings. In an injured tone Dahl wrote: 'Your accusations were so horrible I've had tummy trouble for 3 days and went to the doctor,'[18] but the friendship survived. Smith then moved back to a studio in Thurloe Square, and then to a final one in Yeoman's Row within walking distance of his flat.

Dahl's two sisters also became friends and Alfhild remembers visiting Smith in The Cloisters and watching him paint in the studio. They confirmed what their brother had seen – that it left him exhausted, and he recharged himself with raw eggs afterwards, littering the floor with their shells. Nicholas Logsdail, son of Dahl's other sister Else, recalls Smith's grave courtesy with children:

Matthew Smith used to come down and visit at weekends. This was in the early to mid 1950s, from when I was about five. He was a delightful, charming, modest, rather shy old man. Little, frail. He said, you know, children are always better artists than grown-ups. On one occasion we were in the studio and he suggested to my uncle that he left me with him in the studio. 'He's quite happy and I'll give him some paints.' Every now and again he'd come and admire what I was doing. At the end of the day, he selected one of them, which I had told him was the best, and he said, 'You're right, it's far better than I could do. Could you do me the honour of making an exchange?'[19]

Smith never tried to tell young friends like this how to paint and never seems to have imparted any practical advice to other painters who asked for it. However, in July 1950 he was offered the chance to pass on his lifetime's wisdom in a radio broadcast ('I expect my voice will sound dreadful'). This is the nearest he ever came to an artistic statement since his letter to Gwen in 1907 in which he determined to go for 'the beauty of beautiful reality'. Disappointingly, the broadcast adds little to this, merely spinning words and the big Victorian abstractions, Art, Nature, Beauty – though one is surprised to hear him quoting, in that thin weary voice, Constable, Leonardo and Timon of Athens.

Constable maintained that all was made beautiful by light and shade, which seems rather to suggest that a part of Nature might be ugly but rendered beautiful by another. You see I am attempting, only attempting, to insist that ugliness may exist as cruelty exists, but that an artist can make all things beautiful by his vision.[20]

And so he continued, giving little away, concluding, with Leonardo, 'Art struggles with attempts to rival Nature.' The problem for an instinctive artist like Smith was that he had nothing to pass on in terms of theory or method; each new picture was a new gamble, and the losses and winnings were equally unpredictable.

These pensées seem to take some of their style from two of Smith's favourite books: the Nabi Sérusier's *ABC de la Peinture* (1921) and the Symbolist Odilon Redon's *A Soi Même*, a collection of generalities about art and life – though Redon would not have persuaded Smith to his view that Ingres was a sterile artist who 'will never bring life to generous hearts.'[21]

If Smith was not articulate about his own creative processes then he eventually found a man who said it for him: 'It's all there! Everything!' he exclaimed. In 1929 D. H. Lawrence wrote: 'A man has to have a gizzard like an ostrich to digest all the brass-tacks and wire nails of modern art theory,' so Lawrence put them behind him as he tried to paint:

I disappeared into that canvas. It is to me the most exciting moment – when you have a blank canvas and a big brush full of wet colour, and you plunge. It is just like diving into a pond – then you start frantically to swim. So far as I am concerned it is like swimming in a baffling current and being rather frightened and very thrilled, gasping and striking out for all you're worth. The knowing eye watches sharp as a needle; but the picture comes clean out of instinct, intuition and sheer physical action. Once the instinct and intuition get into the brush-tip, the picture happens, if it is to be a picture at all.[22]

This is from 'Making Pictures', a better essay than Lawrence's 'Introduction To His Paintings' which is a sermon about how syphilis has made us all afraid of our own bodies and sexuality. Lawrence writes patronizingly of Renoir, but says 'yet how infinitely better he is than any English equivalent.' What a pity he did not know about Smith's great nudes of the 1920s.

In March 1950 the Redfern Gallery showed sixty-one watercolours and drawings, and more works were on show in the summer of 1951 at Tooth's. Here Smith was now handled by Richard Smart, more interested in contemporary art than Dudley Tooth, who anyway had his hands full trying to stem Stanley Spencer's output of erotica. Later Peter Cochrane, formerly of the Redfern, took over dealings with Smith and found him unpushy and easy to work with in those days before written contracts tied both gallery and artist in lawyer's tape. He recalled that clients preferred the flowers and landscapes to the nudes, which tended to end up in public galleries or were hoarded in Smith's studio for his own pleasure.

Epstein continued his friendship. While Augustus John had been in artistic decline for years, both 'Jake' and 'Matt' seemed able to maintain their intellectual vigour and inventiveness; except that while Epstein continued robust Matthew was looking increasingly frail. Margaret Epstein had died in 1947 and so Epstein could marry his long-time mistress, Kathleen, who tried her best to cosset Smith and wrote him tender letters of encouragement when he was depressed. In return Smith gave her dry champagne and wrote an over-fulsome catalogue introduction to an exhibition of paintings by Kathleen and Epstein's son Theo ('I look on them with wonder, admiration, and even astonishment. Surely this is an event unequalled in British painting since Van Gogh.'[23]) In 1954 Theo died in tragic circumstances and within ten months his sister Esther killed herself. Smith was full of empathy for the bereaved parents and did what he could to comfort them. He also put portrait commissions Epstein's way where he could, and earlier had thrown a dinner party at The Caprice when his friend's retrospective opened at the Tate in October 1952. It seemed at last as if the wolf Epstein was being allowed into the sheepfold of English art – though neither he nor Smith were in favour at the Royal Academy, where Sir Alfred Munnings insisted during his presidency (1944–9) on putting the clock back to the Victorian era.

Nor was Smith much regarded by the hungry generation treading on his heels. Several young artists in the provinces were still working out their post-war deprivations. The Kitchen Sink School were painting drowned chickens, chip friers and cornflakes (remembering, perhaps, Sickert's call for painting to 'stick to the kitchen'). They looked to German Expressionism or Italian, Mexican and Belgian art for inspiration and had no interest in French hedonism. They would never have adopted Smith's invented verb 'to gay up' a painting. John Berger defended their joyless realism on Marxist grounds and John Bratby admitted, 'The painting of my decade was an expression of its Zeitgeist – introvert, grim, khaki in colour often, opposed to prettiness, and dedicated to portraying a stark, raw, ugly reality. The word Angst prevailed in art talk.'[24] At the Borough Polytechnic in London David Bomberg (1890–1957) was teaching students such as Kossoff, Auerbach and Creffield to use thick oil paint and to seek 'the spirit in the mass', but the colour range was narrow and their touch clotted in comparison to Smith's fluidity. Eardly Knollys, with these groups and the Nicholsonian abstractionists in mind, wrote: 'Eyes accustomed to contemporary orgies of understatement, monochrome and restraint get a peculiarly happy shock from the imprudence of Matthew Smith's paintings with their spectacular abandon.'[25]

Smith took up the Leda and the Swan theme again in watercolour and began playing with a few imaginative canvases of lovers[26], but more importantly he began a series of large still lifes of fruit and studio bric-à-brac which were astonishing in their intense heraldic colour, even for him. The old plaster apples and fish, the chipped jugs and the tables supported by putti were no longer of interest in themselves, but they served as departure points for near-abstract colour harmonies and discords. Full purples and a use of pure white are new features and the paint is applied in a less agitated way now, more in flat areas with outlines and decisive edges appearing once more. He was fulfilling Matisse's precept that 'the subject of a picture and its background must have the same value, or to put it more clearly, there is no principal feature, only the pattern is important.'[27] Compositions, too, are offbeat, often seen from above, with the tables tipped up and the perspective subverted in the Cézanne manner. The passion had drained

69

out of his few late nudes, but with still lifes the combinations are infinite and their appeal is not so much to the man as to the painter. Here he could play with composition and space to his heart's content, coming back to them when he had regained his strength. It seemed his eyes were as gluttonous as ever, in spite of ominously thickening cataracts and a failing body.

CHAPTER 20

Winding Down
1951–1954

Smith had never needed to teach for money, and was probably both too diffident and too parsimonious with his own ideas to do so, but this had its drawbacks. He lacked the fraternity of the staff-room and the stimulus of contact with young minds and new theories. Teachers have to clarify their own ideas and give them a social context in order to pass them on, but Smith never attempted this, being content to muddle along alone. Above all, teaching takes artists away from the solitude of the studio and the waiting blank canvas. Smith's loneliness was assuaged by Mary's visits and excursions to Harrods, the parks, galleries, zoo, clubs and restaurants, though he avoided the more obvious watering holes such as the nearby Chelsea Arts Club. In spite of his dithering about times and dates he was constantly invited out to the theatre or for weekends in the country by the Hallidays (where he once arrived bearing two live lobsters), the Hugheses, the Michaelises, Julian and Mary Trevelyan, Valerie Hobson, the Dahls, or Vanessa Bell and Duncan Grant. Because he looked so helpless and was known never to have cooked a meal people seemed to compete to fuss over him.

Sometimes, in the last years of his life, he went to more cultural events such as the musical evenings held by Sheridan Russell at 100 Cheyne Walk. Russell and his saintly wife Kit were also friends of Vera Cuningham and she painted some of the quartets playing there. Matthew drew the violinists, and in 1957 did a series of sketches of the flautist Elaine Shaffer. Smith, Cuningham and Epstein, who all knew Sheridan before the war, had earlier contributed works to his Pictures in Hospitals scheme and each given him pictures for his own collection.

The musical and discussion evenings in Epstein's house also continued.

In the summer of 1951 Augustus John somehow just missed meeting Smith in Aix as his daughter steered him down towards Saint-Tropez. John had recently finished his memoirs,[1] but Matthew only got a passing mention amidst all the other name-dropping. Elsewhere though, when asked who were the three greatest living English painters, John told people 'Matthew Smith, M. Smith and Smith, M.' Augustus was now deaf and a bore, and though still in demand as a portrait painter he was better known for his eccentricities. His biographer placed him in English art as 'a transitional figure in an age of transition, but moving diagonally.'[2] Like Smith he had been born at the turn of the tide and there were disconcerting signs that both of them were now going to be left high and dry. Neither had featured amongst the prizewinners of the 1951 Festival of Britain competition for British artists. This was won by Lucian Freud and Smith took him and his current girlfriend out to tea but, he reported to Mary, 'he could not bring himself to say anything about my effort so assumed he did not think much of it'.[3] Freud probably did not.

In 1952 he was back in his old favourites Nice, Cagnes and Aix, though he found time in London to paint yet another portrait of Valerie Hobson. He turned up in full white tie and tails to present it to her, still tacky, in the star dressing-room of the musical *The King and I*. Smith was obviously very fond of her and she of him and so when she married Jack Profumo in 1954 he turned up with another wet offering of *Peonies* as a wedding gift. To his delight she introduced him to other actors such as the Oliviers and Gielgud, who with many theatre and some film people such as Richard Attenborough, Stewart Granger and John Mills, began to collect his work.

When Dahl married the glamorous American film-star Patricia Neal in 1953 he wrote to Smith 'You will be crazy about this Pat' and invited him to join them on the honeymoon drive from Italy. Smith had the tact not to accept, but he soon charmed Patricia into sitting for him.[4] She remembers him as fussy, fastidious and 'persnickety', though amusing to be with. Once the three were at a fashionable restaurant when 'Pat took a liking to a pair of silver sugar tongs and Roald pocketed them for her. As they left, a waiter unsuccessfully accosted the shifty-looking

67

painter, but didn't dare to confront Dahl himself.'⁵ However, Patricia Neal now seems to think it was Smith who did the stealing.

During these years Smith became a friend of Henry Moore (a neighbour of the Hugheses), got to know the poet Stephen Spender through the Garrick Club, and met the writers Laurie Lee and Thomas Good. He visited T. S. Eliot for tea and afterwards ruefully told friends how he had been so clumsy that he knocked a table over. He did more portraits of his friend Henry Yorke who, in spite of being born into wealth and privilege, thought of himself primarily as 'a businessman whose pastime was romancing over a bottle to a good band,' which is where he and Smith saw eye to eye.⁶ Smith himself was still romancing and confessed he felt tempted to ask the Queen out when he met her at a party. He continued to cast a roving eye over waitresses and diners in restaurants, and elsewhere he was avoided by secretaries in art galleries as a pouncer and bottom-pincher.⁷

His attentions were not always repulsed. In 1954 he went with the Hallidays to visit his old friend Cholerton, now home from Russia and divorced from his Russian wife. He and his new wife Charlotte, an Austrian Jewess of charm and strong character, lived in the Villa Elizabeth at the foot of a cliff at Cap Martin. They all visited Monte Carlo together but Matthew boasted he 'did not play at the tables being a shrewd Yorkshireman,' and he could not work because there was 'hardly anything to look at but the Mediterranean,' as he told Gwen.⁸ What he did not add was that he was having an affair with his hostess. Back in Aix he received a letter from Charlotte saying how betrayed Chol felt by 'the man he liked and admired most' and 'You can imagine how distressed I am about it all, because it is all my fault. I had no right to make Chol unhappy, he does not deserve it. On the other hand I could not help loving you. My passion was stronger than anything else. I am completely in love with you and I shall stay so whatever happens.'⁹

A former model, and presumed lover, Simone Kenyon (neé Renwick) also kept up a stream of letters and invitations from exotic places round the world such as Tanganyika, Dominica and Iran, where her husband, a freelance pilot, worked or farmed. 'I do miss you so much,' she wrote from Africa and described the hours she spent 'recalling fragments of your conversation, the times we spent together, what you said, how annoyed you used to get when I said "what" and you had to repeat a sentence.'[10] Smith treasured the letters but seems not to have met her in the flesh again until possibly the last year of his life when she came home from Iran to sort out her mother's estate.

In London he had a wild but brief enthusiasm for a dancer in Antonio's Spanish Dancers troupe, then appearing in the West End, and some mildly erotic drawings of a pretty young woman called Grace show that even in old age he could still charm women out of their clothes and into posing for him. Iris Hughes remembers Smith being constantly on the telephone from her home to his latest young woman, perhaps this same Grace, and asking her husband anxiously whether he was making an old fool of himself in pursuing a twenty-five-year-old so ardently.

There were other female friends of this time including Mary Sorrell, a writer on art, who published a couple of articles on him,[11] and Cathleen Mann (1896–1959), herself a Slade-trained artist, whose 1952 portrait of Smith is now in the National Portrait Gallery. Cathleen kept a journal in which she recorded some of their many conversations, observing: 'As usual Matthew hates you to argue. He is so fascinating to listen to although he talks about nothing but himself.'[12] And, 'How naïve he is but full of quiet amusement about himself and so happy alone. I even feel he is happy when he is unhappy.'[13] She sat for a portrait: 'We both felt very nervous, it was all rather too exciting for me. The picture was not a likeness but a good Smith.'[14] She also sat for nudes and did not feel shy because 'painters with nudes are like "honour among thieves."' Smith tactfully scrubbed these out with turps when the sessions were over. She found it 'wonderfully interesting to watch the deliberate way he slashes on the paint, dropping brushes, not finding the right colours etc. . . . He paints by looking at me for 5 seconds then furiously working at canvas walks back and looks at canvas and back to it again without looking at subject – does not copy.'[15] Cathleen was subject to self-doubt and depression herself but Smith was charming to her, saying she was essential to him 'even in his painting'; 'when people treat you as he does as if you were still young you give up acting a part which you do when you know you are old and don't feel it. Then you are very happy and natural again.'[16]

Yet through all these affairs he kept up his almost daily flow of letters addressed to Mrs Mary Keene, enclosing cheques, asking after Alice, boosting her writing and apologizing when she scolded him. Once he took her abroad, to Paris, but spoiled it by booking her into a hotel inferior to his own and so got a sound telling off.

One person he still saw occasionally in London was Vera Cuningham. In September 1946 Smith had written to Vera to congratulate her on an exhibition of her paintings and offer her a cheque which he hoped would buy one of her works. In London she had exhibited at the Redfern and in various mixed shows with the Royal Society of British Artists, the Royal Academy and others, and been admired by the Constable scholar Graham Reynolds and the critic Eric Newton (who with his wife took her to Venice in 1948). However, it was a Paris dealer, Raymond Creuze, who offered her solo exhibitions in 1948, 1951 and 1954. By this time she painted tortured surreal figures with cup-shaped heads, often in religious settings, which were more appreciated in post-war Paris than London. She specialized in gouache rather than oils and her colours became darker and her distortions more extreme as she explored her tortured id and sought, in her own words, 'to convey the existence on the other side of the mountain, the bed of the lake, the penetrable flesh enclosing the impenetrable bones.'[17]

Vera was now essentially wedded to painting and pursued it single-mindly, after 1950 in Log Cottage, Well Road, Hampstead, which she shared only with her vicious parrots. She developed a temper (once thumping her lover Denis Matthews) and a taste for weird hats. Now and again she threw wild parties, but was soon back at the easel pursuing her dark images of predatory females gutted and pulled shapeless by the vehemence of her visions.

On his Aix journeys in the 1950s Smith joined up occasionally with Meraud Guinness, Guevara, and their sadly neglected daughter Nini. Meraud had initially run a kind of salon in Aix at 61 Cours Mirabeau, but then in 1948 she bought a country house near La Tour de César (a Knights Templar watchtower once painted by Cézanne) high on a wooded hill outside the town. It had no plumbing, electricity or approach road but she attracted a mixed bunch of gypsies, poseurs like Brian Howard, the Swiss writer Cingria, the poet David Gascoyne, and Smith himself. His old friend Zawado was also a frequent visitor. In summer life there seems to have been a permanent picnic with fresh game cooked over camp fires, whilst the winters passed in complex and explosive hetero and homosexual love affairs. There were not enough women around and too many cats and dogs for Smith's taste, and he also drank too much and fell down the stone stairs. Nearby lived French artists such as André Masson and Pierre Talcoat, and the American sculptor Alexander Calder (whom Smith had known through Brooks since about 1935) came in 1952, and then in 1953 bought a house called Malvalat to work on gouaches, which he exhibited in Aix at the Christian Zervos gallery.

Meraud still painted, but her once talented husband no longer bothered and declined steadily until he died in 1951, aged fifty-seven, of cancer of the liver and lungs. As a last service to his friend Smith helped arrange a retrospective exhibition of his works at the Mayor Gallery in November 1952. Meraud stayed on at Aix and we know that Smith visited her there again in 1954 because he made dated drawings of her in biro, a new instrument he seemed to enjoy. Matthew also saw Cecil Michaelis at L'Harmas and was driven by him or his son to various locations where he would be dropped, disappear into the woods, and reappear with a wet canvas an hour later. He still hated to be watched at work.

Back in London Smith dined frequently with Rothenstein, who surreptitiously kept notes on many of their conversations. These formed the basis of his chapter on Smith in the first volume of his *Modern English Painters*, published in 1952. All the biographical details came from Smith himself, including the exaggerated story of his terrible childhood struggles against his father, and he checked the manuscript over, saying only 'I take no responsibility for your *praise*.' However, on publication Smith was distressed and told Rothenstein 'When I re-read the piece, early one morning, when I felt wretched anyhow, I could see no course but suicide. But it's all right now. Don't worry about it.'[18] Rothenstein was baffled, but concluded that Smith must have thought his privacy violated.

It is more likely that he resented the repetition of the judgement Hendy had made in 1944 that he was an indecisive wimp who painted bold extrovert pictures to compensate for his inadequacies, and that 'he was one of those artists whose work is the fulfilment of all that they themselves are not.' This judgement was based on such utterances by Smith as the following, made to Rothenstein before one of his own works on display in Tooth's:

'I always work in a state of almost complete nervous prostration and exhaustion,' he said, 'I say *almost* complete, because until I've conquered it to some extent, regained some sort of self-possession, you know, I can't even begin. I worry so appallingly when I think about a picture that I'm intending to paint – I worry so, if you understand,' and his voice died away in a whisper. . . The hollow voice sounded again: 'I used to draw a lot but lately I've almost given up drawing, in any case I never thought very much of my drawings . . .'Again it died slowly away.[19]

Smith worried about his health too, and tried periodically to break his habit of smoking the minute he woke up. He was still an insomniac and passed the night reading in his cell-like room, often the works of Dickens, though print was increasingly difficult to decipher because, as he said, 'I found I was very slowly and carefully going blind.'[20] In January 1953 he at last agreed to have an operation to remove a cataract, which restored the right eye, but he refused further surgery on the left. Michaelis found him very depressed on the grounds that 'Now I've got to go back and see all those awful paintings I've done recently.'

Aged painters, Titian, Rembrandt and Monet for example, often showed a degree of fuzziness in their work because of the natural weakening of the eyes with age (presbyopia), and if in addition they had cataracts the red end of the spectrum came to dominate their vision – as in the late nudes of Renoir. Smith, however, must have gradually compensated for his fading sight because the post-war works retain their brightness of hue and boldness of facture and are no longer particularly 'hot' in tone. He thought the operation would make little difference to his colour sense since 'It's all up here you know' he told Halliday, tapping his head. One immediate delight was being able to read the numbers on the buses and see the birds in the trees. Dahl was thankful that it had improved his handwriting too: 'Legible for a change, no longer like a crazy cardiograph across the page.'[21] Rothenstein thought Smith's broad handling of paint had originally stemmed from his inability to see details but became habitual, and after the operation it was no longer so spontaneous and had to be worked at.

Later Smith painted a portrait of Vera Barry which he seemed not entirely satisfied with, but the man who was to become her third husband, the art critic John Russell, reassured him, 'It seems to me to continue an original and monumental design with an inspired perception of what she was like. Please do not turn against it therefore . . . It is the best portrait of a person known to me that I have ever seen.'[22] Indeed, it captures the autocratic and flamboyant spirit of Vera very well. Renoir had said 'My models don't think at all' and Smith's very largely give the same impression, but Vera was a woman of formidable intellect and character and this comes across. It was painted in his studio at Thurloe Square, rented in 1951. Vera had insisted on scrubbing the floor because 'It's far too rough for a charwoman, but she should be able to manage it now.' Vera, who was of aristocratic Russian origin, was used to getting her peremptory way with writers and artists of the stature of Moore, Auden, Jasper Johns, Beckett, Ernst, Bacon and Tobey in her capacity as entrepreneur and exhibition organizer. She had known Smith since 1929 when she was touring as an actress and had met him in Aix, she informed me, and though she had the kind of beauty that Smith liked, their intimacy was not physical. Later she would be involved in organizing the 1983 Barbican Gallery show of Smith's work and would return from researching his activities in the south of France shocked to have discovered some of his peccadilloes: 'I must say I am very angry with the old boy,' she wrote to Halliday.[23]

A friend of Vera Barry and John Russell was Stephen Spender, who became another of Smith's dining companions around this time. Spender observed:

He is extremely mild and gentle yet uncompromising and acute, reminding me a little of E. M. Forster. Over luncheon he talked gently of many things, including painting and France and girls. He said that Morandi must be an interesting man, but he did not really altogether care for his painting, which he found affected. He said he liked some of the paintings of Jack Yeats but found the large canvases which were exhibited at the Tate Gallery some years ago rather empty. He thought that Yeats should have been advised not to show them. He was very reserved also about Wyndham Lewis. Obviously, despite his gentle manner, he is not easy to please.

Back at the studio Spender was surprised by Smith's energy in dragging out flower canvases to show him but then Smith confessed 'Nowadays I don't seem able to paint flowers. When I was younger I could do so. I used to get so tremendously excited by flowers I saw that I wanted to take them home at once and start working on them.'[24]

In Rothenstein's company Smith trawled the twilight world of Soho, in particular the Colony and Gargoyle drinking clubs where it was impossible to avoid the company of Francis Bacon and his hangers-on. Smith was swept into this maelstrom and survived remarkably well:

The more Francis drank, the more physically helpless his condition, the more marked his imperious dignity. We [Rothenstein and Smith] were joined at the Gargoyle by the painter Robert Colquhoun, a wasted and very drunk Don Quixote, and Robert MacBryde, his rotund, no soberer Sancho Panza, who accompanied noisy demands for whisky with abusive remarks about members of the party that had assembled in the meanwhile. Francis, though unable to rise from the chair at the head of the table, instantly quelled them with the grave authority of a judge.[25]

Evidently there was a mutual respect and affection between Smith and Bacon, no matter how different their work, age, personalities and sexual orientations. Rothenstein wrote: 'Matthew used to say of the work of Francis that even at its least successful it never lacked absorbing interest, and Francis, who admires the work of few of his contemporaries, admires Matthew's with little qualification.' Both were socially mobile in upward and downward directions, sexually obsessed, and in artistic terms had made drawing and painting one simultaneous act.

Rothenstein had his chance to repair the breach in their friendship caused by his book when he arranged a Smith retrospective exhibition at the Tate Gallery in September 1953. There were eighty-one oils on show, and in spite of Smith's dread of the occasion beforehand the exhibition was a triumph. The catalogue has a glowing tribute from Bacon which deserves lengthy quotation since it articulates how a young painter (and gambler) looked upon Smith's *oeuvre* and valued that very risky hit-or-miss quality which the other critics saw as a fault:

He seems to me to be one of the very few English painters since Constable and Turner to be concerned with painting – that is, with attempting to make idea and technique inseparable. Painting in this sense tends towards a complete interlocking of image and paint, so that the image is the paint and vice versa. Here the brush-stroke creates the form and does not merely fill it in. Consequently, every movement of the brush on the canvas alters the shape and implications of the image. That is why real painting is a mysterious and continuous struggle with chance – mysterious because the very substance of the paint, when used in this way, can make such a direct assault upon the nervous system; continuous because the medium is so fluid and subtle that every change that is made loses what is already there in the hope of making a fresh gain.

I think that painting today is pure intuition and luck and taking advantage of what happens when you splash the stuff down, and in this game of chance Matthew Smith seems to have the gods on his side.[26]

Rothenstein wrote the introduction and quoted encomia by Roger Fry and Augustus John. A. J. L. McDonnell made out a case that Smith was after all more English than French on the dubious grounds that 'The English contribution to both the visual and literary arts has so often been inspired by an immediate, emotional reaction to the shapes and colours of the outward visible world.' Henry Yorke extolled the nudes and claimed to detect a vivid sense of humour in his friend's works. Smith told Mary, 'of course his over-praise is painful . . . but it is so far away better than the usual professional criticism or adulation.'[27]

There were loans from public galleries, private collectors, the British Council, the Queen Mother, and the Hallidays, whilst Epstein lent the great 1924 picture of Vera, *Woman With Fan*. Even Smith had to admit, 'It's not so bad as I thought it was going to be – not so bad, you know.'

All his friends (except Vera Cuningham and Mary Keene) came to the launch party and coaxed Smith out of his embarrassment at being in the limelight. Valerie Hobson had Gwen pointed out to her and exclaimed 'But they're alike as two sticks!' Also present were Nye Bevan and Jenny Lee, the former having perhaps the strongest artistic experience he ever had and the latter being so impressed she began an interest in art which eventually led her to becoming the Minister for Arts in the Labour government.[28]

Epstein told his daughter Peggy-Jean: 'It is the finest exhibition by any living artist ever held in London and will finally place Smith where he belongs as our foremost painter. Somewhat late but what can you expect if the Tate shows such dull and uninteresting painters as Braque and Léger, and such frauds as Graham Sutherland.'[29]

The critics could now survey Smith's whole *oeuvre*. The *Times* man disliked the Cornish works as 'too harsh a departure from straightforward vision' and preferred the 1920s nudes where Smith 'had done Matisse over from nature.'[30] Bryan Robertson thought him 'practically the only artist of real stature *painting* in England today, for it is impossible to think of him as a writer or poet, as a psychologist or propagandist of any kind: all of his pictures bring about an acute consciousness of the totally unambiguous and extraordinary process of painting.'[31] The painter Patrick Heron was still an enthusiast and thought Smith's use of 'structure and form [which] are actually begotten of colour in its fullest saturation and vice versa' had permeated English art and led to a lightening of colour, and plastic freedom compared to the 'tepid, timid tidiness of all but a few of Smith's own generation.'[32]

All this praise was too much and Matthew fled to Aix, but before he went the Americans interviewed him for *Time* magazine and were told he was slowing up: 'You have to think about what you've done by the end of the year – not at the end of the week or the day. If you think about that you get panic-stricken.'[33] They admired the way 'his nudes glow with warm reds, swirl with rich curves and rumpled hair; sometimes they are asleep but often they gaze out at the world with impudent eyes and pouting lips. Usually there is a chemise indolently shrugged half off.' They were therefore surprised to find him a frail old man. 'Mornings he potters about "doing the things that have to be done" – sending out laundry, answering the letters and the telephone. Afternoons he paints with the same old sureness of line, every stroke certain and in its place.' But, at seventy-four, how much longer could he keep this up?

CHAPTER 21

The Last Years
1954–1959

In January 1954 Smith's home town of Halifax displayed fifty of his works in the Bankfield Museum. Matthew returned for the first time in forty years and was given a celebrity welcome which he found 'amusing and embarrassing.' The chimneys were nearly all gone now (though one still had Smith written on it) and the pall of smoke long dispersed. An illuminated book was presented to him and he responded with the only public speech he is ever known to have made: 'It is the first time I have ever come more than a mile to see my own paintings. Thank you.'

The local paper then asked a sample of visitors what they thought of the show. Most had come to see the Queen Mother's 1938 *Still Life, Jugs and Apples* (bought from Tooth's for £145), but only eleven out of seventeen said they liked it, and only three of those would bother to carry it home if given it. Many reacted positively to the landscapes and still lifes, but the nudes shocked the puritanical burghers of Halifax. 'Disgusting – it's the models we don't like,' said a group of housewives. One reader warned visitors not to waste their time: 'I came away disgusted, in no way inspired or uplifted by any of the pictures seen. To laud such a collection is, to me, just plain humbug.'[1] So much for the prodigal son's return.

Smith's paintings were better received in the London galleries, where his wife loyally went to view them. She wrote to him in a very shaky hand: 'Dear wonderful boy, you are all I sincerely felt you were. Of course you are, and far more, but every now and again you give us a lift-up to see it. My love and blessings, your old Gwenny.'[2] This letter was written from her room in the Glendower Hotel, Glendower Place, now her permanent home and uncomfortably close to Smith's own flat.

Gwen had moved to London after she realized she was getting too frail to keep house alone in Norfolk. She had packed up her treasures, including a box of Guy Maynard's drawings which must have dated from the Brittany days of 1908, Matthew's own drawings of Mark and Dermot as boys, and their sons' letters from school, Cranwell, and their time in the RAF, though she could not bear to reread any of them. She consulted her husband on what they jointly owned: 'Have you any suggestions about the Daumier, the John drawing or the Epstein etc. *Of course* I am keeping your cockatoo. I do so hope your back is well again. Do write *I love you* you know.'[3] She had not bothered with her own works, and anyway she had sold most of the finished ones in a jumble sale to try and save the crumbling belfry of Overy Staithes church. Matthew had gone over and bought half a dozen for £44 to save her from humiliation. Her life's work fetched a total of £120 and is now scattered beyond recall.

Halliday and Smith went to Norfolk to clear the house and have a bonfire in the garden. It was unusual for Smith to discard anything, but this time he was ruthless. Halliday managed to salvage Smith's own *Tulips with Striped Cloth* which Smith was ready to toss on the fire. Even a passing villager managed to save something of Matthew's from this conflagration.

Smith spent some time that spring in Marseilles and Roquebrune with the Cholertons and also in Aix seeing Michaelis and Zawado. He returned by June because the Honours List proclaimed that plain Matthew Smith was now Sir Matthew, Knight Bachelor. Other ageing innovators, Jacob Epstein, Somerset Maugham and Edith Sitwell, were also honoured for their past contributions to Britain's culture – though Augustus John as a holder of the Order of Merit still outranked them all, and he had been honoured with a huge Tate retrospective show in 1954. All their bohemian lifestyles could now be forgiven and they were welcomed into the establishment.

Phyllis shopped for his suit and took him to the ceremony, where the Queen evidently did not know who he was. Letters of congratulation flooded into Chelsea Cloisters, and Smith threw none away. T. S. Eliot sent his felicitations, and made the surprising claim: 'I take particular satisfaction in the fact that I have known Matthew Smith the painter longer than most people in the world of art and letters today.' (Perhaps they had met in the Valmont Clinic in 1922 after all?) Harold wrote to say he wished their father could have known about it and added 'Well, well. As long as he had already been made a Baronet he might have forgiven you!' Gwen, now Lady Smith, who was too weak to go to the ceremony, wrote 'I think it is too gratifying for words – but *you* are the only painter who should have it since Tintoretto. There! Dear Brave Beautiful Painter. Gwen.' The family historian, George, pointed out that Matthew was now the third member of the Halifax Smiths to be knighted, though the others were tycoons not artists, and of course Gwen's two brothers and her father has also been Sirs. At last Frederic Smith's ambition to make his most wayward son into a gentleman had been accomplished.

Mary Keene rather dampened any euphoria he might have felt with her comment: 'Don't know what to truly think about your being knighted except that an honour of this kind will bring with it many false honours and on the whole more pain than pleasure. I hope anyway this honour may prove useful disgusting though this may be in getting you a two roomed flat.'[4]

He did not seek more rooms but moved two floors up in Chelsea Cloisters to number 921, exactly the same size as his previous one but cockroach free. It, too, was soon stuffed full with pictures and bric-à-brac. He also soon took over Catherine Mann's studio in nearby Yeoman's Row.

In early 1955 he heard that Vera Cuningham was terminally ill with lung cancer. She had always been an incessant smoker, so much so that her parrot had learned to imitate her cough, and a late switch to herbal tobacco had not saved her. Smith took her a pot plant and was one of her last visitors in the Middlesex Hospital before she died, reputedly in his arms, on 3 May 1955, aged fifty-seven. She was still wearing the blue necklace he had given her when they first became lovers. Her biographer tell us 'a few minutes after her death one of her supposed beneficiaries [perhaps Eve Disher] snatched the keys to Vera's house, went to ransack the apartment and in particular to burn Matthew

Smith's letters.'[5] This destruction must have been by mutual agreement since no intimate letters remain from Vera either. Smith wrote to tell both Gwen and Marion about his sorrow, and to say that she had only suffered for about a fortnight. Her main beneficiary was Eve Disher, the artist friend with whom she had been sharing a flat when she so fatefully met Smith at Meninsky's studio in 1922.

Mary, too, was ill and needed visiting in hospital, which was a strain for both parties. Soon after, Smith's nervous affliction struck him down again and as usual when he was under stress he returned to the Valmont Clinic in Switzerland – 'a good place to be when one does not feel too well,' he wrote to Gwen in August.[6] Before he left London he gave Mary some saleable drawings to help with expenses. 'I was about zero when I arrived here' he wrote back to her.[7] From the clinic he went to stay with the Mornays on the shore of Lake Geneva and found the affection still flowed strongly between him and Marion. They would meet twice more before he died. From there he went on to Roquebrune where presumably Chol had long forgiven him for the affair with Charlotte.

Death seemed to be crowding in on all sides now. Matisse, Derain, Léger, Rouault and Vlaminck all died in the 1950s. Only Picasso survived of that heroic School of Paris which had so inspired Smith in his youth. At home all his Slade cohort were gone, too. Roderick O'Conor had died back in 1940, but his widow Renée remained alive until January 1955. Because the claims on the O'Conor estate were numerous it was decided to auction all the studio works in Paris in February 1956, many of them as job lots displayed in laundry baskets. So little was his work known that Smith's *Nude on a Red Divan* of 1924, which O'Conor had owned, received the atelier stamp along with others by Renée herself, Seguin and Bernard. Fortunately the English dealer Henry Roland knew about O'Conor's paintings through Smith and flew over for the sale. He later wrote:

I went to view the things on the morning before the sale. The pictures hung around the wall with only numbers attached to them . . . I was overwhelmed by their beauty. They were the most marvellous 'Fauve' pictures painted well before the Fauves themselves . . . They were absolutely wonderful pictures, and I noticed the French dealers went through the room not giving the pictures much attention. I walked around Paris that afternoon as if on clouds, and at

2.30 punctually, when the doors opened, I was at the Drouot, taking my seat in one of the front rows . . . I bought about 120 pictures in that sale.[8]

Predictably the French buyers snapped up only the modern French masterpieces O'Conor had owned and scorned the rest.

Later, in April 1956, the Roland, Browse and Delbanco gallery put on an exhibition called *Two Masters of Colour* with Smith displayed at the front to tempt customers in, and the lesser known O'Conor at the back. Even Smith was deceived into thinking one of the O'Conor nudes on display was his own work, which demonstrates how potent the Irishman's influence must once have been. This was the beginning of O'Conor's still continuing rise in reputation and Smith must have been pleased to repay his debt to his '*maître*', even if it was posthumously.

Matthew's own work was now tailing off. Still lifes in pastels or watercolour predominate in these final years, the last perhaps being the drawing of two dead pheasants on a table which is now in the Victoria and Albert Museum. His use of oils diminished as his strength and libido declined. He was much feebler and undergoing tests for various alarming symptoms, and the more his health declined the more frantic his journeys became, as if he knew he must visit the scenes of past happiness before he died.

Vera and John Russell (now married) drove Smith through France, starting in Dieppe, then entertained him during late August 1956 at their holiday home in Villeneuve-lès-Avignon, and from there Russell took him to see Ingres' *Venus Anadyomène* at Chantilly. 'Marvellous, you know, REALLY. So much punch in the colour' was Smith's response.[9] Augustus John appeared for a few days, having been passed down France like a badly tied parcel by a chain of admirers and former lovers. From there the two old friends continued unsteadily south to Aix, where John saw a Cézanne exhibition and was taken in hand by his daughter Poppet. When he returned to Fryern he wrote to Smith: 'The Cézanne show was overwhelming and painting seems more mysterious than ever if not utterly impossible. Only the appearance of a young woman outside, with very little on, restored me more or less to normality and hope. But she belonged to an earlier and more fabulous age than ours.'[10] It was John's last trip abroad.

Russell later recalled of this holiday, 'Once, during a period where we watched every evening the fall of light on the Palais des Papes at Avignon, I ventured to comment on Nature's virtuosity in this regard. "Yes" he [Smith] said, "but I can't bear it. It's too fugitive, you know, too fugitive".'[11]

Matthew had refused to join Gwen on a holiday in Sicily in the spring so she went alone, taking oxygen cylinders to boost her failing heart and help her bronchial troubles. 'I want you just as badly,' she had pleaded, but he sent her some crayons as a substitute for himself. He journeyed on to spend September and October with the Cholertons and Hallidays at Cap Martin and Menton, and then persuaded the Chols to drive him to Aix for a wonderful month-long reunion with Marion Monay.

He was due back in Manchester in October to judge the Art College students' summer work, an event organized by the students themselves, that year by the future novelist Glyn Hughes. Smith pointed out that 'I am not a good critic, secondly I could not give an address should that be required of me.'[12] Nevertheless, he was interested to see the current state of painting in his old college and would waive the fee of £5 to do so. The delighted Hughes then put up posters, only to have the visit cancelled by a furious Principal because 'at the same time I was receiving a generous response from Smith, the college wasn't getting on very well in wooing him to make a more grand visit and accept an honour. Holden's attitude was that I had upset his strategies, though I guess the truth was that Smith was without sympathy for the official side of the college.'[13] Perhaps Smith had heard that the head of the Painting School there was telling his students, in Tonks-like tones, that '"modern art" was alright as an interest "in their spare time" – and by modern art he didn't mean anything as devilish as abstract expressionism, he meant Picasso and Matisse.' If any honours were officially offered to Smith he did not accept them, remembering, perhaps, his four wasted years in the college.

Instead, in 1956 he received a Doctorate from London University, in effect conferred by the Slade, which through Tonks had once condemned him as having 'no sense of drawing, no ability to paint.' He wrote to Gwen: 'Well I am now an Honorary Fellow of London University . . . I was spoken of as having been a distinguished student at the Slade – not quite true.'[14]

The honours were coming fast now because people could see that Smith was getting weaker and had little time left. Around Christmas 1956 he had written to Alden Brooks confessing he felt he was 'on his last gasp', but Brooks replied heartily and enclosed a press cutting about a man who was still alive at 103, and 'anyway I have heard the same old refrain since I first knew you.'[15] Brooks was still wondering whether he could come to Europe, or Smith to California, but concludes, 'Well it is but a dream, I realise it now and we shall never meet again. So let's face it.' He chides Smith for his smoking, and then recommends a reading of Clive Bell's book *Old Friends* which mentions them both and is 'very fair' on O'Conor, though full of that Bloomsbury snobbery they both hated.[16]

As a titled celebrity Matthew was now photographed by Douglas Glass, Felix Man and various press photographers, though for none of them did he manage a smile. For the first time this secretive man allowed reporters into his tiny flat and the studio in Yeoman's Row.[17] From their articles we can build up a picture of the 'idiosyncratic disorder' in which he lived and worked. The flat was littered with treasures such as an Epstein cherub, a buddha, a sketch by Delacroix of fiery horses picked up in a Paris junk shop, and over the bed an unframed Van Gogh of cottages from the dark Neunen period, for which he had paid £160 in the 1930s (after his death Mary Keene sold it for £7,000). Beside the window was a small Gauguin pencil sketch and over the desk a drawing by Adrian Daintrey. His own works were stacked round the walls, face out, or stuffed under the bed.

A short walk away was the studio, one of several in this Yeoman's Row cul-de-sac, purpose-built with large windows. Here hogshair brushes and paints were laid out on a table and there were various easels, his 'Leda' screens, and stacks of his own works, many already framed in the heavy gilt frames he favoured. A notice for the charlady's benefit said 'Do not sweep or dust anything if you please.' He liked to pose for photographs beside his copy of Ingres' *Charity*, thus stating his loyalties and baffling the reporters who could see little connection between this cool master and the near-incandescent works around them. Scattered round on small tables (one of them supported by carved cherubs) lay all the objects he painted again and again: the jugs, vases, bowls, plaster fruit and fish, nude statuette, the torso of Christiane, and the wooden figure he had rescued from the debris of Abbeville so long ago.

After his death Mary Keene made an inventory of the works of art he owned and listed originals by Gwen Salmond, Meninsky, William Roberts, Modigliani, Van Dongen, Dufresnay, Moore, Sickert, Augustus John, Epstein, Vera Cuningham, and Segonzac. Prints of three of Matisse's Odalisques are also recorded. The artistic and personal allegiances of his lifetime are encapsulated in this list, as they are also in his library with its French classics, particularly Stendhal, volumes on Ingres and Matisse, and works on most European masters except Picasso.[18]

The year 1957 was rather flat, with no trips across the Channel, though he managed extended stays with both the Hallidays and the Hughes where he was fed and spoiled in ways the undomesticated Mary could never manage. The following year began terribly on 18 January with Gwen's death from coronary thrombosis in her hotel room, though the doctor assured Smith that 'she had a pleasurable exit.' Matthew himself registered the death and Augustus John, who had known her longer even than her husband, wrote the obituary for *The Times*.[19] Halliday wrote an unpublished tribute, too, which told how she had kept on painting to the end, though 'about her painting she was curiously modest, almost shy, perhaps because it came from her innermost self.'[20] She had rarely exhibited her work and when Matthew inherited what little was left he distributed it amongst her nieces. He was full of remorse because he had not turned up for their wedding anniversary the week before: 'I couldn't do it, I couldn't do it. She always played on my emotions then,' he told Catherine Mann. She thought Smith had given Gwen everything but love 'which is out of one's control' and summed her up as 'a bright-coloured person, kind and cruel, always making startling comments.'[21]

In spring 1958 he endured an exploratory operation for cancer in Guy's Hospital and suffered jaundice. ('He looks as if he were dead, yellow skin over a skull. My heart ached with pity for him though he seemed full of fun and little jokes,' Catherine wrote in her diary.)[22] Nevertheless, he had rallied enough for the Russells to take him to

Venice in June. He had tried to get there on his honeymoon in 1912 but had had to cancel the trip because of the death of his mother, though he did visit briefly with Vera Cuningham in the 1920s. He had always admired the Venetian painters and now, too late, when he was ill and tetchy, he saw them *in situ*. Vera Russell wrote to the Hallidays to arrange for them to meet him off the plane at Nice and warned them he was weak and walking badly but 'there's no sign that he knows how seriously ill he is – always speaks of when he will be completely recovered.' The Russells had also been struck by his meanness; 'one can be terribly out of pocket being with him,' Vera complained.[23] On the way home he called one last time on the Chols in Roquebrune and the Monays in Switzerland and said his farewells to Charlotte and Marion. By October he was back in hospital for more desperate surgery.

As Smith lost strength John Russell offers us one last glimpse of him as he was in 1958:

With his downturned hat and very good tweeds he looks, in the street, like a distinguished antiquary who has come to London for the day; fine manners, an unhurried step and a voice like that of a very intelligent moth may convince a chance acquaintance that he is going nowhere in particular. But we must not be deceived; it is he, and not the swashbuckler in the velveteens, who will be remembered as long as there are paintings in England, and walls to hang them on.[24]

After this Smith's illness sapped his strength unrelentingly and his friends rallied round with invitations or comforting letters. John wrote, 'I hope you have some agreeable young woman to look after you. It makes all the difference.'[25] Smith had several. His confidante Cathleen Mann was very attentive (though she too would die within the year), and so was Betty Newmarch, a young and pretty dress designer, who lived along the corridor at 907 and had been his close friend for some years now. She had sat for a portrait and accompanied him on some of his travels. Other devoted ladies came in, such as Barbara Goudge his secretary and Mrs Murphy his cleaner. Mary Keene was still doing her best though she agitated as much as soothed him, and when she asked if he would finally marry her he hissed '*Jamais*.'[26] Other favourites also offered solace, such as Valerie Hobson who took him out for meals and to the theatre as long as he could go, and then for a last trip to the

Regent's Canal with her two sons. Matthew was so weak at the end that he had to be carried into her house near Regent's Park.

Obviously he would soon be getting to the stage when he could no longer live alone. He rallied sufficiently to paint a watercolour of a rose to be bound in a golden-wedding gift volume to Winston Churchill in September 1958. Smith had long admired Churchill the politician and Churchill the painter.

Rothenstein claims that for a long time Smith did not realize what was wrong with him, but, '"Matthew" said a woman friend of his, "must be crucified before he dies" and she repaired his ignorance.'[27] This may be a reference to the now devout Mary, whom Rothenstein disliked. She in turn was being tortured by the doctors' veto on her talking to Smith about his illness or discussing his last wishes. He said to her, 'You suffer for your sins in your own lifetime,' and moaned what an unworthy father he had been to his two sons. He must have known he was near the end, however, because he wrote his will and revised it twice within the year.

On 5 January 1959 Smith told Brooks that he had jaundice again, his weight was down to 6st 4lbs and 'I now know what it's like to feel old.'[28] In the same month he received a letter from Mary saying she was planning to sell some of his works for £450, £550 and £800 each because 'Dear Math Alice and I are very happy to have the extra money, it is like sweet summer coming in.'[29] He had obviously not confided in her when making his will. Miraculously Smith rallied and took a spring holiday with Gwen's brother, Air Marshal Sir Jack Salmond, himself now a frail old man. They had always got on well together and Matthew had painted a fine portrait of his distinguished brother-in-law in 1947, the sitter wrapped in his blue-mauve RAF greatcoat against a blue background relieved only by a crimson sash behind his head.[30] The two knights sailed to Tenerife on the *Venus*. This was to be Smith's only contact with Spain. He disliked its 'sugar-coated modernity' and arid landscape and was glad to get home.

On his return Smith was yet weaker, but still made an appearance at the Royal Academy annual banquet, and so at last was reconciled to that institution. John, who had long ago made his peace with the Academy, wrote to Smith that his life was, as usual, harassed but 'the

RA is beginning to take on the aspect of an asylum for the aged with its sympathetic secretary and its complete immunity from the interference of rapacious tradesmen.'[31]

By summer 1959 Smith was sinking fast and the Russells leased him their home at 23 Acacia Road, St John's Wood, while they were away. Night and day nurses attended for the final six weeks of his life and there his friends came bearing gifts: Iris Hughes, for example, brought him orchids. Then on 17 August Jacob and Kathleen Epstein brought an exquisite little Renoir landscape to have by his bed to cheer him up. They talked together for several hours, smoked, drank champagne and then left. The sculptor seemed as robust as ever and Smith felt envious of 'the two iron grips of the hand' with which they parted. Two days later Epstein collapsed and died of a heart attack.

Smith wrote to Brooks in Topanga, 'I am very upset by the death of Epstein, he seemed to have a very special feeling of friendship for me and I for him though I expressed it less well.' Smith rose and attended the quiet funeral, his eye noting 'the rich vermilion cloak' of the Dean of Canterbury as he officiated. Smith was now only six stone in weight and fed on slops, he told Brooks. 'I have had a long life and some good patches among it all so no reason to complain, but I have many regrets about one thing and another and there has been much sadness and I have never been very good. Well there it is.' He enclosed a sketch of a gaunt face and in a shaky hand the words 'Calling on O'Conor.'[32]

Brooks dropped all his former pretence of jollying Matthew along with jokes about hypochondria and his sex life and replied on 9 September:

So you are dying? Only a little more to go you say. It's all rather sad, depressing – especially as your letter is written with such mental control, even vigour . . . Well, Matthew, if it must be goodbye, let's face it, and here's my hand, even if the grip is not so firm as Epstein's. And if you are not to survive in the living, you will always survive in my memory. And each of my rooms happily carries an image of you . . . Well Matthew, my lad, there may be something in the Great Beyond. And if there is, keep me a place at your table. I won't be long. Alden.[33]

Stephen Spender walked round from his house nearby, and years later still reproached himself for his scruples in not buying a Smith painting as his friend lay dying:

Two days before he died, Matthew said 'I do so wish you had an oil painting by me.' Later, thinking things over, I saw what I should have done. I should have brought the picture to his beside, and said: 'See what I have of yours, which I shall always remember you by' . . . something of the sort.

In the same week he asked me a question which I failed to answer. It was: 'Do you believe there is life after death?' I replied that I didn't know, but I added, I think, that a dear friend of mine was a firm believer in immortality. The next day when I called to see him, the nurse opened the door and told me that Matthew had died during the night. What should I have answered? It is the kind of question which keeps one awake years after the event.[34]

Dr Herbert had come and given him a last morphine injection and Matthew Smith died on 29 September of cancer of the pancreas, a few weeks short of his eightieth birthday.

He was buried beside Gwen in St Jude's churchyard, Gunnersbury, both having after their names and dates the proud title PAINTER. At the memorial service in St James's Piccadilly on 22 October Sir Philip Hendy recalled how Smith had regarded the works of his friends Epstein and John with 'a kind of reverend awe, never imagining that his own pictures would be considered on the same plane.' But, he concluded, 'wherever there is a picture by Matthew Smith in a room, there is a warm fire in that room.' Spender read 'Thoughts' by Thomas Traherne and 'The Retreat' by Henry Vaughan to the assembled Smiths, Salmonds, Mary Keene, titled aristocrats, Heads of the Slade and Arts Council, the President of the Royal Academy, John Rothenstein, Director of the Tate, Kenneth Clark, Henry Moore, Duncan Grant, Dudley Tooth, representatives of Giggleswick School and all those friends who had supported and loved him through his long career. Augustus John then went up and down the aisles heartily kissing the young girls.

The obituaries told of Smith's progress from riches to riches, of his Yorkshire tenacity, personal modesty, and most mentioned, but no longer overstressed, his artistic debts to Matisse. They seemed happy now to call him an English painter, though an isolated one, founding no school and belonging to none. In describing his colour they trowelled on a thick impasto of adjectives: gorgeous, plummy, riotous, opulent, voluptuous, tempestuous, sumptuous, orchestrated, Fauve, Expressionist and Venetian. 'A banquet for the eye, never a stimulus for the mind,' seemed to be the gist of it. The very un-Englishness of such bright colour and 'orgiastic enthusiasm' was commented on by several who took the opportunity to denigrate all other English art as tight-lipped, puritanical, insular, restrained, hesitant, and 'a little wan from mental agitation.' Two (Russell and Sutton) made passing, but provocative, comparisons between his work and that of Alexei von Jawlensky (1864–1941), a Russian painter similarly obsessed with saturated colour harmonies whose work Smith must have known in Paris.

David Piper speculated that 'the root of many of his failures, or rather his near misses, may have lain in a failure of physique. It is as though sometimes he lacked the brute muscular power to sustain the sensuous exuberance of his colour; the heavy contours sag, and thick paint slows.' But Piper saw him off with a flourish: 'From his modest and arduous life he hoisted many triumphant banners, and they remain.'[35] Only one writer ventured an outright criticism of the dead man's *oeuvre*. Eric Newton thought Smith too little concerned with the architecture of his works: 'His forms, broad and noble though they were, and whether they described a bank of trees, a bunch of peonies, were seldom satisfactorily composed. They suggested a tumult within the frame and often they infuriatingly collided with it. Yet his opulence silenced one's demand for structure or a mathematical basis of design.'[36]

It had been a family joke that Smith always forgot his wallet when he took one of his brothers out to lunch at the Royal Court. When Smith's will was published and his nephew Peter read that he had left £173,948 gross he remarked to his father: 'Uncle Matthew must really have been very mean making you pay for everything when all the time he had so much money.' 'I don't think the poor lad knew he had it,' Harold replied.[37] He had lived a comfortable but not epicurean life, his main expenses being rented properties, extensive travels in France, and buying treats for the many woman he loved. When the will was read it was found (to the consternation of some) that, apart from a few bequests to friends and charities, he had left all his money, paintings and copyright to Mary Keene, and after her death, to her daughter Alice.

Epilogue

Mary Keene used some of her inherited money to subsidize a book on her benefactor which, after much negotiation, appeared in 1962 as *Matthew Smith*, with fifty-two colour plates, and contributions by Hendy, Halliday and Russell.[1] Not to be outdone, in the same year Rothenstein produced a rival *Matthew Smith*, with sixteen colour reproductions and thirty-three black and whites.[2]

In February 1960, Tooth's did their best to keep Smith's name before the public with a retrospective exhibition, *Homage to Matthew Smith*, though the critics who had used up their best adjectives in the obituaries were unable to say much new about it. The Royal Academy, to which Smith had never even submitted a picture, gave him a huge exhibition (six rooms crowded with 255 oils) from 15 October to 7 December 1960, obviously intending it to be a chronological survey of his career. Augustus John shambled through the galleries exclaiming 'Stupendous! Marvellous!' though in a letter to *The Times* he claimed 'on a recent visit to the Academy, when called upon by my fellow members to express an opinion, I found myself completely dumb, though God knows I had plenty to say!'[3]

The Academy exhibition was well received, with the usual things repeated in the reviews, and Russell explained to his *Sunday Times* readers Smith's affinities with (rather than borrowings from) Modigliani, Rouault, Matisse, and the contribution to his nudes of Rembrandt's *Danaë* and *Bathsheba*, and to his landscapes those of Rubens.[4] David Carritt in *The Evening Standard* patriotically thought he stood comparison with Dufy, Vlaminck and Derain, and far surpassed Segonzac. However, once again Eric Newton had reservations, this time about the narrowness of Smith's emotional span: 'All his paintings are acts of homage, never studies in drama, so that when he paints an interpretation of Rubens or El Greco one suddenly realises that action and tension are beyond his range . . . There are no agonies, no self-searchings, no disillusionments in his simple but skilful art. Untroubled splendour was his only theme.'[5]

Smith's work was thus available in the early 1960s, in exhibitions, in books and in reviews. However, when one comes to survey these one realizes that the same advocates keep appearing and saying the same things: Rothenstein, Hendy, Russell, Halliday, Newton, Dahl, Sutton, Spender, Yorke – all cultured middle-aged men who knew Smith and owned some of his work. These were writers rather than painters and perhaps temperamentally out of sympathy with newer trends in the visual arts. What young artists were excited about now was not Smith's plump girlfriends, or fruits, or Provençal sunsets, but the onset of Pop Art and the invasion of Abstract Expressionism. Both of these had appeared before Smith's death, though we have no record of his reactions to them, apart from this shrewd aside in an interview: 'Nor did he withhold interest from the "action painting" and "tachisme" of very recent appearance, though mildly remarking that they do "give an opening to various kinds of charlatanism." '[6]

English Pop artists looked to American cars, singers, comics and advertising for inspiration, whilst the New York Abstract Expressionists taught others to research single aspects of traditional painting, such as gesture, accident, size or colour for its own, unrepresentational, sake. Patrick Heron, for example, realized he had seen the future and declared, 'Colour is the only direction in which painting can now travel.' Of these new transatlantic heroes only de Kooning still painted the female nude because he believed that 'Flesh was the reason why oil painting was invented.' But his carnivorous harpies ('They really scare the pants off me,' he admitted) are no relatives of Vera Cuningham, voluptuously curled on her warm sheets.

Many English art colleges abandoned life classes, broke up those antique casts Smith had practised on, and stopped teaching drawing and craft skills. There were now no orthodoxies, only a compulsion to be original. New 'isms' proliferated, even more rapidly than in Paris at the beginning of the century: Minimalism, Conceptualism, Super-Realism, Neo-Expressionism, Post-Modernism, to name but a few. Aestheticians raised political, gender, sociological, philosophical, ethnic and linguistic issues which Fry or Kenneth Clark had never even thought of. Painting in oils on a rectangular canvas was abandoned for new media such as chocolate, blood, formaldehyde, neon, rocks, sump oil, urine and video. Many of these products were so large they could only be displayed in specialist galleries, and it no longer made sense to ask if they were in an English, French, American or Japanese style, because magazines, exhibitions and scholarships disseminated the latest ideas round the globe as soon as they appeared.

All these developments were exciting and necessary, but they inevitably moved avant-garde art beyond the kind of Modernism to which Impressionism, Post-Impressionism, Cubism, Fauvism and Surrealism gave rise, and within which Matthew Smith was happy to work all his life. His was a simpler time and the criteria for success more generally agreed.

Predictably, Smith's paintings fell from fashion in this world avid for novelty, with only half a dozen small exhibitions devoted solely to his work between 1960 and 1983. It was clear that a full-scale retrospective was needed if he was to revive and take up his rightful niche in the history of English art, but this did not come until the Barbican exhibition of 15 September to 30 October 1983. This had a luxurious catalogue with the usual quotes and contributors (Russell, Spender, Fry, Dahl, Hendy, Bacon, Keene). A new generation of reviewers met Smith's work for the first time in this exhibition though, predictably, the radical art magazines chose to ignore it.

Frances Spalding under the odd headline 'Searching and Seedy' thought his 'blowzy' nudes by their very colour and sensuality were calculated to offend against the English love of restraint:

He evidently shared Sickert's belief that the chief source of pleasure in a nude arose from it being 'in the nature of a gleam – a gleam of light and warmth and life.' This, however, suggests a spryness that Smith's nudes do not have. Instead they wallow amid drapery and across divans in standard poses descended from Ingres, Delacroix, Rubens and Courbet. They are painted at speed with undeniable conviction, even though the forms spill out, like roses in his still-lifes, over-blown and over-spelt.

She preferred the Cornish landscapes which revealed 'that he produced his most original work when his own loneliness and pain became an aspect of the subject he treated.'[7]

John Russell Taylor in *The Times* found the show an unexpected revelation both of Smith's variety and the evidence for consistent development right up to his last years, and

some of the drawings, such as the remarkable series of First World War prisoners, indicate that, when he needed it, [he had] a masterly grasp of draughtsmanship and of the bare, stripped essentials of composition: for all their sensuous surface these paintings are rigorously thought out. Many of the paintings in the show make the whole process look as easy as falling off a log, but now one can sense also the fundamental brainwork which went into getting Smith to this state of actual as (opposed to) apparent ease and spontaneity.[8]

That would have pleased Smith, who never thought he received enough credit for his brains.

Another lull followed, though Smith's works continued to hold their value in the salerooms. Then in the definitive 1987 survey exhibition, *British Art of the Twentieth Century*, held in the Royal Academy, Smith was generously represented by eight works, though perversely paired with the minor Mark Gertler as exemplifying 'The Resilient Figure'. (August John, by now deeply unfashionable, was omitted altogether.) In the catalogue no French influence was mentioned, but Smith's Fitzroy Street nudes were closely related to 'Gilman's solidly coordinated planes of colour' and, it is claimed,

his early painting both here and in the Cornish landscapes is not very far distant from Camden Town and Bloomsbury, for he belonged to the London Post-Impressionist development rather than to France. His radical attack on colour, which had been reinforced by friendship with the erratic Roderic O'Conor, singled him out as a positive and extraordinary artistic personality.[9]

Mary Keene had received instructions from Matthew that, if possible, all the pictures he had bequeathed to her should be kept together, so in 1974 she donated over a thousand paintings, drawings, watercolours, pastels and sketchbooks to the Corporation of London. She died in

1981 before all this treasure could be properly sorted and catalogued, and it was only in the summer of 1995 that a public exhibition could be mounted at the Barbican to show four hundred of these works.[10] In some ways this was an unrepresentative display of Smith's capability since his studio leavings were a mixture of masterpieces and failures, early works, those which he could not sell, and unfinished canvases. His important Cornish period, French landscapes and flower paintings were all under-represented. The best were images of the women he had loved and wished to keep by him: glowing works still radiating enough heat to warm his blood in old age. Here are Lucy, Elizabeth, Lorretta, Aniése, Patricia, Catherine, Simone, Poppet, Valerie, Sunita, Christiane, Marion, Vera Cuningham and Mary Keene herself. His wife was not represented, except in a slight drawing of her suckling one of their sons.

Reviewers raised some old topics, amongst them the status in the history of British art of a painter who so obviously loved all things French. William Packer puts the problem in these terms:

We seem to catch our painters in a double-bind. On the one hand, we talk down our native school for the insularity and singularity, if not downright eccentricity, of its members. On the other, the moment an artist betrays the faintest interest in what is going on elsewhere, we condemn him outright as but the palest imitation of the superior foreign model.[11]

We have seen that as fashions and cultural nationalism waxed and waned he was alternately praised for being almost French, then condemned for being merely French, next acclaimed for being wholly English and finally seen as not cosmopolitan enough. The only people who did not try to recruit him to their camp were the French themselves whose critics are still largely unaware of his existence.

Critics of the 1995 exhibition were similarly ambivalent: 'Citoyen Smith', 'The English Fauve', 'The Most French of English Painters', 'His spiritual home was France', 'The most European painter of his generation', 'His closeness to contemporary French painting, and to Matisse most of all, is unarguable', they proclaimed. He still suffered by the comparison too: 'He had neither the nervous system of Soutine nor the gallic insouciance of Segonzac; Dufy makes him clodhopping.'[12] A few, however, disagreed. One thought him 'more francophile than

French,' and another declared: 'Smith was often hailed as a kind of English Matisse. In fact he was a repressed Englishman. Even his most voluptuous nude is restrained by a recognisably English palette and tonal range. These are not the light, airy, playful works of Matisse or Dufy.'[13]

Smith's possible influence on painters who came after him was also raised by the reviewers. Was he a dead end or did he open up a new route for others? Smith never taught and hated the idea that anyone might steal his ideas and develop further what he had acquired for himself with so much labour. He could borrow but not lend, being determined to go out on a limb and then saw it off behind him. We know he was admired by Bacon for the way he made 'idea and technique inseparable' but what of the next generation? Is he still a 'painter's painter' for them? Several critics now claim to be able to detect his direct descendants, particularly Iain Gale in a catalogue essay subtitled, 'Matthew Smith's work and its influences on 20th Century British painting.'[14] Gale suggests we might detect 'a borrowing of the abstract qualities' in Smith in the early work of Gillian Ayres, who admired him, and it is true she has based a whole career on celebrating the physical nature of vigorously applied paint. Recently she said, 'I don't see why you shouldn't be filling yourself up, making yourself happy. Enjoying yourself. Feasting on beauty.'[15] This is certainly near to Smith's intention, but for him the effort was always frustrated by a sense of failure. Gale also traces Smith's 'celebration of worldliness' in the paintings of Patrick Heron. Reviewer Richard Shone, too, sees specific traces of Smith in Heron's still lifes of the 1940s and his early *Delia* portrait.[16]

I wrote to Heron and several others to put Gale's claims to the test, and indeed Heron still does consider Smith, together with Sickert, 'the first British painter of international status since the deaths of Constable and Turner.'[17] The 'often apparently puerperal eroticism' of Heron's friend Roger Hilton is seen by Gale as nodding in Smith's direction, too, but Smith, who was raised a Victorian, would have averted his eyes from Hilton's pictorial indiscretions: his own works were sensual, but discreetly posed, and for him bawdiness was confined to late night jokes over brandy in the Café Royal.

John Hoyland is a contemporary artist whose forte is dynamic colour, but he found Smith only an indirect inspiration in so far as he proved that brilliant paintings could be done by someone else raised in a grey Yorkshire industrial city.[18] The landscapes and flowers of Ivon Hitchens share a gestural freedom with Smith's, but were arrived at by an independent route. Howard Hodgkin's imagery and Eastern inspirations make any painterly similarities no more than incidental, though he told me that as a schoolboy he had been enthusiastic about Hendy's book and loved the two Fitzroy Street Nudes and the Tate's *Cornish Church* with its black sky. The less firmly structured 'sloppy' pictures which came later he had less time for, and overall could not say that his own practice had been influenced by Smith. He did, though, consider him to be vastly superior to Hitchens. Curiously, when Smith's works were shown at the Knoedler Gallery in New York in 1979 Hodgkin designed the all-black frames in which they were displayed.[19] Another colourist, Adrian Berg, does admit he was so enthusiastic about Smith in his student days that he copied a still life and found the nudes 'interesting and influential.' He concludes, 'Smith was of practical use as well as being an English artist up to [that] date better than any other in that field.'[20]

'Something of Smith's sensuality or paint quality is reflected in the work of such apparently diverse artists as John Bratby, Frank Auerbach, Sheila Girling and Eileen Cooper, all of whom have the ability to make the most mundane subject matter resonate with the possibilities of life,' Gale tells us confidently. Shone, too, thinks 'there are passages in his landscapes and nudes that seem to have a mainline connection with Auerbach in his more colourful mode, paint slashed and swirled against the expected rhythm of the object portrayed.'[21] We can perhaps allow a tenuous thread from Smith to some of these minor artists, but surely Auerbach is in a different league and an odd choice? He, along with Kossoff and Creffield, take their descent from Sickert, and their tutor Bomberg's later style, and owe nothing to Smith's high-pitched colours, or thin, one-touch application of paint. Nevertheless, Auerbach wrote, 'I have always admired the independence, tenacity and appetite of Matthew Smith, have on various occasions paid especial attention to the courage and intelligence in his work, and have never quite tired of it.[22] Which is generous, but not the same thing as being influenced by Smith. Leon Kossoff, too, admits Smith's importance: 'He kept painting alive during a very fallow period. He knew you had to move the paint around, he intuitively understood the bond between drawing and painting. And yet I can't say that I was much influenced by his work when I was a student nor do I know if today's young painters pay him much attention.'[23] A more Impressionistic painter of nudes, Ken Howard, would disagree. He was 'knocked out' by a Smith exhibition when a student and very influenced until 'I realised there was a strong expressionist streak in his work which wasn't part of my make up.' However, 'I think he is very relevant to young painters today where there has been a return to figurative painting with a strong underlying expressionist influence.'[24]

On balance then, Smith seems still to be respected amongst our straw poll of mainly figurative painters, though none sees him as a major force in their mature work. If Smith in his turn opened a porthole for our reserved and over-tasteful British painters it was one which showed them, in the most general way, the possibilities of saturated colour, free handling, and that they need not be furtive about having an appetite for the good things in life. As the *Guardian* critic put it: 'Smith seems to survive as one of the few genuine sensualists of twentieth century British art' with his 'unashamed celebration of the flesh.'[25] But David Lee's claim that 'there is hardly a British painter who would not doff his cap to Matthew Smith. It seems that when Smith's name is mentioned praise is automatic,' is mere hyperbole.[26] There is no School of Smith, and he remains one of those artists like Spencer, Collins, Burra or Bacon who have many admirers, but no direct heirs.

The Barbican exhibition catalogue had an outline of his life, entitled 'The Two Mr Smiths' and nearly all the reviewers picked up on the title's implied contrast between the 'fogeyish' grey recluse who appeared in the family photographs and his crimson paintings of fat women sprawled across tousled beds. Jeremy Treglown writes perceptively under the headline 'From girl to girl, studio to studio': 'There was in fact only one Mr Smith: a nervous man in love with beauty and especially with women, on whom he depended, most of whom couldn't depend on him, and some of whom he cost in terms of their own art.'[27] Elsewhere

Martin Gayford offers the insight that 'Smith was a master psychic escapologist, and his vagueness, nervousness and elusiveness aided him in this respect.'[28] It certainly got him out of any kind of emotional commitment which would interfere with his painting.

Andrew Lambirth wrote: 'Although admired and liked, his work isn't really up there in the big league. Why? Perhaps we want our art to be a little more testing.' He quotes Wyndham Lewis's dismissal of Smith's work as 'the taste of the stupid', but then unlike Lewis's it had no pretentions to be 'intellectual, philosophical, literary or particularly metaphysical. It is deliberately pleasurable, but it also has a formal flexibility and strength which has always attracted the attention of many fellow artists. Smith deserves to be reconsidered, and better known.'[29] Only one or two reviewers looked deeper into the 'radiantly optimistic' works and their bravura painting, and hinted that this exultant sensuality is not just self-indulgent. It had been earned through suffering in two wars and in his private life, and 'thus his splendidly affirmative art was perhaps a braver gesture than at first might appear.'[30] The nudes and still lifes answered to needs deeper than merely sensuous ones and so 'a deep and unresolved emotional ferment was let loose, at once a vibrant celebration of life and an expression of its deepest pain.'[31]

David Lee blames the dip in Smith's posthumous reputation on several factors which have nothing to do with the merits of his painting. Firstly, he was knighted in 1954 and so appeared to join 'the ranks of those flairless, plodding "academics" who are usually thus honoured.' Then again, 'maybe the problem is that there is no immediately great masterpiece by Smith; there is no famous portrait or other commission by him, no great war works.' Then, more seriously, 'because he had no particular painterly ideology or intellectual axe to grind, he cannot be conveniently pigeon-holed, which is a drawback when it comes to establishing reputations, postures and stances.'[32] Indeed, Charles Harrison in his survey of *English Art and Modernism: 1900–1939* felt it necessary to apologize for not being able to find a suitable label: 'The need to advance this narrative is offered for the scant attention paid to those artists such as Matthew Smith whose work was pursued during the period in question in circumstances of comparative isolation, apart from group activities.'[33]

Nicholas Serota, Director of the Tate Gallery, thinks that today 'Smith's reputation is secure, but perhaps not advancing. He occupies a unique place within early and mid-twentieth-century British art in his response to the School of Paris. His singular approach to the human form, to still life and the use of colour left him, perhaps, in a more isolated position than artists like Sickert or Bomberg.'[34]

This book has been an attempt to show how Smith came to occupy this 'unique place' in British art, and how he evolved his 'singular approach' to painting. He never painted to illustrate a theory, or allowed himself to be recruited to any grouping, English or French, which might have lessened the travail of creation. From his integrity and individualism sprang a body of work which is one of the glories of British art.

References

Several people accumulated Smith's letters and associated papers during his lifetime. Their collections are now to be found as follows: Francis Halliday's in the possession of Christopher Halliday; Mary Keene's in the possession of Alice Keene; Marion Monay's in the possession of Alice Keene; Phyllis Royde-Smith's in the possession of Michael Royde-Smith; Frederic Smith: copies of six letters from Matthew to his father were given by Paul Birkett-Smith to the Tate Gallery; Gwen Smith's (née Salmond) in the possession of Alice Keene. Matthew Smith's own papers are in the possession of Alice Keene.

In addition, valuable sources of information are: Alden Brooks's diaries in the possession of Corinne Cornish; Cathleen Mann's diaries in the possession of Lord Queensberry; Fanny Smith's diaries in the possession of Michael Royde-Smith; Arthur Tooth's archive in the possession of Simon Matthews.

In quoting from the above sources I have corrected Smith's occasional spelling errors but retained his idiosyncratic punctuation.

The main critical and biographical texts on Smith are, in order of publication:

Hendy, Philip, *Matthew Smith*, Penguin, 1944
Rothenstein, John, *Modern English Painters*, Vol. 1 (Chapter on Smith), 1952 [I have made use of the revised Macdonald and Jane edition, 1976, Vol. 2]
Rothenstein, John, *Matthew Smith*, Beaverbrook Newspapers, 1962
Halliday, Francis, and Russell, John, *Matthew Smith*, introduction by Sir Philip Hendy, Allen & Unwin, 1962
Royde-Smith, Sophie, 'The early paintings of Matthew Smith', unpublished M.Phil. dissertation, Courtauld Institute, London, 1991
Keene, Alice, *The Two Mr Smiths*, Lund Humphries, Corporation of London, 1995

Also helpful is the thesis: Knott, D. H., 'A Matthew Smith Bibliography', Diploma in Librarianship, London University, 1966. Detailed reference is made to catalogues and reviews within the text.

Notes

Introduction

1 Spoken to Mary Keene and told to the author by Alice Keene.
2 J. M. Whistler, a letter of 1878 published in his *The Gentle Art of Making Enemies*, 1890, pp. 127–8.

1 A Yorkshire Youth: 1879–1898

1 J. Rothenstein, *Time's Thievish Progress*, 1970, p. 3.
2 Catherine Mann diaries, 23 February 1958.
3 Matthew Smith (hereafter MS) to Alden Brooks, 17 February 1954.
4 *Halifax Courier and Guardian*, 23 July 1927.
5 G. H. Smith, 'The Smiths of Halifax', paper delivered on 1 November 1941 and then published in the *Proceedings of the Halifax Antiquarian Society*, 1949, pp. 73–91.
6 J. Fletcher, *Memories of a Spectator*, 1912, p. 7.
7 H. Whone, *The Essential West Riding*, 1987, p. 163.
8 These and other Smith documents are held by The West Yorkshire Archive Service, Calderdale, Halifax.
9 F. Smith, *A Chest of Viols and Other Verses*, 1896.
10 Details from auction catalogue of Dunham Lawn, Bowdon, 2–5 June 1919, by Messrs C. W. Provis & Sons.
11 F. Halliday and J. Russell, *Matthew Smith*, 1962, p. 4; Alden Brooks diaries, 19 June 1919.
12 J. Rothenstein, *Matthew Smith*, 1962, p. 2.
13 J. Rothenstein, *Modern English Painters*, Vol. 1, 1976, p. 230.
14 J. Russell, 'Matthew Smith: Master Painter', *England*, Journal of the Royal Society of St George, Spring 1958, p. 20.
15 Catherine Mann diaries, 17 March 1958.
16 *Halifax Courier and Guardian*, 23 July 1927.
17 For most of the Giggleswick materials I am indebted to the Second Master, Warwick Brooks, and the Secretary, Mrs F. Hargreaves.
18 Alden Brooks diaries, 19 June 1919.

2 Manchester: 1899–1904

1 Briton Rivière, RA (1840–1920), specialist in animal pictures.
2 Dendy Sadler, RBA (1854–1923), specialist in historical and genre subjects.
3 George Frederic Watts (1817–1904), painter of portraits and allegories. Fanny Smith's diary for 14 June 1905 reads: 'Met Fred. Went to see Watts' pictures. Our favourite is Hope.'
4 Catherine Mann diaries, 5 March 1953.
5 F. Halliday and J. Russell, catalogue introduction to Memorial Exhibition of Works by MS, Royal Academy, 1960, p. v.
6 Henri Moret (1856–1913), French painter of land and seascapes. Worked with Gauguin at Pont Aven.
7 Emil Claus (1849–1924), Belgian genre and landscape painter.
8 Presumably Norman Prescott Davies, RBA (1862–1915), popular genre painter.
9 J. Rothenstein, *Modern English Painters*, Vol. 1, 1976, p. 229.
10 *Halifax Courier and Guardian*, 9 January 1954.
11 Rothenstein, op. cit., p. 229.
12 F. Halliday and Russell, op. cit., p. 229.
13 W. M. Thackeray, *The Newcomes*, 1853–5, quoted in P. Gillett, *The Victorian Painter's World*, 1990, p. 19.
14 G. S. Messenger, *Manchester in the Victorian Age*, 1985, p. 129.
15 E. Fenby, *Delius*, 1971, p. 14.
16 S. Royde-Smith, 'The Early Paintings of Matthew Smith', 1981, quoting R. Glazier who was himself trained in the Technical School, p. 7.
17 Ibid., p. 9.
18 MS to Phyllis Smith, 5 March 1905.
19 M. Levy, *Painters of Today: L. S. Lowry*, 1961, p. 9
20 *Halifax Courier and Guardian*, 9 January 1954.
21 D. Jeremiah, *A Hundred Years and More*, 1980, p. 36.
22 MS also told Catherine Mann this happened at the Slade (diaries, 19 December 1955).
23 Alden Brooks to Francis Halliday, 29 August 1960.
24 MS to Phyllis Smith, 6 January 1905.
25 Now in the City of London Collection.
26 *Halifax Courier and Guardian*, 9 January 1954.

3 London: 1905–1908

1 W. Coldstream, in *Henry Tonks and the Art of Pure Drawing*, ed. L. Morris, 1985, p. 11.
2 Catherine Mann diaries, 5 March 1953.
3 A. L. Balby, *The Studio*, Vol. 35, 1905, p. 37.
4 E. J. Poynter, 'Ten Lectures on Art', quoted in P. Gillett, *The Victorian Painter's World*, 1990, p. 10.
5 H. Lessor, in *Henry Tonks and the Art of Pure Drawing*, op. cit., p. 8.
6 W. Rothenstein, *Men and Memories*, Vol. 1, 1931, p. 23.
7 M. Holroyd, *Augustus John: A Biography*, 1987, p. 56.
8 D. S. MacColl, 'Professor Brown, Teacher and Painter', *The Magazine of Art*, 1893, p. 407.
9 J. Rothenstein, *Modern English Painters*, op. cit., p. 88.
10 J. Hone, *The Life of Henry Tonks*, 1939, p. xvi.

11 Ibid., p. 75.
12 Ibid., p. 75.
13 Ibid., p. 272.
14 Ibid., p. xvii.
15 M. Lilly, *Sickert: The Painter and His Circle*, 1971, p. 118.
16 J. Rothenstein, op. cit., p. 230.
17 C. Bell, *Daily Telegraph*, 11 October 1959.
18 A. Daintrey, *I Must Say*, 1963, p. 61.
19 Ibid., p. 53.
20 W. Coldstream, in *Henry Tonks and the Art of Pure Drawing*, op. cit., p. 11.
21 A. Daintrey, op. cit., p. 63.
22 See for example plates 7, 10, 96, 168, 170, 171 in A. Keene, *The Two Mr Smiths*, 1995.
23 R. A. M. Stevenson, *Velázquez*, 1900.
24 MS to Gwen Salmond, September 1907.

4 Whitby: 1906–1907

1 cf. R. Schwabe, 'Reminiscences of Fellow Students', *Burlington Magazine*, Vol. 82, 1943, pp. 6–9.
2 MS to Gwen Salmond (hereafter GS), summer 1907.
3 A. John, Obituary of Gwen Smith (née Salmond), *The Times*, 1 February 1958.
4 MS to GS, autumn 1907 (many of the letters are undated and the envelopes lost).
5 MS to GS, 14 October 1907.
6 MS to GS, autumn 1907.
7 MS to GS, autumn 1907.
8 Possibly Esther George, a friend of Gwen's who exhibited at the Royal Academy in 1896, 1899, 1906.
9 MS to GS, autumn 1907.
10 D. S. MacColl, *The Life Work and Setting of Wilson Steer*, 1945, p. 31.
11 MS to GS, autumn 1907
12 MS to GS, autumn 1907
13 MS to GS, autumn 1907.
14 MS to GS, autumn 1907.
15 GS to MS, 19 September 1907.
16 MS to GS, summer 1908.

5 Brittany: 1908–1909

1 M. Jacobs, *The Good and Simple Life*, 1985, p. 44.
2 Ibid., p. 85.
3 M. Denis, 'Definition of Neo-Traditionalism', 1890, in H. B. Chipp, *The Theories of Modern Art*, 1968, p. 100.
4 W. Jaworska, *Gauguin and the Pont Aven School*, 1972, p. 8.
5 Accounts of this incident vary but I have taken this version from A. Cariou, *Painting in Brittany: Gauguin and his Friends*, catalogue of the exhibition at the Laing Art Gallery, Newcastle on Tyne, 1992.
6 Chipp, op. cit., p. 94.
7 F. Halliday and J. Russell, *Matthew Smith*, exh. cat., Royal Academy, 1960, p. vi.
8 D. Sutton (ed.), *Letters of Roger Fry*, 1972, No. 496, 15 February 1921.
9 J. Rothenstein, *Modern English Painters*, 1976, p. 231.

10 Alden Brooks to Francis Halliday, 28 August 1960.
11 T. H. Thomas to MS, undated 1918.
12 cf. J. Benington, *Roderic O'Conor*, 1992, Plate 14.
13 J. Rothenstein, op. cit., p. 231.

6 Paris: 1909–1911

1 J. Lyman, 'Matisse as Teacher', *Studio International*, Vol. 176, 1968, pp. 2–3.
2 MS to Francis Halliday, *c.* 1950.
3 Q. Bell, *Elders and Betters*, 1995, p. 158.
4 J. Elderfield, *Pleasuring Painting: Matisse's Feminine Representations*, 1995, p. 13.
5 J. Lyman, op. cit., p. 2.
6 'Matisse Speaks to his Students', trans. S. Stein, in A. H. Barr, *Matisse: His Art and His Public*, 1975, p. 550.
7 Ibid., p. 550.
8 J. Lyman, op. cit., p. 2.
9 J. Elderfield, *Henry Matisse: A Retrospective*, Museum of Modern Art, New York, 1992, p. 181.
10 H. Matisse, 'Notes of a Painter', in H. B. Chipp, *Theories of Modern Art*, 1968, p. 135.
11 J. Flam, *Matisse on Art*, 1973, p. 82.
12 Ibid., p. 86.
13 C. Holland, 'Lady Art Students' Life in Paris', *Studio*, Vol. XXX, 1903, p. 230.
14 Ibid., p. 230.
15 City of London Collection, reproduced in A. Keene, *The Two Mr Smiths*, 1995, Plate 2.
16 G. Picon, *Jean August Dominic Ingres*, 1980, p. 122.
17 The original is now in the collection of Alice Keene. For the copy cf. *Matthew Smith*, exh. cat., Barbican Art Gallery, 1983, p. 63.
18 J. Rothenstein, *Time's Thievish Progress*, p. 11.
19 *Barn with Trees, Varengeville*, 1911, owned by Michael Royde-Smith but displayed in the Central Museum, Northampton.
20 *Still Life with Forget-Me-Nots, c.* 1910, 13 × 16 in., exh. cat., Barbican Art Gallery, 1983, p. 8.

7 Grez-sur-Loing: 1912–1914

1 *The Queen: The Lady's Newspaper*, 20 January 1912, p. 110.
2 MS to GS, 12 February 1912.
3 S. Royde-Smith, 'The Early Paintings of Matthew Smith', p. 53.
4 Roger Fry, 'The French Post-Impressionists' (1912), *Vision and Design*, 1920, p. 157.
5 MS to Frederic Smith, 30 December 1913.
6 cf. J. Rothenstein, *Matthew Smith*, 1962, Plate 3.
7 cf. A. Keene, *The Two Mr Smiths*, 1995, Plate 5.
8 Ibid., Plate 6.
9 F. Sadler, 'L'Hôtel Chevillon et les Artistes de Grez-sur-Loing', privately published, no date.
10 M. Jacobs, *The Good and Simple Life: Artists' Colonies in Europe and America*, 1985, p. 33.
11 R. L. Stevenson, 'Fontainebleau Village Communities of Painters', quoted in *Sir John Lavery*, exh. cat. by K. McConkey, 1985, p. 11.
12 A. Brooks, *Will Shakespeare and the Dyer's Hand*, 1943.
13 Alden Brooks to Francis Halliday, 1960.

14 O. Sitwell (ed.), *A Free House: Being the Writings of W. R. Sickert*, 1947, p. 327.
15 G. Picon, *Jean August Dominic Ingres*, 1980, p. 128.
16 F. Halliday and J. Russell, op. cit., p. 6.
17 cf. P. Hendy, *Matthew Smith*, 1944, Plate 4, and A. Keene, *The Two Mr Smiths*, 1995, Plate 8.
18 P. Hendy, ibid., p. 7.
19 cf. A. Keene, op. cit., Plate 7.
20 S. Royde-Smith, op. cit., p. 65.
21 Alden Brooks diaries, 31 August 1912.
22 Alden Brooks to Francis Halliday, 31 August 1960.

8 Fitzroy Street: 1914–1916

1 MS to John Lyman, 28 February 1915.
2 Ibid.
3 Guy Maynard to MS, undated.
4 Some of these are in the Victoria and Albert Museum Drawings Collection. Also cf. A. Keene, *The Two Mr Smiths*, p. 37.
5 Ibid., Plates 7, 9, 10.
6 M. Lilly, *Sickert: The Painter and His Circle*, 1971, p. 146.
7 Ibid., p. 78.
8 Ibid., p. 138.
9 MS to Alden Brooks, 26 November 1915.
10 'Futurist Painting Technical Manifesto', 11 April 1910, in H. B. Chipp, *Theories of Modern Art*, 1968, p. 293.
11 cf. *Matthew Smith*, exh. cat., Barbican Art Gallery, 1983, No. 10, now in Southampton Art Gallery.
12 A. Keene, op. cit., Plate 14.

9 War: 1917–1919

1 M. and S. Harries, *The War Artists*, 1983, p. 112.
2 P. Nash, 'To His Wife', *Outline*, 1949, p. 210.
3 MS to Alden Brooks, 26 November 1915.
4 J. Rothenstein, *Modern English Painters*, 1976, p. 232.
5 MS to Phyllis Smith, November 1916.
6 MS to Phyllis Smith, undated 1916.
7 MS to Phyllis Smith, 17 March 1917.
8 MS to Phyllis Smith, 27 May 1917.
9 MS to Hilma Brooks, 7 August 1918.
10 M. and S. Harries, op. cit., p. 290, note 62.
11 See J. Benington, *Roderic O'Conor: A Biography*, 1992, Plate 61.
12 John Lyman to his father, 8 June 1919, in *Inédits de John Lyman*, 1980.
13 Alden Brooks diaries, 20 May 1919.
14 Alden Brooks diaries, 17 June 1919.
15 Quoted by A. Keene in *Matthew Smith*, exh. cat., Barbican Art Gallery, 1983, p. 22.
16 Ibid., p. 22.
17 MS broadcast on BBC Radio 1950; see part transcription in exh. cat., Barbican Art Gallery, 1983, p. 15.
18 J. Rothenstein, op. cit., p. 234.

19 T. H. Thomas to MS, 12 July 1919.
20 cf. P. Hendy, *Matthew Smith*, 1944, Plate 5. Now in Leeds Art Gallery.
21 J. Rothenstein, *Matthew Smith*, 1962, Plate 3.
22 S. Royde-Smith, 'The Early Paintings of Matthew Smith', p. 78, and exh. cat., Barbican Art Gallery, 1983, p. 16.

10 Cornwall: 1920–1922

1 MS to Alden Brooks, 17 October 1920.
2 Ibid.
3 F. Halliday and J. Russell, *Matthew Smith*, 1962, p. 7.
4 J. Russell, 'Matthew Smith in France', *Apollo* 76, 1962, p. 372.
5 E. Zola, *My Hatreds*, trans. P. and J. Yashinsky, 1991, p. 150.
6 cf J. Benington, *Roderic O'Conor: A Biography*, 1992, Plate 19, and exh. cat., Barbican Art Gallery, 1983, No. 26.
7 G. Grigson, 'Two London Art Exhibitions', *Listener*, 17 February 1949, p. 282.
8 cf. P. Hendy, *Matthew Smith*, 1944, Plate 7.
9 J. Rothenstein, *Modern English Painters*, 1976, p. 235.
10 D. Piper, Obituary, *Listener*, 8 October 1959
11 cf. *Matthew Smith*, exh. cat., Barbican Art Gallery, 1983, No. 28.
12 R. Fry, review in *Nation and Atheneum*, 1 May 1926, p. 126.
13 Alden Brooks, quoted by F. Halliday and J. Russell in *Matthew Smith*, exh. cat., Royal Academy, 1960, p. ix.
14 J. Rothenstein, *Matthew Smith*, 1962, Plate 3.
15 V. Eliot (ed.), *The Letters of T. S. Eliot, 1898–1922*, footnote p. 480.
16 R. Gathorne-Hardy (ed.), *The Early Memoirs of Lady Ottoline Morrell*, 1963, p. 237.
17 J. Huxley, *Memories*, 1970, p. 124.
18 A. Keene, in *Matthew Smith*, exh. cat., Barbican Art Gallery, 1983, p. 23.
19 A. Daintrey, *I Must Say*, 1963, p. 107.
20 A. Keene, *The Two Mr Smiths*, 1995, p. 45.
21 See J. Rothenstein, *Matthew Smith*, 1962, Plate 17.
22 See Crane Kalman catalogue, July 1990, Plate 8.
23 Barbara Whelpton interviewed MS for the Eastern Service of the BBC, 19 April 1946. See also exh. cat., Barbican Art Gallery, 1983, p. 70, note 31.
24 M. Lilly, *Sickert the Painter and His Circle*, 1971, p. 103.

11 Paris Again: 1922–1925

1 R. Creuze, *Vera Cuningham*, 1984, p. 14.
2 J. Rothenstein, *Matthew Smith*, 1962, p. 4.
3 P. Trevor-Roper, *The World Through Blunted Sight*, 1971.
4 P. Quennell, 'Augustus John', *Harper's Bazaar*, February 1952, p. 45.
5 K. Clark, *The Nude*, 1956, p. 1.
6 D. Hálevy, *Degas Parle*, 1960, p. 14.
7 J. Rothenstein, *Modern English Painters*, 1976, p. 235.
8 'Painter's Pilgrimage' in *Time*, 21 September 1953, p. 88.
9 K. Clark, op. cit., p. 1.
10 H. Green, 'Matthew Smith: A Personal Tribute', exh. cat., Tate Gallery, 1953, p. 9.
11 A. Daintrey, *I Must Say*, 1963, p. 109.
12 J. Hobhouse, *The Bride Stripped Bare*, 1988, p. 76.

13 J. Russell, 'Matthew Smith in France', *Apollo* 76, 1962, p. 372.
14 R. Thompson, *Degas: The Nudes*, 1988, p. 70.
15 See J. Rothenstein, *Matthew Smith*, 1962, Plate 7.
16 P. Hendy, *Matthew Smith*, 1944, p. 12.
17 N. Watkins, *Bonnard*, 1994, p. 171.
18 J. Bell, *Bonnard*, 1994, p. 86.
19 R. Creuze, *Vera Cuningham*, 1984.
20 The oil portraits are in private collections but see Creuze, op. cit., p. 26 for 'Portrait of Joe', and *Drawing and Design*, Vol. IV, No. 19, January 1928, for a Cuningham drawing of Smith (p. 18) and a nude (p. 13).

12 The First Exhibition: 1926–1928

1 Alden Brooks to D. Sutton, 12 July 1956 (Tate archives).
2 cf. A. Keene, *The Two Mr Smiths*, 1995, Plates 25, 26.
3 MS to Harold Smith, 15 April 1928.
4 J. Benington, *Roderic O'Conor: A Biography*, 1992, p. 148.
5 A. Daintrey, *I Must Say*, 1963, p. 101.
6 See J. Rothenstein, *Matthew Smith*, 1962, Plate 20.
7 Quoted in C. Connolly, 'Matthew Smith: Job and Prospero', exh. cat., Barbican Art Gallery, 1983, p. 51.
8 A. Bertram, *Saturday Review*, 24 April 1926, p. 535.
9 P. Konody, *Observer*, 11 April 1926.
10 R. Fry, *Nation and Atheneum*, 1 May 1926, p. 127.
11 J. Rothenstein, *Modern English Painters*, 1976, p. 239.
12 Anon, *The Times*, 3 December 1927.
13 cf. A. Thomas, *Portraits of Women*, 1994, Plate 42.
14 MS to GS, undated.
15 Alden Brooks diaries, 9 November 1929.
16 Alden Brooks to Francis Halliday, 28 August 1960.
17 Alden Brooks to Francis Halliday, 28 August 1960.

13 Growing Fame: 1928–1932

1 A. John, *Vogue*, 8 October 1928, p. 76.
2 Lady Epstein, Foreword to the catalogue of the 1966 Arts Council exhibition of Smith's work, Cardiff.
3 P. Hendy, Introduction to F. Halliday and J. Russell, *Matthew Smith*, 1962, p. 2.
4 Margaret Epstein to MS, 9 January 1929.
5 J. Epstein, *Let There Be Sculpture*, 1942, p. 109.
6 F. Rutter, *Sunday Times*, 27 October 1929.
7 S. Gardiner, *Epstein*, 1993, p. 303.
8 See P. Hendy, *Matthew Smith*, 1944, Plate 24.
9 R. Ingleby, *Christopher Wood: An English Painter*, 1995, p. 213.
10 P. Hendy, Introduction to *Matthew Smith*, 1962, p. 3.
11 MS to Phyllis Smith, 18 December 1929.
12 Anon, *New Statesman*, 17 December 1927.
13 P. Konody, *Observer*, 18 December 1927.
14 Anon, 'Eccentricity in Art: Mr Matthew Smith's Colour Schemes', *Morning Post*, 6 December 1927.

15 W. Gaunt, *Drawing and Design*, Vol. 3, No. 16, October 1927, p. 107. This edition also contains a drawing of Smith by Vera Cuningham.
16 P. Konody, 'The art of Matthew Smith', *Apollo*, Vol. X, No. 59, November 1929, p. 260.
17 MS to Francis Halliday, undated.
18 T. G. Dowson to MS, November 1929.
19 Quoted in R. Hughes, *The Shock of the New*, 1980, p. 127.
20 A. Keene in *Matthew Smith*, exh. cat., Barbican Art Gallery, 1983, p. 26.
21 Alden Brooks to Francis Halliday, 17 September 1960.
22 MS to Alden Brooks, 10 April 1930.
23 See F. Halliday and J. Russell, *Matthew Smith*, 1962, Plate 31.
24 Ibid., Plates 35, 36.
25 Ibid., Plate 33.
26 See J. Rothenstein, *Matthew Smith*, 1962, Plate 14.
27 H. Green, 'Matthew Smith: A Personal Tribute', exh. cat., Tate Gallery, 1953, p. 10.
28 H. Furst, 'An exhibition of Matthew Smith's new paintings at Messrs Tooth's Gallery', *Apollo* 15, April 1932, p. 185.
29 F. Rutter, 'A Feast of Colour', *Sunday Times*, 11 April 1932.
30 F. Rutter, *Modern Masterpieces*, 1940, p. 248.
31 MS quoted in exh. cat., Barbican Art Gallery, 1983, p. 26.
32 F. Rutter, 'Fireworks in Paint: A Question of Colour', *Sunday Times*, 27 February 1937.
33 Alden Brooks to Francis Halliday, 29 August 1960, quoting diary entry of 8 February 1931.
34 MS to GS, 17 September 1932.
35 MS to GS, 30 July 1927.

14 Southern France: 1933–1936

1 A. Thomas, *Portraits of Women*, 1994, p. 204.
2 Ibid., p. 206.
3 L. Larguier, *Le Dimanche Avec Paul Cézanne*, 1925, p. 138.
4 MS to GS, 13 December 1934.
5 Anon, *Sunday Times*, 20 May 1934.
6 See A. Keene, *The Two Mr Smiths*, Plates 65 to 69.
7 R. Chiappini, *Chaim Soutine*, 1995, p. 191.
8 H. Miller, *My Life and Times*, 1972, p. 165.
9 MS to Eric Fenby, dated Tuesday, November 1936.
10 MS to Dudley Tooth, undated 1936.
11 MS to GS, 16 September 1934.
12 J. Russell, Introduction to catalogue of MS's work, Waddington Gallery, January 1968.
13 T. W. Earp, 'A Stimulant to Modern Art', *Daily Telegraph*, 14 November 1936.

15 Aix-en-Provence: 1937–1939

1 Anecdote from Anthony Smith.
2 J. Rothenstein, *Time's Thievish Progress*, 1970, p. 9.
3 I. Hughes, notes sent to author.
4 MS to Marion Monay, January 1939.
5 See J. Russell and F. Halliday, *Matthew Smith*, 1962, Plate 43.
6 XXI Esposizione Biennale Internationale D'Arte, 1938, Venice, pp. 273–4.
7 Anon, *The Times*, 12 January 1939.

8 MS to Francis Halliday, 25 April 1940.
9 Mark Smith to MS, undated.
10 GS to Dermot Smith, 31 May 1940.

16 Another War: 1940–1941

1 MS to Phyllis Smith, 8 December 1940.
2 GS to Phyllis Smith, 14 December 1940.
3 K. Clark, 'War Artists at the National Gallery', *Studio*, CXXIII, January 1942, p. 586.
4 Alden Brooks to MS, 12 July 1940.
5 Alden Brooks to MS, 8 March 1941.
6 Vivien John to MS, 11 April 1941.
7 R. Keene, 'Famous Artists: Matthew Smith', *Artist*, September 1934, p. 22.
8 J. Stallworthy, *Louis MacNeice*, 1995, p. 238.
9 R. Wyndham, 'Matthew Smith', *Horizon* 6, 1942, pp. 108–12.
10 MS to Mary Keene (hereafter MK), 29 July 1945.
11 MS to MK, 27 August 1947.
12 MS to Vera Cuningham, 10 December 1940.
13 MS to GS, 29 December 1942.
14 MS to Francis Halliday, 13 January 1942.
15 M. Lilly, *Sickert: The Painter and His Circle*, 1971, p. 104.

17 A Slow Revival: 1942–1944

1 E. Newton, *Sunday Times*, 19 July 1942.
2 For details of this movement, see M. Yorke, *The Spirit of Place: Nine Neo-Romantic Artists and Their Times*, 1988.
3 cf. A. Keene, *The Two Mr Smiths*, 1995, Plates 77, 80, 81, 82.
4 MS to MK, undated 1952.
5 Augustus John to MS, undated.
6 MK to MS, undated. See A. Keene, op. cit., Plate 152.
7 R. Dahl, 'Searching for Mr Smith' (1979), in exh. cat., Barbican Art Gallery, 1983, pp. 54–5.
8 C. Beaton, *Photobiography*, 1951, pp. 118–19.
9 J. Rothenstein, *Modern English Painters*, 1976, p. 241.
10 J. Rothenstein, *Time's Thievish Progress*, 1970, p. 4.
11 J. Rothenstein, *Modern English Painters*, p. 2.

18 A Book and a Return: 1944–1947

1 P. Hendy, *Matthew Smith*, 1944, p. 5.
2 Ibid., p. 14.
3 Ibid., p. 16.
4 J. Rothenstein, *Time's Thievish Progress*, 1970, p. 5.
5 cf. E. Kris and O. Kurz, *Legend, Myth and Magic in the Image of the Artist*, 1979.
6 R. W. Alston, *Nineteenth Century and After*, August 1945.
7 J. Rothenstein, op. cit., p. 7.
8 MS to Francis Halliday, 4 August 1944.
9 cf. *Matthew Smith*, exh. cat., Barbican Art Gallery 1983, No. 76.
10 MS to Alden Brooks, 20 November 1944.

11 MS to Alden Brooks, 3 January 1944.
12 Alden Brooks to MS, 24 June 1947.
13 MS to Henry Yorke, September 1948. Quoted in A. Keene, *The Two Mr Smiths*, 1995, p. 68.
14 S. de Beauvoir, 'Force of Circumstance', quoted in F. Morris, Introduction to *Paris Post-War: Art and Existentialism*, exh. cat., Tate Gallery, 1993, p. 15.
15 *Horizon*, Vol. XII, No. 17, 1945, p. 337.
16 J. Rothenstein, *Time's Thievish Progress*, 1970, p. 8.
17 Ibid, p. 8.
18 MS to Dig Yorke, September 1946, quoted in A. Keene, op. cit., p. 70.
19 MS to MK, 20 December 1946.
20 MS to Francis Halliday, March 1946.
21 MS to MK, undated.
22 P. Heron, *New Statesman and Nation*, 8 November 1947, p. 368.
23 P. Heron, letter to author, 24 May 1995.

19 Late Maturity: 1948–1950

1 cf. A. Keene, *The Two Mr Smiths*, 1995, Plates 99, 100.
2 E. Knollys, *New Statesman and Nation*, 5 February 1949.
3 Anon, *Sunday Times*, 6 February 1949.
4 M. Middleton, 'The Wild Man of Art', *Picture Post*, 8 October 1949, pp. 25–7.
5 M. Ayrton, *British Drawings*, 1946, p. 46.
6 R. Ironside, *Painting Since 1939*, 1948, p. 158.
7 H. Read, *Contemporary British Art*, 1951, p. 17.
8 MK to MS, undated.
9 MK to MS, undated.
10 MS to MK, 19 November 1949.
11 MS to Alden Brooks, 23 February 1950.
12 A. Keene, Epilogue to *Mrs Donald* by Mary Keene, 1983, p. 121.
13 MK to MS, undated.
14 M. Keene, *Mrs Donald*, 1983.
15 E. Newton, *Sunday Times*, 25 June 1950.
16 J. Treglown, *Roald Dahl: A Biography*, 1994, p. 90.
17 Diana Marsh to MS, 6 December 1950. cf. also A. Keene, *The Two Mr Smiths*, 1995, Plate 101.
18 R. Dahl to MS, incomplete and undated letter.
19 N. Logsdail, *Modern Painters*, Summer 1993, p. 80.
20 Partly reprinted in exh. cat., Barbican Art Gallery, 1983, p. 15.
21 O. Redon, *To Myself: Notes on Life, Art and Artists*, 1986, p. 79.
22 D. H. Lawrence, 'Making Pictures', *Phoenix*, Vol. II, ed. W. Roberts and H. Moore, 1968, pp. 603–7.
23 Redfern Gallery, 10 January 1950.
24 *The Forgotten Fifties*, exh. cat., Graves Art Gallery, Sheffield, Spring 1984, p. 46.
25 E. Knollys, *New Statesman and Nation*, 5 February 1949.
26 See A. Keene, *The Two Mr Smiths*, Plates 116, 118, 119, 112, 113, 115.
27 J. Flam, *Matisse on Art*, 1973, p. 72.

20 Winding Down: 1951–1954

1 A. John, *Chiaroscuro*, 1952.
2 M. Holroyd, *Augustus John: A Biography*, 1987, p. 422.
3 MS to MK, 16 April 1951.
4 cf. A. Keene, *The Two Mr Smiths*, 1995, Plate 153.
5 J. Treglown, *Roald Dahl*, 1994, p. 118.
6 cf. H. Green, *Pack My Bag: A Self-Portrait*, 1940.
7 Told to author by Lilian Browse.
8 MS to GS, 26 April 1954.
9 Charlotte Cholerton to MS, 29 May 1954.
10 Simone Kenyon to MS, undated.
11 M. Sorrell, 'Matthew Smith', *Apollo* 48, 1948, pp. 30–32, and 'Portrait of the Artist', *Art News and Review*, No. 16, 10 September 1949.
12 Catherine Mann diaries, 14 July 1953.
13 Ibid., 31 August 1954.
14 Ibid., 29 August 1952; see also A. Keene, *The Two Mr Smiths*, Plate 125.
15 Ibid., 27 July 1952.
16 Ibid., 27 July 1952.
17 E. Newton, Introduction to *Vera Cuningham*, exh. cat., Barbican Art Gallery, 1956.
18 J. Rothenstein, *Time's Thievish Progress*, 1970, p. 14.
19 Ibid., p. 1.
20 'Painter's Pilgrimage', *Time*, 21 September 1953, p. 88.
21 Roald Dahl to MS, 4 May 1953.
22 John Russell to MS, April 1958.
23 Vera Russell to Francis Halliday, undated.
24 Stephen Spender, *The Thirties and After*, 1978, p. 183.
25 J. Rothenstein, op. cit., p. 12.
26 *Matthew Smith: Paintings from 1909 to 1952*, exh. cat., Tate Gallery, 1953, p. 12.
27 MS to MK, 5 August 1953.
28 cf. Jenny Lee, 'My Life with Nye', extract, *Observer* magazine, 8 December 1972.
29 S. Gardiner, *Epstein*, 1993, p. 445.
30 Anon, *The Times*, 3 September 1953.
31 B. Robertson, 'A Tribute to Matthew Smith', *Listener*, 10 September 1953.
32 P. Heron, *New Statesman and Nation*, 19 November 1953, p. 313.
33 *Time*, 21 September 1953.

21 The Last Years: 1954–1959

1 *Halifax Courier and Guardian*, 9 January 1954.
2 GS to MS, undated.
3 GS to MS, undated.
4 MK to MS, undated.
5 R. Creuze, letter to author.
6 MS to GS, 2 August 1955.
7 MS to MK, August 1955.
8 H. Roland, *Behind the Façade: Recollections of an Art Dealer*, 1991, p. 103.
9 J. Russell, *Sunday Times*, 26 August 1956.
10 Augustus John to MS, 5 September 1956.
11 J. Russell, 'Matthew Smith in France', *Apollo* 76, 1962, pp. 372–6.

12 MS to Glyn Hughes, 19 July 1956.
13 Glyn Hughes to author, 5 February 1994.
14 MS to GS, undated 1956.
15 Alden Brooks to MS, 15 January 1957.
16 C. Bell, *Old Friends*, 1956.
17 cf. *Sunday Times*, 26 August 1956, and *The Times*, 17 September 1957.
18 The library is now in the possession of Alice Keene.
19 A. John, *The Times*, 1 February 1958.
20 Francis Halliday, in the collection of Christopher Halliday.
21 Catherine Mann diaries, 18 January 1958.
22 Ibid., 22 April 1958.
23 Vera Russell to Francis Halliday, undated.
24 J. Russell, *England*: Journal of the Royal Society of St George, 1958, p. 20.
25 Augustus John to MS, 17 April 1958.
26 Told by Alice Keene to the author.
27 J. Rothenstein, *Time's Thievish Progress*, 1970, p. 17.
28 MS to Alden Brooks, 5 January 1959.
29 MK to MS, 20 January 1959.
30 cf. F. Halliday and J. Russell, *Matthew Smith*, 1962, Plate 51.
31 Augustus John to MS, 1 July 1959.
32 MS to Alden Brooks, 5 September 1959.
33 Alden Brooks to MS, 9 September 1959.
34 S. Spender, 'Reminiscences', exh. cat., Barbican Art Gallery, 1983, p. 58.
35 D. Piper, *Listener*, 8 October 1959.
36 E. Newton, *Guardian*, 30 September 1959.
37 Told by Peter Birkett-Smith to author.

Epilogue

1 *Matthew Smith*, 1962.
2 J. Rothenstein, *Matthew Smith*, 1962.
3 Augustus John, *The Times*, 14 October 1960.
4 J. Russell, *Sunday Times*, 16 October 1960.
5 E. Newton, *Guardian*, 14 October 1960.
6 Anon, 'In the Studio of Sir Matthew Smith', *The Times*, 17 September 1957.
7 F. Spalding, 'Searching and Seedy', *Times Literary Supplement*, 30 September 1983.
8 J. Russell Taylor, 'The Thoughtful Process of Falling off a Log', *The Times*, 20 September 1983.
9 F. Gore, in *British Art in the Twentieth Century: The Modern Movement*, exh. cat., Royal Academy, 15 January–5 April 1987, p. 172.
10 *Sir Matthew Smith 1879–1959*, Concourse Gallery, Barbican, London, 7 June–23 July 1995, then on tour to Halifax, Aberdeen and Bath.
11 W. Packer, 'Colourful Hedonism', *Financial Times*, 27 June 1995.
12 R. Shone, 'Matthew Smith', *Burlington Magazine*, Vol. CXXXVIII, No. 1117, April 1996, p. 265.
13 T. Roberts, 'Alias Smith and Loans', *Tonight*, 9 June 1995.
14 I. Gale, 'Matthew Smith's work and its influence on 20th century British painting', exh. cat., Montpelier Sandelson Gallery, 3 May–7 June 1995.
15 F. Rocco, 'It's Colour She Loves', *Independent on Sunday*, 24 September 1995.
16 R. Shone, op. cit., p. 267.

17 P. Heron, letter to author, 25 April 1995.
18 J. Hoyland, telephone conversation with author, 10 March 1995.
19 Telephone conversation with author, 8 July 1996.
20 A. Berg, letter to author, 9 July 1995.
21 R. Shone, op. cit., p. 267.
22 F. Auerbach, letter to author, 4 July 1995.
23 L. Kossoff, letter to author, 6 July 1995.
24 K. Howard, letter to author, 3 July 1995.
25 *Guardian*, 12 August 1995.
26 D. Lee, 'Ladies of the Knight', *Art Review*, May 1995.
27 J. Treglown, 'From girl to girl, studio to studio', *Times Literary Supplement*, 23 June 1995.
28 M. Gayford, 'The flowering of Mr Futility', *Sunday Telegraph*, 14 May 1995.
29 A. Lambirth, 'The English Fauve', *What's On*, 31 May 1995.
30 M. Gayford, op. cit.
31 R. Campbell-Johnston, 'The upshot of the affairs', *The Times*, 21 June 1995.
32 D. Lee, op. cit.
33 C. Harrison, *English Art and Modernism: 1900–1939*, 1981, p. 7.
34 N. Serota, letter to the author, 18 December 1995.

List of Illustrations

(Measurements are given in inches)

1 *Self Portrait*, oil on canvas, 28½ x 19½, 1909 (Corporation of London)
2 Frederic Smith, Matthew's father (loaned by Paul Birkett-Smith)
3 Fanny Smith, Matthew's mother (loaned by Paul Birkett-Smith)
4 Frederick Smith & Co, Caledonia Works, Halifax, *c.* 1895 (from *An Illustrated Account of Halifax, Brighouse and District*, W. T. Pike & Co, Brighton, 1895)
5 Noel Arthur Smith aged 8, Matthew aged 6, Harold aged 3, Hilda aged 9 (loaned by Michael Royde-Smith)
6 Dunham Lawn, Bowdon, Cheshire, showing drawing room and library windows (loaned by Michael Royde-Smith)
7 Matthew Smith as a young man (loaned by Michael Royde-Smith)
8 *Gwendolen Smith*, red chalk on paper, 10½ x 7¾, *c.* 1908 (private collection)
9 Matthew Smith in Breton costume at Pont Aven, *c.* 1909; the bearded figure on the right is labelled Maynard on the back of the photograph (loaned by Alice Keene)
10 *Portrait of a Young Boy*, oil on panel, 13 x 12½, 1908 (private collection)
11 *Self Portrait in a Mirror*, oil on panel, 8¾ x 7½, 1908–9 (private collection)
12 *Portrait of the Artist's Wife, Gwen*, oil on canvas, 12 x 10, 1912 (private collection)
13 *Mme Rivière, after Ingres*, oil on canvas, 45 x 35, 1910–13 (Corporation of London)
14 *Coastal Landscape*, oil on panel, 8½ x 10½, 1911 (private collection, photo Christie's)
15 *Flowers in a Green Vase*, oil on canvas, 18 x 12½, 1913 (Private collection, photo Crane Kalman)
16 *Lilies*, oil on canvas, 30 x 22, 1913 (Leeds City Art Gallery)
17 Matthew Smith and Gwen Salmond at Dunham Lawn, date unknown (loaned by Michael Royde-Smith)
18 Gwen with Mark and Dermot, date unknown (loaned by Michael Royde-Smith)
19 Gwen, Frederic, Geoffrey and Matthew Smith at Swinford Manor, *c.* 1914 (loaned by Michael Royde-Smith)
20 *The Arum Lily*, oil on canvas, 40 x 29, 1916 (private collection)
21 *Fitzroy Street Nude No. 1*, oil on canvas, 34 x 30, 1916 (Tate Gallery)
22 *Fitzroy Street Nude No. 2*, oil on canvas, 40 x 30, 1916 (The British Council)
23 *Portrait of a German P.O.W.*, pencil on paper, 19¾ x 12¾, 1918–19 (City of London)
24 *Steeple in Cornwall*, oil on canvas, 20 x 15½, 1920 (private collection)
25 *Cornish Garden with Monkey-Puzzle Tree*, oil on canvas, 24 x 20, 1920 (private collection)
26 *The Wet Road*, oil on canvas, 21 x 25, 1920 (private collection)

27 *Cornish Landscape*, oil on canvas, 16 x 19¾, 1920 (Browse and Darby)

28 Vera Cuningham, date unknown (loaned by Tony Estill)

29 Matthew Smith and Vera Cuningham in the garden of the Villa Brune, *c.* 1923 (loaned by Alice Keene)

30 *Reclining Nude*, oil on canvas, 24 x 25½, 1925 (Browse and Darby)

31 *Portrait of Vera Cuningham*, oil on canvas, 30 x 25, date unknown (private collection)

32 *The Blue Necklace*, oil on canvas, 28 x 35, 1924 (private collection)

33 *Standing Nude with Fan*, oil on canvas, 52 x 17, 1924–5 (City of London)

34 *Model à La Rose*, oil on canvas, 35½ x 25½, 1924 (private collection)

35 *Model Turning*, oil on canvas, 26 x 32, 1924 (Tate Gallery)

36 *Nude on a Red Divan*, oil on canvas, 18 x 25, 1923–4 (private collection)

37 *Yorkshire Landscape*, oil on canvas, 13½ x 17½, 1926 (private collection)

38 *Laura the Parrot*, oil on canvas, 30 x 25, 1928 (private collection)

39 *Nude*, pencil on paper, 25 x 15, *c.* 1925 (Victoria & Albert Museum)

40 *The Red Sari*, oil on canvas, 23½ x 28¼, *c.* 1931 (private collection, photo Crane Kalman)

41 *Still Life with Blue Jug and Date Box*, oil on canvas, 32 x 25¾, *c.* 1925 (private collection)

42 *The Two Sisters*, oil on canvas, 20 x 27, 1931 (private collection, photo Crane Kalman)

43 *Model Waking*, oil on canvas, 23½ x 28½, 1931 (private collection)

44 *Self Portrait*, oil on canvas, 16¼ x 13, 1932 (National Portrait Gallery)

45 Christiane de Mauberg, date unknown (loaned by Alice Keene)

46 *Nude with Necklace*, oil on canvas, 28½ x 36¼, *c.* 1931 (City of London)

47 *Mont Sainte-Victoire*, oil on canvas, 22 x 30, 1932 (private collection)

48 *Evening Landscape near Aix*, oil on canvas, 20 x 24, date unknown (photo Sotheby's)

49 *Peaches*, oil on canvas, 20 x 29, 1935 (photo Jonathan Clark and Co.)

50 *Portrait of Christiane*, oil on canvas, 24 x 29, 1934–6 (photo Sotheby's)

51 *Vase of Flowers with Apple*, watercolour on paper, 19 x 13½, no date (photo Sotheby's)

52 *Marion Monay*, oil on canvas, 30 x 28½, 1939 (photo Sotheby's)

53 *Nude with Yellow Roses (Aniése Moreau)*, oil on canvas, 36 x 28½, 1936–7 (photo Sotheby's)

54 *The Two Sisters*, oil on canvas, 26 x 32, 1936–7 (Pyms Gallery)

55 *The Two Sisters*, oil on canvas, 25 x 30, *c.* 1941 (City of London)

56 *Francis Halliday*, oil on canvas, 11½ x 8½, 1942 (private collection)

57 *Elizabeth White Holding a Rose*, oil on canvas, 25¼ x 30, 1942–5 (City of London)

58 *Young Actress (Phoebe)*, oil on canvas, 36¼ x 28, 1943 (Bankfield Museum, Halifax)

59 *Young Girl with Arms Folded (Phoebe)*, oil on canvas, 30 x 22, *c.* 1943 (photo Sotheby's)

60 *Valerie Hobson*, oil on canvas, 45¼ x 43, *c.* 1951 (Pyms Gallery)

61 *Roald Dahl*, oil on canvas, 40 x 26, *c.* 1944 (private collection)

62 *Augustus John*, oil on canvas, 30 x 25, 1944 (photo Sotheby's)

63 *Mary Keene*, oil on canvas, 30 x 25, *c.* 1950 (City of London)

64 Mary Keene (loaned by Alice Keene)

65 *Peaches in a Striped Dish*, oil on canvas, 20 x 24, 1950 (private collection)

66 *Fruit in a Blue Dish*, watercolour on paper, 14 x 20, 1950–55 (private collection)

67 *Patricia Neal*, oil on canvas, 36 x 28, 1954 (City of London)

68 *Cathleen Mann*, oil on canvas, 30 x 20, 1952 (City of London)

69 *Large Decoration I*, oil on canvas, 72 x 37½, *c.* 1952–3 (City of London)

70 Matthew Smith in his Yeoman's Row studio (photo by Douglas Glass, 1956)

Index

Note: works of art, etc., are listed under the names of their creators.